# The Expositor's Bible:
## The Gospel According to St. Luke
### By Reverend Henry Burton M.A. D.D.
### Originally Edited Reverend Sir William Robertson Nicoll, M.A. LL.D.
#### This Edition Edited by Anthony Uyl

Woodstock, Ontario, Canada 2018

**The Expositor's Bible: The Gospel According to St. Luke**
**By Reverend Henry Burton M.A. D.D. (1840-?)**
**Originally Edited Reverend Sir William Robertson Nicoll, M.A. LL.D. (1851-1923)**
**This Edition Edited by Anthony Uyl**

Originally Published by:
Hodder and Stoughton Publishers: London

The text of The Expositor's Bible: The Gospel According to St. Luke is all in the Public Domain. The covers, background, layout and Devoted Publishing logo are Copyright ©2018 Devoted Publishing. This edition is published by Devoted Publishing a division of 2165467 Ontario Inc.

**What kind of philosophies do you have?
Let us know!**

Visit our online store: www.devotedpublishing.com
Contact us at: devotedpub@hotmail.com
Visit us on Facebook: @DevotedPublishing

**Published in Woodstock, Ontario, Canada 2018**

For bulk educational rates, please contact us at the above email address.

ISBN: 978-1-77356-201-8

# Table of Contents

CHAPTER I - THE GENESIS OF THE GOSPEL ..... 4
CHAPTER II - THE MUTE PRIEST ..... 9
CHAPTER III - THE GOSPEL PSALMS ..... 14
CHAPTER IV - THE VIRGIN MOTHER ..... 20
CHAPTER V - THE ADORATION OF THE SHEPHERDS ..... 26
CHAPTER VI - THE VOICE IN THE WILDERNESS ..... 30
CHAPTER VII - THE TEMPTATION ..... 38
CHAPTER VIII - THE GOSPEL OF THE JUBILEE ..... 46
CHAPTER IX - A SABBATH IN GALILEE ..... 52
CHAPTER X - THE CALLING OF THE FOUR ..... 57
CHAPTER XI - CONCERNING PRAYER ..... 62
    Footnotes: ..... 67
CHAPTER XII - THE FAITH OF THE CENTURION ..... 68
CHAPTER XIII - THE ANOINTING OF THE FEET ..... 73
    Footnotes: ..... 77
CHAPTER XIV - THE PARABLE OF THE SOWER ..... 78
CHAPTER XV - THE KINGDOM OF GOD ..... 83
CHAPTER XVI - THE MIRACLES OF HEALING ..... 88
CHAPTER XVII - THE MIRACLE OF THE LOAVES ..... 92
CHAPTER XVIII - THE TRANSFIGURATION ..... 96
CHAPTER XIX - THE GOOD SAMARITAN ..... 100
CHAPTER XX - THE TWO SISTERS ..... 104
    Footnotes: ..... 107
CHAPTER XXI - LOST AND FOUND ..... 108
    Footnotes: ..... 113
CHAPTER XXII - THE ETHICS OF THE GOSPEL ..... 114
    Footnotes: ..... 118
CHAPTER XXIII - THE ESCHATOLOGY OF THE GOSPEL ..... 119
    Footnotes: ..... 122
CHAPTER XXIV - THE WATCH IN GETHSEMANE ..... 123
CHAPTER XXV - THE PASSION ..... 127
CHAPTER XXVI - THE FIRST LORD'S DAY ..... 134

# CHAPTER I - THE GENESIS OF THE GOSPEL

The four walls and the twelve gates of the Seer looked in different directions, but together they guarded, and opened into, one City of God. So the four Gospels look in different directions; each has its own peculiar aspect and inscription; but together they lead towards, and unveil, one Christ, "which is, and which was, and which is to come, the Almighty." They are the successive quarterings of the one Light. We call them "four" Gospels, though in reality they form but one, just as the seven arches of colour weave one bow; and that there should be four, and not three or five, was the purpose and design of the Mind which is above all minds. There are "diversities of operations" even in making Testaments, New or Old; but it is one Spirit who is "over all, and in all;" and back of all diversity is a heavenly unity--a unity that is not broken, but rather beautified, by the variety of its component parts.

Turning to the third Gospel, its opening sentences strike a key-note unlike the tone of the other three. Matthew, the Levite Apostle, schooled in the receipt of custom--where parleying and preambling were not allowed--goes to his subject with sharp abruptness, beginning his story with a "genesis," "the book of the generation of Jesus Christ." Mark, too, and John, without staying for any prelude, proceed at once to their portrayals of the Divine Life, each starting with the same word "beginning"--though between the "beginning" of St. Mark and that of St. John there is room for an eternity. St. Luke, on the other hand, stays to give to his Gospel a somewhat lengthy preface, a kind of vestibule, where we become acquainted with the presence and personality of the verger, before passing within the temple proper.

It is true the Evangelist does not here inscribe his name; it is true that after inserting these lines of explanation, he loses sight of himself completely, with a "sublime repressing of himself" such as John did not know; but that he here throws the shadow of himself upon the page of Scripture, calling the attention of all people and ages to the "me also," shows clearly that the personal element cannot be eliminated from the question of inspiration. Light is the same in its nature; it moves only in straight lines; it is governed by fixed laws; but in its reflections it is infinitely varied, turning to purple, blue, or gold, according to the nature of the medium and reflecting substance. And what, indeed, is beauty, what the harmony of colours, but the visible music as the same light plays upon the diverse keys? Exactly the same law rules in inspiration. As the Divine Love needed an incarnation, an enshrining in human flesh, that the Divine Word might be vocal, so the Divine Light needs its incarnation too. Indeed, we can scarcely conceive of any revelation of the Divine Mind but as coming through a human mind. It needs the human element to analyze and to throw it forward, just as the electric spark needs the dull carbon-point to make it visible. Heaven and earth are here, as elsewhere, "threads of the same loom," and if we take out one, even the earthly woof of the humanities, we leave only a tangle; and if it is true of works of art that "to know them we must know the man who produced them," it is equally important, if we would know the Scripture, that we have some knowledge of the scribe. And especially important is it here, for there are few books of Scripture on which the writer's own personality is more deeply impressed than on the Gospel of St. Luke. The "me also" is only legible in the third verse, but we may read it, between the lines, through the whole Gospel.

Concerning the life of St. Luke the facts are few. It has been thought by some that he was one of the "certain Greeks" who came to Jerusalem to worship; while others, again, suppose him to be the nameless one of the two Emmaus travellers. But both these suppositions are set aside by the fact that the Evangelist carefully separates himself from those who were "eye-witnesses," which he could not well have done had he taken part in those closing scenes of the Lord's life, or had he been honoured with that "infallible proof" of the Lord's resurrection. That he was a Gentile is evident; his speech bewrayeth him; for he speaks with a Grecian accent, while Greek idioms are sprinkled over his pages. Indeed, St. Paul speaks of him as not being of the "circumcision" (Col. iv. 11, 14), and he himself, in Acts i. 19, speaks of the dwellers at Jerusalem, and the Aceldama of "their" proper tongue. Tradition, with unanimous voice, represents him as a native of Antioch, in Syria.

Responding to the Divine Voice that bids him "write," St. Luke brings to the task new and special qualifications. Familiar with the Old Testament Scriptures--at least in their Septuagint form, as his many quotations show--intimately acquainted with the Hebrew faith and ritual, he yet brings to his work a mind unwarped by its traditions. He knows nothing of that narrowness of spirit that

Hebraism unconsciously engendered, with its insulation from the great outer world. His mount of vision was not Mount Zion, but a new Pisgah, lying outside the sacred borders, and showing him "all the kingdoms of the world," as the Divine thought of humanity took possession of him. And not only so, we must remember that his connection with Christianity has been mainly through St. Paul, who was the Apostle of the "uncircumcision." For months, if not for years, he has been his close companion, reading his innermost thoughts; and so long and so close together have they been, their two hearts have learned to beat in a perfect synchronism. Besides, we must not forget that the Gentile question--their status in the new kingdom, and the conditions demanded of them--had been the burning question of the early Church, and that it was at this same Antioch it had reached its height. It was at Antioch the Apostle Peter had "dissembled," so soon forgetting the lessons of the Cæsarean Pentecost, holding himself aloof from the Gentile converts until Paul felt constrained to rebuke him publicly; and it was to Antioch came the decree of the Jerusalem Council, that Magna Charta which recognized and enfranchised manhood, giving the privileges of the new kingdom to Gentiles, without imposing upon them the Judaic anachronism of circumcision. We can therefore well understand the bent of St. Luke's mind and the drift of his sympathies; and we may expect that his pen--though it is a reed shaken with the breath of a higher inspiration--will at the same time move in the direction of these sympathies.

And it is exactly this--its "gentility," if we may be allowed to give a new accent and a new meaning to an old word--that is a prominent feature of the third Gospel. Not, however, that St. Luke decries Judaism, or that he denies the "advantage" the Jews have; he cannot do this without erasing Scripture and silencing history; but what he does is to lift up the Son of man in front of their tabernacle of witness. He does not level down Judaism; he levels up Christianity, letting humanity absorb nationality. And so the Gospel of St. Luke is the Gospel of the world, greeting "all nations, and kindreds, and peoples, and tongues" with its "peace on earth." St. Matthew traces the genealogy of Christ back to Abraham; St. Luke goes farther back, to the fountain-head, where all the divergent streams meet and mingle, as he traces the descent to Adam, the Son of God. Matthew shows us the "wise men," lost in Jerusalem, and inquiring, "Where is He that is born King of the Jews?" But St. Luke gives, instead, the "good tidings" to "all people;" and then he repeats the angel song, which is the key-note of his Gospel, "Glory to God in the highest, ... goodwill toward men." It is St. Luke only who records the first discourse at Nazareth, showing how in ancient times, even, the mercy of God flowed out towards a Gentile widow and a Gentile leper. St. Luke alone mentions the mission of the Seventy, whose very number was a prophecy of a world-wide Gospel, seventy being the recognized symbol of the Gentile world, as twelve stood for the Hebrew people. St. Luke alone gives us the parable of the Good Samaritan, showing that all the virtues did not reside in Israel, but that there was more of humanity, and so more of Divinity, in the compassionate Samaritan than in their priest and Levite. St. Luke alone records the call of Zacchæus, the Gentile publican, telling how Jesus cancelled their laws of heredity, passing him up among the sons of Abraham. St. Luke alone gives us the twin parables of the lost coin and the lost man, showing how Jesus had come to seek and to save that which was lost, which was humanity, here, and there, and everywhere. And so there breathes all through this Gospel a catholic spirit, more pronounced than in the rest, a spirit whose rhythm and deep meaning have been caught in the lines--

"There's a wideness in God's mercy,
Like the wideness of the sea."

The only other fact of the Evangelist's life we will here notice is that of his profession; and we notice this simply because it enters as a factor into his work, reappearing there frequently. He was a physician; and from this fact some have supposed that he was a freedman, since many of the Roman physicians were of that class. But this by no means follows. All physicians were not freedmen; while the language and style of St. Luke show him to be an educated man, one, too, who walked in the upper classes of society. Where he speaks natively, as here in the introduction, he uses a pure Greek, somewhat rounded and ornate, in which there is a total absence of those rusticisms common in St. Mark. That he followed his calling at Troas, where he first joined St. Paul, is probable; but that he practised it on board one of the large corn-ships of the Mediterranean is a pure conjecture, for which even his nautical language affords no presumption; for one cannot be at sea for a few weeks--especially with an observant eye and attentive ear, as St. Luke's were-- without falling naturally into nautical language. One's speech soon tastes of salt.

The calling of a physician naturally develops certain powers of analysis and synthesis. It is the art of putting things together. From the seen or felt symptoms he traces out the unseen cause. Setting down the known quantities, by processes of comparison or of elimination he finds the unknown quantity, which is the disease, its nature and its seat. And so on the pages of the third Gospel we frequently find the shadow of the physician. It appears even in his brief preface; for as he sits down with ample materials before him--on one side the first-hand testimony of "eye-witnesses," and on the other the many and somewhat garbled narratives of anonymous scribes--we see the physician-Evangelist exercising a judicious selection, and thus compounding or distilling his pure elixir. Then, too, a skilled and educated physician would find easy access into the higher circles of society, his very calling furnishing him with letters of introduction. And so, indeed, we find it. Our physician dedicates his Gospel, and also the "Acts," to, not the "most excellent," but the "most noble" Theophilus, giving to him the same title that he afterwards gave to Felix and to Festus. Perhaps its English equivalent would be "the honourable." At any rate it shows that this Theophilus was no mere myth, a locution for any "friend of God," but that he was a person of rank and influence, possibly a Roman governor. Then, too, St. Luke's mention of certain names omitted by the other Evangelists, such as Chuza and Manaen, would suggest that probably he had some personal acquaintance with the members of Herod's household. Be this as it may, we recognize the "physician" in St. Luke's habits of observation, his attention to detail, his fondness for grouping together resemblances and contrasts, his fuller reference to miracles of healing, and his psychological observations. We find in him a student of the humanities. Even in his portrayal of the Christ it is the human side of the Divine nature that he emphasizes; while all through his Gospel, his thought of humanity, like a wide-reaching sky, overlooks and embraces all such earthly distinctions as position, sex, or race.

With a somewhat high-sounding word "Forasmuch," which here makes its solitary appearance in the pages of Scripture--a word, too, which, like its English equivalent, is a treble compound--the Evangelist calls our attention to his work, and states his reasons for undertaking it. It is impossible for us to fix either the date or the place where this Gospel was written, but probably it was some time between A.D. 58-60. Now, what was the position of the Church at that date, thirty-five years after the Crucifixion? The fiery tongues of Pentecost had flashed far and wide, and from their heliogram even distant nations had read the message of peace and love. Philip had witnessed the wonderful revival in "the (a) city of Samaria." Antioch, Cæsarea, Damascus, Lystra, Philippi, Athens, Rome--these names indicate, but do not attempt to measure, the wide and ever-widening circle of light. In nearly every town of any size there is the nucleus of a Church; while Apostles, Evangelists, and Christian merchants are proclaiming the new kingdom and the new laws everywhere. And since the visits of the Apostles would be necessarily brief, it would only be a natural and general wish that some permanent record should be made of their narratives and teaching. In other places, which lay beyond the line of Apostles' travel, the story would reach them, passed from mouth to mouth, with all the additions of rumour, and exaggerations of Eastern loquacity. It is to these ephemeral Gospels the Evangelist now refers; and distinguishing, as he does, the "many" from the "eye-witnesses" and "ministers of the word," he shows that he does not refer to the Gospels of St. Matthew and St. Mark--which probably he has not seen--for one was an Apostle, and both were "eye-witnesses." There is no censure implied in these words, nor does the expression "taken in hand" in itself imply failure; but evidently, to St. Luke's mind, these manifold narratives were incomplete and unsatisfactory. They contain some of the truth, but not all that the world should know. Some are put together by unskilled hands, and some have more or less of fable blended with them. They need sifting, winnowing, that the chaff may be blown away, and the seed tares separated from the wheat. Such is the physician's reason for now assuming the rôle of an Evangelist. The "forasmuch," before being entered on the pages of his Scriptures, had struck upon the Evangelist's soul, setting it vibrating like a bell, and moving mind and hand alike in sympathy.

And so we see how, in ways simple and purely natural, Scripture grows. St. Luke was not conscious of any special influence resting upon him. He did not pose as an oracle or as the mouthpiece of an oracle, though he was all that, and vastly more. He does not even know that he is doing any great work; and who ever does? A generous, unselfish thought takes possession of him. He will sacrifice leisure and ease, that he may throw forward to others the light that has fallen upon his own heart and life. He will be a truth-seeker, and a light-bearer for others. Here, then, we see how a human mind falls into gear with the Divine mind, and human thought gets into the rhythm and swing of the higher thought. Simply natural, purely human are all his processes of reasoning, comparing, and planning, and the whole Gospel is but the perfect bloom of this seed-thought. But whence came this thought? That is the question. Did it not grow out of these manifold narratives? and did not the narratives themselves grow out of the wonderful Life, the Life which was itself but a Divine Thought and Word incarnate? And so we cannot separate heaven from earth, we cannot eliminate the Divine from even our little lives; and though St. Luke did not recognize it as such--he was an ordinary man, doing an ordinary thing--yet we, standing a few centuries back, and seeing how the Church has hidden in her ark the omer of manna that he gathered, to be carried on and down till time itself shall be no more, we see another Apocalyptic vision, and we hear a Voice Divine that commands him "write." When St. Luke wrote, "It seemed good to me also," he doubtless wrote the pronoun small; for it was the "me" of his obscure, retiring self; but high above the human thought we see the Divine purpose, and as we watch, the smaller "me" grows into the ME, which is a shadow of the great I AM. And so while the "many" treatises, those which were purely human, have passed out of sight, buried deep in their unknown sepulchres, this Gospel has survived and become immortal--immortal because God was behind it, and God was in it.

So in the mind of St. Luke the thought ripens into a purpose. Since others "have taken in hand" to draw up a narrative concerning those matters which have been "fulfilled among us," he himself will do the same; for has he not a special fitness for the task, and peculiar advantages? He has long been intimately associated with those who from the very first were "eye-witnesses and ministers of the Word," the chosen companion of one Apostle, and doubtless, owing to his visit to Jerusalem and to his prolonged residence at Cæsarea, personally acquainted with the rest. His shall not be a Gospel of surmise or of rumour; it shall only contain the record of facts--facts which he himself has investigated, and for the truth of which he gives his guarantee. The clause "having traced the course of all things accurately from the first"--which is a more exact rendering than that of the Authorized Version, "having had perfect understanding of all things from the very first"--shows us the keen, searching eye of the physician. He looks into things. He distinguishes between the To seem and the To be, the actual and the apparent. He takes nothing for granted, but proves all things. He investigates his facts before he endorses them, sounding them, as it were, and reading not only their outer voice, which may be assumed, and so untrue, but with his stethoscope of patient research listening for the unconscious voices that speak within, and so finding out the reality. He himself is committed to nothing. He is not anxious to make up a story. Himself a searcher after truth, his one concern is to know, and then to tell, the truth, naturally, simply, with no fictitious adornment or dressing up of his own. And having submitted the facts of the Divine Life to a close scrutiny, and satisfied himself of their absolute truth, and having thrown aside the many guesses and fables which somehow have woven themselves around the wonderful Name, he will write down, in historical order as far as may be, the story, so that his friend Theophilus may know the "certainty of the things" in which he has been "instructed," or orally catechized, as the word would mean.

Where, then, it may be asked, is there room for inspiration? If the genesis of the Gospel is so purely human, where is there room for the touch of the Divine? Why should the Gospel of St. Luke be canonized, incorporated into Holy Scripture, while the writings of others are thrown back into an Apocrypha, or still farther back into oblivion? The very questions will suggest an answer. That touch of the Divine which we call inspiration is not always an equal touch. Now it is a pressure from above that is overwhelming. The writer is carried out of himself, borne up into regions where Sight and Reason in their loftiest flights cannot come, as the prophet foretells events no human mind could foresee, much less describe. In the case of St. Luke there was no need for this abnormal pressure, or for these prophetic ecstasies. He was to record, for the most part, facts of recent occurrence, facts that had been witnessed, and could now be attested, by persons still living; and a fact is a fact, whether it is inspired or no. Inspiration may record a fact, while others are omitted, showing that this fact has a certain value above others; but if it is true, inspiration itself cannot make it more true. Nevertheless, there is the touch of the Divine even here. What is the meaning of this new departure? for it is a new and a wide departure. Why does not Thomas write a Gospel? or Philip, or Paul? Why should the Evangelist-mantle be carried outside the bounds of the sacred land, to be thrown around a Gentile, who cannot speak the sacred tongue except with a foreign Shibboleth? Ah, we see here the movings of the Holy Ghost! selecting the separate agents for the separate tasks, and dividing to "every man severally as He will." And not only does the Holy Spirit summon him to the work, He qualifies him for it, furnishing him with materials, and guiding his mind as to what shall be omitted and what retained. It is the same Spirit, who moved "holy men of old" to speak and write the things of God, who now touches the mind and heart of the four Evangelists, enabling them to give the four versions of the one Story, in different language, and with sundry differences of detail, but with no contradiction of thought, each being, in a sense, the complement of the rest, the four quarters making one rounded and perfect whole.

Perhaps at first sight our subject may not seem to have any reference to our smaller lives; for who of us can be Evangelists or Apostles, in the highest meaning of the words? And yet it has, if we look into it, a very practical bearing upon our lives, even the commonplace, every-day life. Whence come our gifts? Who makes these gifts to differ? Who gives us the differing taste and nature? for we are not consulted as to our nature any more than as to our nativities. The fact is, our "human" is touched by the Divine at every point. What are the chequered scenes of our lives but the black or the white squares to which the Unseen Hand moves us at will? Earth's problem is but Heaven's purpose. And are not we, too, writing scriptures? putting God's thoughts into words and deeds, so that men may read them and know them? Verily we are; and our writing is for eternity. In the volume of our book are no omissions or erasures. Listen, then, to the heavenly call. Be obedient to your heavenly vision. Leave mind and heart open to the play of the Divine Spirit. Keep self out of sight. Delight in God's will, and do it. So will you make your lowlier life another Testament, written ever with Gospels and Epistles, and closing at last with an Apocalypse.

Henry Burton

# CHAPTER II – THE MUTE PRIEST

*Luke i. 5-25, 57-80.*

After his personal prelude, our Evangelist goes on to give in detail the pre-Advent revelations, so connecting the thread of his narrative with the broken-off thread of the Old Testament. His language, however, suddenly changes its character and accent; and its frequent Hebraisms show plainly that he is no longer giving his own words, but that he is simply recording the narratives as they were told him, possibly by some member of the Holy Family.

"There was in the days of Herod, king of Judæa." Even the surface-reader of Scripture will observe how little is made in its pages of the time-element. There is a purposed vagueness in its chronology, which scarcely accords with our Western ideas of accuracy and precision. We observe times and seasons. We strike off the years with the clang of bells or the hush of solemn services. Each day with us is lifted up into prominence, having a personality and history all its own, and as we write its history, we keep it clear of all its to-morrows and its yesterdays. And so the day grows naturally into a date, and dates combine into chronologies, where everything is sharp, exact. Not so, however, was it, or indeed is it, in the Eastern world. Time there, if we may speak temporally, was of little moment. To that slow-moving and slow-thinking world one day was a trifle, something atomic; it took a number of them to make an appreciable quantity. And so they divided their time, in ordinary speech, not minutely as we do, due into larger periods, measuring its distances by the shadows of their striking events. Why is it that we have four Gospels, and in fact a whole New Testament, without a date? for it cannot possibly be a chance omission. Is the time-element so subdued and set back, lest the "things temporal" should lead off our minds from the "things spiritual and eternal"? For what is time, after all, but a negative quantity? an empty space, in itself all silent and dead, until our thoughts and deeds strike against it and make it vocal? Nay, even in the heavenly life we see the same losing of the time-element, for we read, "There should be time no longer." Not that it will then disappear, swallowed up in that infinite duration we call eternity. That would make heaven a confusion; for to finite minds eternity itself must come in measured beats, striking, like the waves along the shore, in rhythmic intervals. But our time will be no longer. It must needs be transfigured, ceasing to be earthly, that it may become heavenly in its measurement and in its speech. And so in the Bible, which is a Divine-human book, written for the ages, God has purposely veiled the times, at any rate the "days" of earthly reckoning. Even the day of our Lord's birth, and the day of His death, our chronologies cannot determine: we measure, we guess, but it is randomly, like the blinded men of Sodom, who wearied themselves to find the door. In Heaven's reckoning deeds are more than days. Time-beats by themselves are only broken silences, but put a soul among them, and you make songs, anthems, and all kinds of music. "In those days" may be a common Hebraism, but may it not be something more? may it not be an idiom of celestial speech, the heavenly way of referring to earthly things? At any rate we know this, that while Heaven is careful to give us the purpose, the promise, and the fulfilment, the Divine Spirit does not care to give us the exact moment when the promise became a realization. And that it is so shows that it is best it should be so. Silence sometimes may be better than speech.

But in saying all this we do not say that Heaven is unobservant of earthly times and seasons. They are a part of the Divine order, stamped on all lives, on all worlds. Our days and nights keep their alternate step; our seasons observe their processional order, singing in antiphonal responses; while our world, geared in with other worlds, strikes off our earthly years and days with an absolute precision. So, now, the time of the Advent has been Divinely chosen, for whole millenniums unalterably fixed; nor have the cries of Israel's impatient hopes been allowed to hurry forward the Divine purpose, so making it premature. But why should the Advent be so long delayed? In our off-handed way of thinking we might have supposed the Redeemer would have come directly after the Fall; and as far as Heaven was concerned, there was no reason why the Incarnation and the Redemption should not be effected immediately. The Divine Son was even then prepared to lay aside His glories, and to become incarnate. He might have been born of the Virgin of Eden, as well as of the Virgin of Galilee; and even then He might have offered unto God that perfect obedience by which the "many are made righteous." Why, then, this strange delay, as the months lengthen into years, and the years into centuries? The Patriarchs come and go, and only see the promise "afar off." Then come centuries of oppression, as Canaan is completely eclipsed by the dark shadow of Egypt; then the Exodus, the wanderings, the conquest. The Judges administer a rough-handed justice; Kings play with their little crowns; Prophets rebuke and prophesy, telling of the "Wonderful" who shall be; but still the Messiah delays His coming. Why this strange postponement of the world's hopes, as if prophecy dealt in illusions only? We find the answer in St. Paul's Epistle to the Galatians (chap. iv. 4). The "fulness of the time" was not yet come. The time was maturing, but was not yet ripe. Heaven was long ago prepared for an Incarnation, but Earth was not; and had the Advent occurred at an earlier stage of the world's history, it would have been an anachronism the age would have misunderstood. There must be a leading up to God's gifts, or His blessings cease to be blessings. The world must be prepared for the Christ, or virtually He is no Christ, no Saviour to them. The Christ must come into the world's mind as a familiar thought, He must come into the world's heart as a deep-felt need, before He can come as the Word Incarnate.

And when is this "fulness of the time"? "In the days of Herod, king of Judæa." Such is the phrase that now strikes the Divine hour, and leads in the dawn of a new dispensation. And what dark days were those to the Hebrew people, when on the throne of their David sat that Idumean shadow of the dread Cæsar! Their land swarms with Gentile hordes, and on the soil devoted to Jehovah rise stately, splendid temples, dedicated to strange gods. It is one irruption of Paganism, as if the Roman Pantheon had emptied itself upon the Holy Land. Nay, it seemed as if the Hebrew faith itself would become extinct, strangled by heathen fables, or at any rate that she would survive, only the ghost of her other self, walking like an apparition, with veiled face and sealed lips, amid the scenes of her former glories. "The days of Herod" were the Hebrew midnight, but they give us the Bright and Morning Star. And so upon this dial-plate of Scripture the great Herod, with all his royalties, is nothing more than the dark, empty shadow which marks a Divine hour, "the fulness of the time."

Israel's corporate life began with four centuries of silence and oppression, when Egypt gave them the doubled task, and Heaven grew strangely still, giving them neither voice nor vision. Is it but one of the chance repetitions of history that Israel's national life should end, too, with four hundred years of silence? for such is the coincidence, if, indeed, we may not call it something more. It is, however, just such a coincidence as the Hebrew mind, quick to trace resemblances and to discern signs, would grasp firmly and eagerly. It would revive their long-deferred and dying hopes, overlaying the near future with its gold. Possibly it was this very coincidence that now transformed their hope into expectation, and set their hearts listening for the advent of the Messiah. Did not Moses come when the task was doubled? And was not the four hundred years' silence broken by the thunders of the Exodus, as the I AM, once again asserting Himself, "sent redemption to His people"? And so, counting back their silent years since Heaven's last voice came to them through their prophet Malachi, they caught in its very silences a sound of hope, the footfall of the forerunner, and the voice of the coming Lord. But where, and how, shall the long silence be broken? We must go for our answer--and here, again, we see a correspondence between the new Exodus and the old--to the tribe of Levi, and to the house of Amram and Jochebed.

Residing in one of the priestly cities of the hill-country of Judæa--though not in Hebron, as is commonly supposed, for it is most unlikely that a name so familiar and sacred in the Old Testament would here be omitted in the New--was "a certain priest named Zacharias." Himself a descendant of Aaron, his wife, too, was of the same lineage; and besides being "of the daughters of Aaron," she bore the name of their ancestral mother, "Elisabeth." Like Abraham and Sarah, they were both well advanced in years, and childless. But if they were not allowed to have any lien upon posterity, throwing themselves forward into future generations, they made up the lack of earthly relationships by cultivating the heavenly. Forbidden, as they thought, to look forward down the lines of earthly hopes, they could and did look heavenward; for we read that they were both "righteous"--a word implying a Mosaic perfection--"walking in all the commandments and ordinances of the Lord blameless." We may not be able, perhaps, to give the precise distinction between "commandments" and "ordinances," for they were sometimes used interchangeably; but if, as the general use of the words allows us, we refer the "commandments" to the moral, and the "ordinances" to the ceremonial law, we see how wide is the ground they cover, embracing, as they do, the (then) "whole duty of man." Rarely, if ever, do the Scriptures speak in such eulogistic terms; and that they should here be applied to Zacharias and Elisabeth shows that they were advanced in saintliness, as well as in years. Possibly St. Luke had another object in view in giving us the portraits of these two pre-Advent Christians, completing in the next chapter the quarternion, by his mention of Simeon and Anna. It is somewhat strange, to say the least, that the Gentile Evangelist should be the one to give us this remarkable group--the four aged Templars, who, "when it was yet dark," rose to chant their matins and to anticipate the dawn. Whether the Evangelist intended it or not, his narrative salutes the Old, while it heralds the New dispensation, paying to that Old a high though unconscious tribute. It shows us that Hebraism was not yet dead; for if on its central stem, within the limited area of its Temple courts, such a cluster of beautiful lives could be found, who will tell the harvest of its outlying branches? Judaism was not altogether a piece of mechanism, elaborate and exact, with a soulless, metallic click of rites and ceremonies. It was an organism, living and sentient. It had nerves and blood. Possessed of a heart itself, it touched the hearts of its children. It gave them aspirations and inspirations without number; and even its shadows were the interpreters, as they were the creations, of the heavenly light. And if now it is doomed to pass away, outdated and superseded, it is not because it is bad, worthless; for it was a Divine conception, the "good" thing, preparing for and proclaiming God's "better thing." Judaism was the "glorious angel, keeping the gates of light;" and now, behold, she swings back the gates, welcomes the Morning, and herself then disappears.

It is the autumn service for the course of Abia--which is the eighth of the twenty-four courses into which the priesthood was divided--and Zacharias proceeds to Jerusalem, to perform whatever part of the service the lot may assign to him. It is probably the evening of the Sabbath--the presence of the multitude would almost imply that--and this evening the lot gives to Zacharias the coveted distinction---which could only come once in a lifetime--of burning incense in the Holy Place. At a given signal, between the slaying and the offering of the lamb, Zacharias, barefooted and robed in white, passes up the steps, accompanied by two assistants, one bearing a golden censer containing half a pound of the sweet-smelling incense, the other bearing a golden vessel of burning coals taken from the altar. Slowly and reverently they pass within the Holy Place, which none but Levites are permitted to enter; and having arranged the incense, and spread the live coals upon the altar, the assistants retire, leaving Zacharias alone--alone in the dim light of the seven-branched candlestick, alone beside that veil he may not uplift, and which hides from his sight the Holy of Holies, where God dwells "in the thick darkness." Such is the place, and such the supreme moment, when Heaven breaks the silence of four hundred years.

It is no concern of ours to explain the phenomenon that followed, or to tone down its supernatural elements. Given an Incarnation, and then the supernatural becomes not only probable, but necessary. Indeed, we could not well conceive of any new revelation without it; and instead of its being a weakness, a blemish on the page of Scripture, it is rather a proof of its heavenliness, a hall-mark that stamps its Divinity. Nor is there any need, believing as we do in the existence of intelligences other and higher than ourselves, that we apologize for the appearance of angels, here and elsewhere, in the story; such deference to Sadducean doubts is not required.

Suddenly, as Zacharias stands with uplifted hands, joining in the prayers offered by the silent "multitude" without, an angel appears. He stands "on the right side of the altar of incense," half-veiled by the fragrant smoke, which curling upwards, filled the place. No wonder that the lone priest is filled with "fear," and that he is "troubled"--a word implying an outward tremor, as if the very body shook with the unwonted agitation of the soul. The angel does not at first announce his name, but seeks rather to calm the heart of the priest, stilling its tumult with a "Fear not," as Jesus stilled the waters with His "Peace." Then he makes known his message, speaking in language most homely and most human: "Thy prayer is heard." Perhaps a more exact rendering would be, "Thy request was granted," for the substantive implies a specific prayer, while the verb indicates a "hearing" that becomes an "assenting." What the prayer was we may gather from the angel's words; for the whole message, both in its promise and its prophecy, is but an amplification of its first clause. To the Jew, childlessness was the worst of all bereavements. It implied, at least they thought so, the Divine displeasure; while it effectually cut them off from any personal share in those cherished Messianic hopes. To the Hebrew heart the message, "Unto you a son is born," was the music of a lower Gospel. It marked an epoch in their life-history; it brought the fulfilment of their desires, and a wealth of added dignities. And Zacharias had prayed, earnestly and long, that a son might be born to them; but the bright hope, with the years, had grown distant and dim, until at last it had dropped down beyond the horizon of their thoughts, and become an impossibility. But those prayers were heard, yea, and granted, too, in the Divine purpose; and if the answer has been delayed, it was that it might come freighted with a larger blessing.

But in saying that this was the specific prayer of Zacharias we do not wish to disparage his motives, confining his thoughts and aspirations within a circle so narrow and selfish. This lesser hope of offspring, like a satellite, revolved around the larger hope of a Messiah, and indeed grew out of it. It drew all its brightness and all its beauty from that larger hope, the hope that lighted up the dark Hebrew sky with the auroras of a new and fadeless dawn. When mariners "take the sun," as they call it, reading from its disc their longitudes, they bring it down to their horizon-level. They get the higher in the lower vision, and the real direction of their looks is not the apparent direction. And if Zacharias' thoughts and prayers seem to have an earthward drift, his soul looks higher than his speech; and if he looks along the horizon-level of earthly hopes, it is that he may read the heavenly promise. It is not a son that he is looking for, but the Son, the "Seed" in whom "all the families of the earth shall be blessed." And so, when the silent tongue regains its powers of speech, it gives its first and highest doxologies for that other Child, who is Himself the promised "redemption" and a "horn of salvation;" his own child he sets back, far back in the shadow (or rather the light) of Him whom he calls the "Lord." It is the near realization of both these hopes that the angel now announces.

A son shall be born to them, even in their advanced years, and they shall call his name "John," which means "The Lord is gracious." "Many will rejoice with them at his birth," for that birth will be the awakening of new hopes, the first hour of a new day. "Great in the sight of the Lord," he must be a Nazarite, abstaining wholly from "wine and strong drink"--the two Greek words including all intoxicants, however made. "Filled with the Holy Ghost from his mother's womb"-- that original bias or propensity to evil, if not obliterated, yet more than neutralized--he shall be the Elijah (in spirit and in power) of Malachi's prophecy, turning many of Israel's children "to the Lord their God." "Going before Him"--and the antecedent of "Him" must be "the Lord their God" of the preceding verse, so early is the purple of Divinity thrown around the Christ--he "shall turn the hearts of fathers to their children," restoring peace and order to domestic life, and the "disobedient" he shall incline "to walk in the wisdom of the just" (R.V.), bringing back the feet that have erred and slipped to "the paths of uprightness," which are the "ways of wisdom." In short, he shall be the herald, making ready a people prepared for the Lord, running before the royal chariot, proclaiming the coming One, and preparing His way, then leaving his own little footprints to disappear, thrown up in the chariot-dust of Him who was greater and mightier than he.

We can easily understand, even if we may not apologize for, the incredulity of Zacharias. There are crises in our life when, under profound emotion, Reason herself seems bewildered, and Faith loses her steadiness of vision. The storm of feeling throws the reflective powers into confusion, and thought becomes blurred and indistinct, and speech incoherent and wild. And such a crisis was it now, but intensified to the mind of Zacharias by all these additions of the supernatural. The vision, with its accessories of place and time, the message, so startling, even though so welcome, must necessarily produce a strange pertubation of soul; and what surprise need there be that when the priest does speak it is in the lisping accents of unbelief? Could it well have been otherwise? Peter "wist not that it was true which was done by the angel, but thought he saw a vision;" and though Zacharias has none of these doubts of unreality--it is to him no dream of the moment's ecstasy--still he is not yet aware of the rank and dignity of his angel-visitant, while he is perplexed at the message, which so directly contravenes both reason and experience. He does not doubt the Divine power, let it be observed, but he does seek for a sign that the angel speaks with Divine authority. "Whereby shall I know this?" he asks, reminding us by his question of Jacob's "Tell me thy name." The angel replies, in substance, "You ask whereby you may know this; that is, you wish to know by whose authority I declare this message to you. Well, I am Gabriel, that stand in the presence of God; and I was sent to speak unto you, and to bring you these good tidings. And since you ask for a sign, an endorsement of my message, you shall have one. I put the seal of silence upon your lips, and you shall not be able to speak until the day when these things shall come to pass, because you believed not my words." Then the vision ends; Gabriel returns to the songs and anthems of the skies, leaving Zacharias to carry, in awful stillness of soul, this new "secret of the Lord."

This infliction of dumbness upon Zacharias has generally been regarded as a rebuke and punishment for his unbelief; but if we refer to the parallel cases of Abraham and of Gideon, such is not Heaven's wonted answer to the request for a sign. We must understand it rather as the proof Zacharias sought, something at once supernatural and significant, that should help his stumbling faith. Such a sign, and a most effective one, it was. Unlike Gideon's dew, that would soon evaporate, leaving nothing but a memory, this was ever present, ever felt, at least until faith was exchanged for sight. Nor was it dumbness simply, for the word (ver. 22) rendered "speechless" implies inability to hear as well as inability to speak; and this, coupled with the fact mentioned in ver. 62, that "they made signs to him"--which they would scarcely have done could he have heard their voices--compels us to suppose that Zacharias had suddenly become deaf as well as dumb. Heaven put the seal of silence upon his lips and ears, that so its own voice might be more clear and loud; and so the profound silences of Zacharias' soul were but the blank spaces on which Heaven's sweet music was written.

How long the interview with the angel lasted we cannot tell. It must, however, have been brief; for at a given signal, the stroke of the Magrephah, the attendant priest would re-enter the Holy Place, to light the two lamps that had been left unlighted. And here we must look for the "tarrying" that so perplexed the multitude, who were waiting outside, in silence, for the benediction of the incensing priest. Re-entering the Holy Place, the attendant finds Zacharias smitten as by a sudden paralysis--speechless, deaf, and overcome by emotion. What wonder that the strange excitement makes them oblivious of time, and, for the moment, all-forgetful of their Temple duties! The priests are in their places, grouped together on the steps leading up to the Holy Place; the sacrificing priest has ascended the great brazen altar; ready to cast the pieces of the slain lamb upon the sacred fire; the Levites stand ready with their trumpets and their psalms--all waiting for the priests who linger so long in the Holy Place. At length they appear, taking up their position on the top of the steps, above the rows of priests, and above the silent multitude. But Zacharias cannot pronounce the usual benediction to-day. The "Jehovah bless thee and keep thee" is unsaid; the priest can only "beckon" to them, perhaps laying his finger on the silent lips, and then pointing to the silent heavens--to them indeed silent, but to himself all vocal now.

And so the mute priest, after the days of his ministration are completed, returns to his home in the hill-country, to wait the fulfilment of the promises, and out of his deep silences to weave a song that should be immortal; for the Benedictus, whose music girdles the world to-day, before it struck upon the world's ear and heart, had, through those quiet months, filled the hushed temple of his soul, lifting up the priest and the prophet among the poets, and passing down the name of Zacharias as one of the first sweet singers of the new Israel.

And so the Old meets, and merges into the New; and at the marriage it is the speaking hands of the mute priest that join together the two Dispensations, as each gives itself to the other, never more to be put asunder, but to be "no longer twain, but one," one Purpose, one Plan, one Divine Thought, one Divine Word.

## CHAPTER III - THE GOSPEL PSALMS

Unlike modern church builders, St. Luke sets his chancel by the porch. No sooner have we passed through the vestibule of his Gospel than we find ourselves within a circle of harmonies. On the one side are Zacharias and Simeon, the one chanting his Benedictus, and the other his Nunc Dimittis. Facing them, as if in antiphon, are Elisabeth and Mary, the one singing her Beatitude, and the other her Magnificat; while overhead, in the frescoed and star-lighted sky, are vast multitudes of the heavenly host enriching the Advent music with their Glorias. What means this grand irruption of song? and why is St. Luke, the Gentile Evangelist, the only one who repeats to us these Hebrew psalms? At first it would seem as if their natural place would be as a prelude to St. Matthew's Gospel, which is the Gospel of the Hebrews. But strangely enough, St. Matthew passes them by in silence, just as he omits the two angelic visions. St. Matthew is evidently intent on one thing. Beginning a New Testament, as he is, he seems especially anxious that there shall be no rent or even seam between the Old and the New; and so, in his first pages, after giving us the genealogy, running the line of descent up to Abraham, he laces up the threads of his narrative with the broken-off threads of the old prophecies, so that the written Word may be a vestment of the Incarnate Word, which shall be "without seam, woven from the top throughout." And so really the Advent hymns would not have suited St. Matthew's purpose. Their ring would not have been in accord with the tone of his story; and had we found them in his first chapters, we should instinctively have felt that they were out of place, as if we saw a rose blossoming on a widespread oak.

St. Luke, however, is portraying the Son of man. Coming to redeem humanity, he shows how He was first born into that humanity, making His advent in a purely human fashion. And so the two conceptions form a fit beginning for his Gospel; while over the Divine Birth and Childhood he lingers reverently and long, paying it however, only the homage Heaven had paid it before. Then, too, was there not a touch of poetry about our Evangelist? Tradition has been almost unanimous in saying that he was a painter; and certainly in the grouping of his figures, and his careful play upon the lights and shadows, we can discover traces of his artistic skill, in word-painting at any rate. His was evidently a soul attuned to harmonies, quick to discern any accordant or discordant strains. Nor must we forget that St. Luke's mind is open to certain occult influences, whose presence we may indeed detect, but whose power we are not able to gauge. As we have already seen, it was the manifold narratives of anonymous writers that first moved him to take up the pen of the historian; and to those narratives we doubtless owe something of the peculiar cast and colouring of St. Luke's story. It is with the Nativity that tradition would be most likely to take liberties. The facts of the Advent, strange enough in themselves, would at the hands of rumour undergo a process of developing, like the magnified and somewhat grotesque shadows of himself the traveller casts on Alpine mists. It was doubtless owing to these enlargements and distortions of tradition that St. Luke was led to speak of the Advent so fully, going into the minutiæ of detail, and inserting, as is probable, from the Hebrew tone of these first two chapters, the account as given orally, or written, by some members of the Holy Family.

It must be admitted that to some inquiring and honest minds these Advent psalms have been a difficulty, an enigma, if not a stumbling-block. As the bells that summon to worship half-deafen the ear of the worshipper on a too near approach, or they become merely a confused and unmeaning noise if he climbs up into the belfry and watches the swing of their brazen lips, so this burst of music in our third Gospel has been too loud for certain sensitive ears. It has shaken somewhat the foundations of their faith. They think it gives an unreality, a certain mythical flavour, to the story, that these four pious people, who have always led a quiet, prosaic kind of life, should now suddenly break out into impromptu songs, and when these are ended lapse again into complete silence, like the century plant, which throws out a solitary blossom in the course of a hundred years. And so they come to regard these Hebrew psalms as an interpolation, an afterthought, thrown into the story for effect. But let us not forget that we are dealing now with Eastern mind, which is naturally vivacious, imaginative, and highly poetical. Even our colder tongue, in this glacial period of nineteenth-century civilization, is full of poetry. The language of common every-day life--to those who have ears to hear--is full of tropes, metaphors, and parables. Take up the commonest words of daily speech, and put them to your ear, and they will sing like shells from the sea. There are whole poems in them--epics, idylls, of every sort; and let our colder speech get among the sweet influences of religion, and like the iceberg adrift in the Gulf Stream, it loses its rigidity and frigidity at once, melting in liquid, rhythmic measures, throwing itself away in hymns and jubilates. The fact is, the world is full of music. As the Sage of Chelsea said, "See deep enough, and you see musically, the heart of Nature being everywhere music if you can only reach it." And it is so. You can touch nothing but there are harmonies slumbering within it, or itself is a stray note of some grander song. Dead wood from the forest, dead ore from the mine, dead tusks of the beast--these are the "base things" that strike our music; and only put a mind within them, and a living soul with a living touch before them, and you have songs and anthems without number.

But to Eastern minds poetry was a sort of native language. Its inspiration was in the air. Their ordinary speech was ornate and efflorescent, throwing itself out in simile and hyperbole. It only needed some small excitement, and they fell naturally into the couplet form of utterance. Even to-day the children swing under the mulberry-trees to songs and choruses; hucksters extol their wares in measured verse; and the Bethany fruit-girl sings in the market, "O lady, take of our fruit, without money and without price: it is yours; take all that you will"! And so it need not surprise us, much less trouble us, that Simeon and Elisabeth, Zacharias and Mary, should each speak in measured cadences. Their speech blossomed with flowers of rhetoric, just as naturally as their hills were ablaze with daisies and anemones. Besides, they were now under the direct inspiration of the Holy Spirit. We read, "Elisabeth was filled with the Holy Ghost;" and again, Zacharias was "filled with the Holy Ghost;" Simeon "came in the Spirit into the Temple;" while Mary now seemed to live in one conscious, constant inspiration. It is said that "a poet is born, not made;" and if he be not thus "free-born" no "great sum," either of gold or toil, will ever pass him up within the favoured circle. And the same is true of the poet's creations. Sacred hymns are not the product of the unaided intellect. They do not come at the bidding of any human will. They are inspirations. There is the overshadowing of the Holy Spirit in their conception. The human mind, heart, and lips are but the instrument, a kind of Æolian lyre, played upon by the Higher Breath, which comes and goes--how, the singer himself can never tell; for

"In the song
The singer has been lost."

It was when "filled with the Spirit" that Bezaleel put into his gold and silver the thoughts of God; it was when the Spirit of God came upon him that Balaam took up his parable, putting into stately numbers Israel's forward march and endless victories. And so the sacred psalm is the highest type of inspiration; it is a voice from no earthly Parnassus, but from the Mount of God itself--the nearest approach to the celestial harmonies, the harmonies of that city whose very walls are poetry, and whose gates are praise.

And so, after all, it was but fitting and perfectly natural that the Gospel that Heaven had been so long time preparing should break upon the world amid the harmonies of music. Instead of apologizing for its presence, as if it were but an interlude improvised for the occasion, we should have noted and mourned its absence, as when one mourns for "the sound of a voice that is still." When the ark of God was brought up from Baale Judah it was encircled with one wide wreath of music, a travelling orchestra of harps and psalteries, castanets and cymbals; and as now that Ark of all the promises is borne across from the Old to the New Dispensation, as the promise becomes a fulfilment, and the hope a realization, shall there not be the voice of song and gladness? Our sense of the fitness of things expects it; Heaven's law of the harmonies demands it; and had there not been this burst of praise and song, we should have listened for the very stones to cry out, rebuking the strange silence. But the voice was not silent. The singers were there, in their places; and they sang, not because they would, but because they must. A heavenly pressure, a sweet constraint, was upon them. If Wealth lays down her tribute of gold, with frankincense and myrrh, Poetry weaves for the Holy Child her beautiful songs, and crowns Him with her fadeless amaranth; and so around the earthly cradle of the Lord, as around His heavenly throne, we have angelic songs, and "the voices of harpers, harping with their harps."

Turning now to the four Gospel-psalmists--not, however, to analyze, but to listen to their song--we meet first with Elisabeth. This aged daughter of Aaron, and wife of Zacharias, as we have seen, resided somewhere in the hill-country of Judæa, in their quiet, childless home. Righteous, blameless, and devout, religion to her was no mere form; it was her life. The Temple services, with which she was closely associated, were to her no cold clatter of dead rites; they were realities, full of life and full of music, as her heart had caught their deeper meaning. But the Temple, while it attracted her thoughts and hopes, did not enclose them; its songs and services were to her but so many needles, swinging round on their marble pivot, and pointing beyond to the Living God, the God who dwelt not in temples made with hands, but who, then as now, inhabits the purified temple of the heart. Long past the time when motherly hopes were possible, the fretting had subsided, and her spirit had become, first acquiescent, then quiescent. But these hopes had been miraculously rekindled, as she slowly read the vision of the Temple from the writing-table of her dumb husband. The shadow of her dial had gone backward; and instead of its being evening, with gathering shadows and ever-lessening light, she found herself back in the glow of the morning, her whole life lifted to a higher level. She was to be the mother, if not of the Christ, yet of His forerunner. And so the Christ was near at hand, this was certain, and she had the secret prophecy and promise of His advent. And Elisabeth finds herself exalted--borne up, as it were, into Paradise, among visions and such swells of hosannas that she cannot utter them; they are too sweet and too deep for her shallow words. Was it not this, the storm of inward commotion, that drove her to hide herself for the five months? Heaven has come so near to her, such thoughts and visions fill her mind, that she cannot bear the intrusions and jars of earthly speech; and Elisabeth passes into a voluntary seclusion and silence, keeping strange company with the dumb and deaf Zacharias.

At length the silence is broken by the unexpected appearance of her Nazareth relative. Mary, fresh from her hasty journey, "entered into the house of Zacharias and saluted Elisabeth." It is a singular expression, and evidently denotes that the visit of the Virgin was altogether unlooked for. There is no going out to meet the expected guest, as was common in Eastern hospitalities; there was even no welcome by the gate; but like an apparition, Mary passes within, and salutes the surprised Elisabeth, who returns the salutation, not, however, in any of the prescribed forms, but in a benediction of measured verse:--

> *"Blessed art thou among women,*
> *And blessed is the fruit of thy womb!*
> *And whence is this to me,*
> *That the mother of my Lord should come unto me?*
> *For, behold, when the voice of thy salutation came into mine ears*
> *The babe leaped in my womb for joy.*
> *And blessed is she that believed,*
> *For there shall be a fulfilment of the things which have been spoken to her from the Lord."*

The whole canticle--and it is Hebrew poetry, as its parallelisms and strophes plainly show--is one apostrophe to the Virgin. Striking the key-note in its "Blessed art thou," the "thou" moves on, distinct and clear, amid all variations, to the end, reaching its climax in its central phrase, "The mother of my Lord." As one hails the morning star, not so much for its own light as for its promise of the greater light, the dayspring that is behind it, so Elisabeth salutes the morning star of the new dawn, at the same time paying homage to the Sun, whose near approach the star heralds. And why is Mary so blessed among women? Why should Elisabeth, forgetting the dignity of years, bow so deferentially before her youthful relative, crowning her with a song? Who has informed her of the later revelation at Nazareth? It is not necessary to suppose that Elisabeth, in her seclusion, had received any corroborative vision, or even that she had been supernaturally enlightened. Had she not the message the angel delivered to Zacharias? and was not that enough? Her son was to be the Christ's forerunner, going, as the angel said, before the face of "the Lord." Three times had the angel designated the Coming One as "the Lord," and this was the word she had carried with her into her seclusion. What it meant she did not fully understand; but she knew this, that it was He of whom Moses and the prophets had written, the Shiloh, the Wonderful; and as she put together the detached Scriptures, adding, doubtless, some guesses of her own, the Christ grew as a conception of her mind and the desire of her heart into such colossal proportions that even her own offspring was dwarfed in comparison, and the thoughts of her own maternity became, in the rush of greater thoughts, only as the stray eddies of the stream. That such was the drift of her thoughts during the five quiet months is evident; for now, taught of the Holy Ghost that her kinswoman is to be the mother of the expected One, she greets the unborn Christ with her lesser Benedictus. Like the old painters, she puts her aureole of song around the mother's head, but it is easy to see that the mother's honours are but the far-off reflections from the Child. Is Mary blessed among women? it is not because of any wealth of native grace, but because of the fruit of her womb. Does Elisabeth throw herself right back in the shade, asking almost abjectly, "Whence is this to me?" it is because, like the centurion, she feels herself unworthy that even the unborn "Lord" should come under her roof. And so, while this song is really an ode to the Virgin, it is virtually Elisabeth's salute of the Christ who is to be, a salute in which her own offspring takes part, for she speaks of his "leaping" in her womb, as if he were a participant in her joy, interpreting its movements as a sort of "Hail, Master!" The canticle thus becomes invested with a higher significance. Its words say much, but suggest more. It carries our thought out from the seen to the unseen, from the mother to the Holy Child, and Elisabeth's song thus becomes the earliest "Hosannah to the Son of David," the first prelude to the unceasing anthems that are to follow.

*Henry Burton*

It will be observed that in the last line the song drops out of the first and the second personals into the third. It is no longer the frequent "thy," "thou," "my," but "she:" "Happy is she that believed." Why is this change? Why does she not end as she began--"Happy art thou who hast believed"? Simply because she is no longer speaking of Mary alone. She puts herself as well within this beatitude, and at the same time states a general law, how faith ripens into a harvest of blessedness. The last line thus becomes the "Amen" of the song. It reaches up among the eternal "Verilies," and sets them ringing. It speaks of the Divine faithfulness, out of which and within which human faith grows as an acorn within its cup. And who could have better right to sing of the blessedness of faith, and to introduce this New Testament grace--not unknown in the Old Testament, but unnamed--as she who was herself such an exemplification of her theme? How calmly her own heart reposed on the Divine word! How before her far-seeing and foreseeing vision valleys were exalted, mountains and hills made low, that the way of the Lord might appear! Elisabeth sees the unseen Christ, lays before Him the tribute of her song, the treasures of her affection and devotion; even before the Magi had saluted the Child-King, Elisabeth's heart had gone out to meet Him with her hosannas, and her lips had greeted Him "My Lord." Elisabeth is thus the first singer of the New Dispensation; and though her song is more a bud of poetry than the ripe, blossomed flower, enfolding rather than unfolding its hidden beauties, it pours out a fragrance sweeter than spikenard on the feet of the Coming One, while it throws around Him the purple of new royalties.

Turning now to the song of Mary, our Magnificat, we come to poetry of a higher order. Elisabeth's introit was evidently spoken under intense feeling; it was the music of the storm; for "she lifted up her voice with a loud cry." Mary's song, on the other hand, is calm, the hymn of the "quiet resting-place." There is no unnatural excitement now, no inward perturbation, half mental and half physical. Mary was perfectly self-possessed, as if the spell of some Divine "peace" were upon her soul; and as Elisabeth's "loud cry" ceased, Mary "said"--so it reads--her response. But if the voice was lower, the thought was higher, more majestic in its sweep. Elisabeth's song was on the lower heights. "The mother of my Lord," this was its starting-place, and the centre around which its circles were described; and though its wings beat now and again against the infinities, it does not attempt to explore them, but returns timidly to its nest. But Elisabeth's loftiest reach is Mary's starting-point; her song begins where the song of Elisabeth ends. Striking her key-note in the first line, "The Lord," this is her one thought, the Alpha and Omega of her psalm. We call it the Magnificat; it is a Te Deum, full of suggested doxologies. Beginning with the personal, as she is almost compelled to do by the intense personality of Elizabeth's song, Mary hastes to gather up the eulogies bestowed upon herself, and to bear them forward to Him who merits all praise, as He is the Source of all blessing. Her soul "magnifies the Lord," not that she, by any weak words of hers, can add to His greatness, which is infinite, but even she may give the Lord a wider place within her thoughts and heart; and whoever is silent, her song shall make "the voice of His praise to be heard." Her spirit "hath rejoiced in God her Saviour," and why? Has He not looked down on her low estate, and done great things for her? "The bondmaid of the Lord," as she a second time calls herself, glorying in her bonds, such is her promotion and exaltation that all generations shall call her blessed. Then, with a beautiful effacement of self, which henceforth is not even to be a mote playing in the sunshine, she sings of Jehovah--His holiness, His might, His mercy, His faithfulness.

Mary's song, both in its tone and language, belongs to the Old Dispensation. Thoroughly Hebraic, and all inlaid with Old Testament quotations, it is the swan-song of Hebraism. There is not a single phrase, perhaps not a single word, that bears a distinctive Christian stamp; for the "Saviour" of the first strophe is the "Saviour" of the Old Testament, and not of the New, with a national rather than an evangelical meaning. The heart of the singer is turned to the past rather than to the future. Indeed, with the solitary exception, how all generations shall call her blessed, there is no passing glimpse into the future. Instead of speaking of the Expected One, and blessing "the fruit of her womb," her song does not even mention Him. She tells how the Lord hath done great things for her, but what those "great things" are she does not say; she might, as far as her own song tells us, be simply a later Miriam, singing of some family or personal deliverance, a salvation which was one of a thousand. A true daughter of Israel, she dwells among her own people, and her very broadest vision sees in her offspring no world-wide blessing, only a Deliverer for Israel, His servant. Does she speak of mercy? it is not that wider mercy that like a sea laves every shore, bearing on its still bosom a redeemed humanity; it is the narrower mercy "toward Abraham and his seed for ever." Mary recognizes the unity of the Godhead, but she does not recognize the unity, the brotherhood of man. Her thought goes back to "our fathers," but there it halts; the shrunken sinew of Hebrew thought could not cross the prior centuries, to find the world's common father in Paradise. But in saying this we do not depreciate Mary's song. It is, and ever will be, the Magnificat, great in its theme, and great in its conception. Following the flight of Hannah's song, and making use of its wings at times, it soars far above, and sweeps far beyond its original. Not even David sings of Jehovah in more exalted strains. The holiness of God, the might supreme above all powers, the faithfulness that cannot forget, and that never fails to fulfil, the Divine choice and exaltation of the lowly--these four chief chords of the Hebrew Psalter Mary strikes with a touch that is sweet as it is clear.

Mary sang of God; she did not sing of the Christ. Indeed, how could she? The Christ to be was part of her own life, part of herself; how could she sing His praise without an appearance of egotism and self-gratulation? There are times when silence is more eloquent than speech; and Mary's silence about the Christ was but the silence of the winged cherubim, as they bend over the ark, beholding and feeling a mystery they can neither know nor tell. It was the hush inspired by a near and glorious presence. And so the Magnificat, while it tells us nothing of the Christ, swings our thoughts around towards Him, sets us listening for His advent; and Mary's silence is but the setting for the Incarnate WORD.

The song of Zacharias follows that of Mary, not only in the order of time, but also in its sequence of thought. It forms a natural postlude to the Magnificat, while both are but different parts of one song, this earliest "Messiah." It is something remarkable that our first three Christian hymns should have their birth in the same nameless city of Judah, in the same house, and probably in the same chamber; for the room, which now is filled with the priest's relatives, and where Zacharias breaks the long silence with his prophetic Benedictus, is doubtless the same room where Elisabeth chanted her greeting, and Mary sang her Magnificat. The song of Mary circled about the throne of Jehovah, nor could she leave that throne, even to tell the great things the Lord had done for her. Zacharias, coming down from his mount of vision and of silence, gives us a wider outlook into the Divine purpose. He sings of the "salvation" of the Lord; and salvation, as it is the key-note of the heavenly song, is the key-note of the Benedictus. Does he bless the Lord, the God of Israel? it is because He has "visited" (or looked upon) "His people, and wrought redemption for" them; it is because He has provided an abundant salvation, or a "horn of salvation," as he calls it. Has God remembered His covenant, "the oath He sware unto Abraham"? has He "shown mercy towards their fathers"? that mercy and faithfulness are seen in this wonderful salvation--a salvation "from their enemies," and "from the hand of all that hate" them. Is his child to be "the prophet of the Most High," going "before the face of the Lord," and making "ready His ways"? it is that he may "give knowledge of" this "salvation," in "the remission of sins." Then the psalm ends, falling back on its key-note; for who are they who "sit in darkness and the shadow of death," but a people lost? And who is the Day-spring who visits them from on high, who shines upon their darkness, turning it into day, and guiding their lost feet into the way of peace, but the Redeemer, the Saviour, whose name is "Wonderful"? And so the Benedictus, while retaining the form and the very language of the Old, breathes the spirit of the New Dispensation. It is a fragrant breeze, blowing off from the shores of a new, and now near world, a world already seen and possessed by Zacharias in the anticipations of faith. The Saviour whose advent the inspired priest proclaims is no mere national deliverer, driving back those eagles of Rome, and rebuilding the throne of his father David. He might be all that--for even prophetic vision had not sweep of the whole horizon; it only saw the little segment of the circle that was Divinely illumined--but to Zacharias He was more, a great deal more. He was a Redeemer as well as Deliverer; and a "redemption"--for it was a Temple word--meant a price laid down, something given. The salvation of which Zacharias speaks is not simply a deliverance from our political enemies, and from the hand of all that hate us. It was a salvation higher, broader, deeper than that, a "salvation" that reached to the profound depths of the human soul, and that sounded its jubilee there, in the remission of sin and deliverance from sin. Sin was the enemy to be vanquished and destroyed, and the shadow of death was but the shadow of sin. And Zacharias sings of this great redemption that leads to salvation, while the salvation leads into the Divine peace, to "holiness and righteousness," and a service that is "without fear."

The ark of Israel was borne by four of the sons of Kohath; and here this ark of song and prophecy is borne of four sweet singers, the sexes dividing the honours equally. We have listened to the songs of three, and have seen how they follow each other in a regular, rhythmic succession, the thought moving forward and outward in ever-widening circles. Where is the fourth? and what is the burden of his song? It is heard within the precincts of the Temple, as the parents bring the Child Jesus, to introduce Him to the visible sanctities of religion, and to consecrate Him to the Lord. It is the Nunc Dimittis of the aged Simeon. He too sings of "salvation," "Thy salvation" as he calls it. It is the "consolation of Israel" he has looked for so ardently and so long, and which the Holy Ghost had assured him he should behold before his promotion to the higher temple. But the vision of Simeon was wider than that of Zacharias, as that in turn was wider and clearer than the vision of Mary. Zacharias saw the spiritual nature of this near salvation, and he described it in words singularly deep and accurate; but its breadth he did not seem to realize. The theocracy was the atmosphere in which he lived and moved; and even his vision was theocratic, and so somewhat narrow. His Benedictus was for the "God of Israel," and the "redemption" he sang was "for His people." The "horn of salvation" is "for us;" and all through his psalm these first personal pronouns are frequent and emphatic, as if he would still insulate this favoured people, and give them a monopoly even of "redemption." The aged Simeon, however, stands on a higher Pisgah. His is the nearer and the clearer vision. Standing as he does in the Court of the Gentiles, and holding in his arms the Infant Christ, "the Lord's Christ," he sees in Him a Saviour for humanity, "the Lamb of God, who taketh away the sin of the world." Still, as ever, "the glory of God's people Israel," but likewise "a light for the unveiling of the Gentiles." Like the sentry who keeps watch through the night till the sunrise, Simeon has been watching and longing for the Day-spring from on high, reading from the stars of promise the wearing of the night, and with the music of fond hopes "keeping his heart awake till dawn of morn." Now at length the consummation, which is the consolation, comes. Simeon sees in the Child Jesus the world's hope and Light, a salvation "prepared before the face of all people." And seeing this, he sees all he desires. Earth can give no brighter vision, no deeper joy, and all his request is--

*"Now lettest Thou Thy servant depart, O Lord,*
*According to Thy word, in peace;*
*For mine eyes have seen Thy salvation."*

And so the four psalms of the Gospels form in reality but one song, the notes rising higher and still higher, until they reach the very pinnacle of the new temple--God's purpose and plan of redemption; that temple whose altar is a cross, and whose Victim is "the Lamb slain from the foundation of the world;" that temple where courts and dividing-lines all disappear; where the Holiest of all lies open to a redeemed humanity, and Jews and Gentiles, bond and free, old and young, are alike "kings and priests unto God." And so the Gospel psalms throw back, as it were, in a thousand echoes, the Glorias of the Advent angels, as they sing--

*"Glory to God in the highest,*
*And on earth peace."*

And what is this but earth's prelude or rehearsal for the heavenly song, as all nations, and kindreds, and peoples, and tongues, falling down before the Lamb in the midst of the throne, sing, "Salvation unto our God, which sitteth upon the throne, and unto the Lamb"?

## CHAPTER IV – THE VIRGIN MOTHER

The Beautiful Gate of the Jewish Temple opened into the "Court of the Women"--so named from the fact that they were not allowed any nearer approach towards the Holy Place. And as we open the gate of the third Gospel we enter the Court of the Women; for more than any other Evangelist, St. Luke records their loving and varied ministries. Perhaps this is owing to his profession, which naturally would bring him into more frequent contact with feminine life. Or perhaps it is a little Philippian colour thrown into his Gospel; for we must not forget that St. Luke had been left by the Apostle Paul at Philippi, to superintend the Church that had been cradled in the prayers of the "river-side" women. It may be a tinge of Lydia's purple; or to speak more broadly and more literally, it may be the subtle, unconscious influences of that Philippian circle that have given a certain feminity to our third Gospel. St. Luke alone gives us the psalms of the three women, Anna, Elisabeth, and Mary; he alone gives us the names of Susanna and Joanna, who ministered to Christ of their substance; he alone gives us that Galilean idyll, where the nameless "woman" bathes His feet with tears, and at the same time rains a hot rebuke on the cold civilities of the Pharisee, Simon; he alone tells of the widow of Zarephath, who welcomed and saved a prophet men were seeking to slay; he alone tells us of the widow of Nain, of the woman bent with infirmity, and of the woman grieving over her lost piece of silver. And as St. Luke opens his Gospel with woman's tribute of song, so in his last chapter he paints for us that group of women, constant amid man's inconstancies, coming ere the break of day, to wrap around the body of the dead Christ the precious and fragrant offering of devotion. So, in this Paradise Restored, do Eve's daughters roll back the reproach of their mother. But ever first and foremost among the women of the Gospels we must place the Virgin Mother, whose character and position in the Gospel story we are now to consider.

We need not stay to discuss the question--perhaps we ought not to stay even to give it a passing notice--whether there might have been an Incarnation even had there been no sin. It is not an impossible, it is not an improbable supposition, that the Christ would have come into the world even had man kept his first estate of innocence and bliss. But then it would have been the "Christ" simply, and not Jesus Christ. He would have come into the world, not as its Redeemer, but as the Son and Heir, laying tribute on all its harvests; He would have come as the flower and crown of a perfected humanity, to show the possibilities of that humanity, its absolute perfections. But leaving the "might-have-beens," in whose tenuous spaces there is room for the nebulæ of fancies and of guesses without number, let us narrow our vision within the horizon of the real, the actual.

Given the necessity for an Incarnation, there are two modes in which that Incarnation may be brought about--by creation, or by birth. The first Adam came into the world by the creative act of God. Without the intervention of second causes, or any waiting for the slow lapse of time, God spake, and it was done. Will Scripture repeat itself here, in the new Genesis? and will the second Adam, coming into the world to repair the ruin wrought by the first, come as did the first? We can easily conceive such an advent to be possible; and if we regarded simply the analogies of the case, we might even suppose it to be probable. But how different a Christ it would have been! He might still have been bone of our bone, flesh of our flesh; He might have spoken the same truths, in the same speech and tone; but He must have lived apart from the world. It would not be our humanity that He wore; it would only be its shadow, its semblance, playing before our minds like an illusion. No, the Messiah must not be simply a second Adam; He must be the Son of man, and He cannot become Humanity's Son except by a human birth. Any other advent, even though it had satisfied the claims of reason, would have failed to satisfy those deeper voices of the heart. And so, on the first pages of Scripture, before Eden's gate is shut and locked by bolts of flame, Heaven signifies its intention and decision. The coming One, who shall bruise the serpent's head, shall be the woman's "Seed"--the Son of woman, that so He may become more truly the Son of man; while later a strange expression finds its way into the sacred prophecy, how "a Virgin shall conceive, and bear a son." It is true these words primarily might have a local meaning and fulfilment--though what that narrower meaning was no one can tell with any approach to certainty; but looking at the singularity of the expression, and coupling it with the story of the Advent, we can but see in it a deeper meaning and a wider purpose. Evidently it was that the virgin-conception might strike upon the world's ear and become a familiar thought, and that it might throw backwards across the pages of the Old Testament the shadow of the Virgin Mother. We have already seen how the thought of a Messianic motherhood had dropped deep within the heart of the Hebrew people, awaking hopes, and prayers, and all sorts of beautiful dreams--dreams, alas! that vanished with the years, and hopes that blossomed but to fade. But now the hour is coming, that supreme hour for which the centuries have all been waiting. The forerunner is already announced, and in twelve short weeks he who loved to call himself a Voice will break the strange silence of that Judæan home. Whence will come his Lord, who shall be "greater than he"? Where shall we find the Mother-elect, for whom such honours have been reserved--honours such as no mortal has ever yet borne, and as none will ever bear again? St. Luke tells us, "Now in the sixth month the angel Gabriel was sent from God unto a city of Galilee, named Nazareth, to a virgin betrothed to a man whose name was Joseph, of the house of David; and the virgin's name was Mary" (R.V.). And so the Mother-designate takes her place in this firmament of Scripture, silently and serenely as a morning star, which indeed she is; for she shines in a borrowed splendour, taking her glories all from Him around whom she revolves, from Him who was both her Son and her Sun.

It will be seen in the above verse how particular the Evangelist is in his topographical reference, putting a kind of emphasis upon the name which now appears for the first time upon the pages of Scripture. When we remember how Nazareth was honoured by the angel visit; how it was, not the chance, but the chosen home of the Christ for thirty years; how it watched and guarded the Divine Infancy, throwing into that life its powerful though unconscious influences, even as the dead soil throws itself forward and upward into each separate flower and farthest leaf; when we remember how it linked its own name with the Name of Jesus, becoming almost a part of it; how it wrote its name upon the cross, then handing it down to the ages as the name and watchword of a sect that should conquer the world, we must admit that Nazareth is by no means "the least among the cities" of Israel. And yet we search in vain through the Old Testament for the name of Nazareth. History, poetry, and prophecy alike pass it by in silence. And so the Hebrew mind, while rightly linking the expected One with Bethlehem, never associated the Christ with Nazareth. Indeed, its moralities had become so questionable and proverbial that while the whole of Galilee was too dry a ground to grow a prophet, Nazareth was thought incapable of producing "any good thing." Was, then, the Nazareth chapter of the Christ-life an afterthought of the Divine Mind, like the marginal reading of an author's proof, put in to fill up a blank or to be a substitute for some erasure? Not so. It had been in the Divine Mind from the beginning; yea, it had been in the authorized text, though men had not read it plainly. It is St. Matthew who first calls our attention to it. Writing, as he does, mainly for Hebrew readers, he is constantly looping up his story with the Old Testament prophecies; and speaking of the return from Egypt, he says they "came and dwelt in a city called Nazareth: that it might be fulfilled which was spoken by the prophets, that He should be called a Nazarene." We said just now that the name of Nazareth was not found in the Old Testament. But if we do not find the proper name, we find the word which is identical with the name. It is now regarded by competent authorities as proved that the Hebrew name for Nazareth was Netser. Taking now this word in our mind, and turning to Isaiah xi. 1, we read, "And there shall come forth a shoot out of the stock of Jesse, and a branch [Netser] out of his roots shall bear fruit: and the Spirit of the Lord shall rest upon Him." Here, then, evidently, is the prophetic voice to which St. Matthew refers; and one little word--the name of Nazareth--becomes the golden link binding in one the Prophecies and the Gospels.

Returning to our main subject, it is to this secluded, and somewhat despised city of Nazareth the angel Gabriel is now sent, to announce the approaching birth of Christ. St. Luke, in his nominative way of speaking, says he came "to a Virgin betrothed to a man whose name was Joseph, of the house of David; and the Virgin's name was Mary." It is difficult for us to form an unbiased estimate of the character before us, as our minds are feeling the inevitable recoil from Roman assumptions. We are confused with the childish prattle of their Ave Marias; we are amused at their dogmas of Immaculate Conceptions and Ever Virginities; we are surprised and shocked at their apotheosis of the Virgin, as they lift her to a throne practically higher than that of her Son, worshipped in devouter homage, supplicated with more earnest and more frequent prayers, and at the blasphemies of their Mariolatry, which make her supreme on earth and supreme in heaven. This undue exaltation of the Virgin Mother, which becomes an adoration pure and simple, sends our Protestant thought with a violent swing to the extreme of the other side, considerably over the line of the "golden mean." And so we find it hard to dissociate in our minds the Virgin Mother from these Marian assumptions and divinations; for which, however, she herself is in no way responsible, and against which she would be the first to protest. Seen only through these Romish haloes, and atmospheres highly incensed, her very name has been distorted, and her features, spoiled of all grace and sweet serenity, have ceased to be attractive. But this is not just. If Rome weights one scale with crowns, and sceptres, and piles of imperial purple, we need not load down the other with our prejudices, satires, and negations. Two wrongs will not make a right. It is neither on the crest of the wave, nor yet in the deep trough of the billows, that we shall find the mean sea-level, from which we can measure all heights, running out our lines even among the stars. Can we not find that mean sea-level now, hushing alike the voices of adulation and of depreciation? Laying aside the traditions of antiquity and the legends of scribulous monks, laying aside, too, the coloured glasses of our prejudice, with which we have been wont to protect our eyes from the glare of Roman suns, may we not get a true portraiture of the Virgin Mother, in all the native naturalness of Scripture? We think we can.

She comes upon us silently and suddenly, emerging from an obscurity whose secrets we cannot read. No mention is made of her parents; tradition only has supplied us with their names--Joachim and Anna. But whether Joachim or not, it is certain that her father was of the tribe of Judah, and of the house of David. Having this fact to guide us, and also another fact, that Mary was closely related to Elisabeth--though not necessarily her cousin--who was of the tribe of Levi and a daughter of Aaron, then it becomes probable, at least, that the unnamed mother of the Virgin was of the tribe of Levi, and so the connecting link between the houses of Levi and Judah--a probability which receives an indirect but strong confirmation in the fact that Nazareth was intimately connected with Jerusalem and the Temple, one of the cities selected as a residence of the priests. May we not, then, suppose that this unnamed mother of the Virgin was a daughter of one of the priests then residing at Nazareth, and that Mary's relatives on the mother's side--some of them--were also priests, going up at stated times to Jerusalem, to perform their "course" of Temple services? It is certainly a most natural supposition, and one, too, that will help to remove some subsequent difficulties in the story; as, for instance, the journey of Mary to Judæa. Some honest minds have stumbled at that long journey of a hundred miles, while others have grown pathetic in their descriptions of that lonely pilgrimage of the Galilean Virgin. But it is neither necessary nor likely that Mary should take the journey alone. Her connection with the priesthood, if our supposition be correct, would find her an escort, even among her own relatives, as least as far as Jerusalem; and since the priestly courses were half-yearly in their service, it would be just the time the "course of Abijah," in which Zacharias served, would be returning once again to their Judæan homes. It is only a supposition, it is true, but it is a supposition that is extremely natural and more than probable; and if we look through it, taking "Levi" and "Judah" as our binocular lenses, it carries a thread of light through otherwise dark places; while throwing our sight forward, it brings distant Nazareth in line with Jerusalem and the "hill-country of Judæa."

Betrothed to Joseph, who was of the royal line, and as some think, the legal heir to David's throne, Mary was probably not more than twenty years of age. Whether an orphan or not we cannot tell, though the silence of Scripture would almost lead us to suppose that she was. Papias, however, who was a disciple of St. John, states that she had two sisters--Mary the wife of Cleophas, and Mary Salome the wife of Zebedee. If this be so--and there is no reason why we should discredit the statement--then Mary the Virgin Mother would probably be the eldest of the three sisters, the house-mother in the Nazareth home. Where it was that the angel appeared to her we cannot tell. Tradition, with one of its random guesses, has fixed the spot in the suburbs, beside the fountain. But there is something incongruous and absurd in the selection of such a place for an angelic appearance--the public resort and lounge, where the clatter of feminine gossip was about as constant as the flow and sparkle of its waters. Indeed, the very form of the participle disposes of that tradition, for we read, "He came in unto her," implying that it was within her holy place of home the angel found her. Nor is there any need to suppose, as some do, that it was in her quiet chamber of devotion, where she was observing the stated hours of prayer. Celestials do not draw that broad line of distinction between so-called secular and sacred duties. To them "work" is but another form of "worship," and all duties to them are sacred, even when they lie among life's temporal, and so-called secular things. Indeed, Heaven reserves its highest visions, not for those quiet moments of still devotion, but for the hours of busy toil, when mind and body are given to the "trivial rounds" and the "common tasks" of every-day life. Moses is at his shepherding when the bush calls him aside, with its tongues of fire; Gideon is threshing out his wheat when God's angel greets him and summons him to the higher task; and Zacharias is performing the routine service of his priestly office when Gabriel salutes him with the first voice of a New Dispensation. And so all the analogies would lead us to suppose that the Virgin was quietly engaged in her domestic duties, offering the sacrifice of her daily task, as Zacharias offered his incense of stacte and onycha, when Gabriel addressed her, "Hail, thou that art highly favoured, the Lord is with thee" (R.V.). The Romanists, eager to accord Divine honours to the Virgin Mother as the dispenser of blessing and of grace, interpret the phrase, "Thou that art full of grace." It is, perhaps, not an inapt rendering of the word, and is certainly more euphonious than our marginal reading "much graced;" but when they make the "grace" an inherent, and not a derived grace, their doctrine slants off from all Scripture, and is opposed to all reason. That the word itself gives no countenance to such an enthronement of Mary, is evident, for St. Paul makes use of the same word when speaking of himself and the Ephesian Christians (Eph. i. 6), where we render it "His grace, which He freely bestowed on us in the Beloved." But criticism apart, never before had an angel so addressed a mortal, for even Daniel's "greatly beloved" falls below this Nazareth greeting. When Gabriel came to Zacharias there was not even a "Hail;" it was simply a "Fear not," and then the message; but now he gives to Mary a "Hail" and two beatitudes besides: "Thou art highly favoured;" "the Lord is with thee." And do these words mean nothing? Are they but a few heavenly courtesies whose only meaning is in their sound? Heaven does not speak thus with random, unmeaning words. Its voices are true, and deep as they are true, never meaning less, but often more than they say. That the angel should so address her is certain proof that the Virgin possessed a peculiar fitness for the Divine honours she was now to receive--honours which had been so long held back, as if in reserve for herself alone. It is only they who look heavenward who see heavenly things. There must be a heart aflame before the bush burns; and when the bush is alight it is only "he who sees takes off his shoes."

The glimpses we get of the Virgin are few and brief; she is soon eclipsed--if we may be allowed that shadowy word--by the greater glories of her Son; but why should she be selected as the mother of the human Christ? why should her life nourish His? why should the thirty years be spent in her daily presence, her face being the first vision of awaking consciousness, as it was in the last earthward look from the cross?--why all this, except that there was a wealth of beauty and of grace about her nature, a certain tinge of heavenliness that made it fitting the Messiah should be born of her rather than of any woman else? As we have seen, the royal and the priestly lines meet in her, and Mary unites in herself all the dignity of the one with the sanctity of the other. With what delicacy and grace she receives the angel's message! "Greatly troubled" at first--not, however, like Zacharias, at the sight of the messenger, but at his message--she soon recovers herself, and "casts in her mind what manner of salutation this might be." This sentence just describes one prominent feature of her character, her reflective, reasoning mind. Sparing of words, except when under the inspiration of some Magnificat, she lived much within herself. She loved the companionship of her own thoughts, finding a certain music in their still monologue. When the shepherds made known the saying of the angel about this child, repeating the angelic song, perhaps, with sundry variations of their own, Mary is neither elated nor astonished. Whatever her feelings--and they must have been profoundly moved--she carefully conceals them. Instead of telling out her own deep secrets, letting herself drift out on the ecstasies of the moment, Mary is silent, serenely quiet, unwilling that even a shadow of herself should dim the brightness of His rising. "She kept," so we read, "all these sayings, pondering them in her heart;" or putting them together, as the Greek word means, and so forming, as in a mental mosaic, her picture of the Christ who was to be. And so, in later years, we read (ii. 51) how "His mother kept all these sayings in her heart," gathering up the fragmentary sentences of the Divine Childhood and Youth, and hiding them, as a treasure peculiarly her own, in the deep, still chambers of her soul. And what those still chambers of her soul were, how heavenly the atmosphere that enswathed them, how hallowed by the Divine Presence, her Magnificat will show; for that inspired psalm is but an opened window, letting the music pass without, as it throws the light within, showing us the temple of a quiet, devout, and thoughtful soul.

With what complacency and with what little surprise she received the angel's message! The Incarnation does not come upon her as a new thought, a thought for which her mind cannot possibly find room, and human speech can weave no fitting dress. It disturbs neither her reason nor her faith. Versed in Scripture as she is, it comes rather as a familiar thought--a heavenly dove, it is true, but gliding down within her mind in a perfect, because a heavenly naturalness. And when the angel announces that the "Son of the Most High," whose name shall be called Jesus, and who shall reign over the house of Jacob for ever, shall be born of herself, there is no exclamation of astonishment, no word of incredulity as to whether this can be, but simply a question as to the manner of its accomplishment: "How shall this be, seeing that I know not a man?" The Christ had evidently been conceived in her mind, and cradled in her heart, even before He became a conception of her womb.

And what an absolute self-surrender to the Divine purpose! No sooner has the angel told her that the Holy Ghost shall come upon her, and the power of the Most High overshadow her, than she bows to the Supreme Will in a lowly, reverential acquiescence: "Behold, the handmaid [bondmaid] of the Lord; be it unto me according to thy word." So do the human and the Divine wills meet and mingle. Heaven touches earth, comes down into it, that earth may evermore touch heaven, and indeed form part of it.

The angel departs, leaving her alone with her great secret; and little by little it dawns upon her, as it could not have done at first, what this secret means for her. A great honour it is, a great joy it will be; but Mary finds, as we all find, the path to heaven's glories lies through suffering; the way into the wealthy place is "through the fire." How can she carry this great secret herself? and yet how can she tell it? Who will believe her report? Will not these Nazarenes laugh at her story of the vision, except that the matter would be too grave for a smile? It is her own secret yet, but it cannot be a secret long; and then--who can defend her, and ward off the inevitable shame? Where can she find shelter from the venomed shafts that will be hurled from every side--where, save in her consciousness of unsullied purity, and in the "shadow of the Highest"? Was it thoughts like these that now agitated her mind, deciding her to make the hasty visit to Elisabeth? or was it that she might find sympathy and counsel in communion with a kindred soul, one that age had made wise, and grace made beautiful? Probably it was both; but in this journey we will not follow her now, except to see how her faith in God never once wavered. We have already listened to her sweet song; but what a sublime faith it shows, that she can sing in face of this gathering storm, a storm of suspicion and of shame, when Joseph himself will seek to put her away, lest his character should suffer too! But Mary believed, even though she felt and smarted. She endured "as seeing Him who is invisible." Could she not safely leave her character to Him? Would not the Lord avenge His own elect? Would not Divine Wisdom justify her child? Faith and hope said "Yes;" and Mary's soul, like a nightingale, trilled out her Magnificat when earth's light was disappearing, and the shadows were falling thick and fast on every side.

It is on her return to Nazareth, after her three months' absence, that the episode occurs narrated by St. Matthew. It is thrown into the story almost by way of parenthesis, but it casts a vivid light on the painful experience through which she was now called to pass. Her prolonged absence, most unusual for one betrothed, was in itself puzzling; but she returns to find only a scant welcome. She finds herself suspected of shame and sin, "the white flower of her blameless life" dashed and stained with black aspersions. Even Joseph's confidence in her is shaken, so shaken that he must put her away and have the betrothal cancelled. And so the clouds darken about the Virgin; she is left almost alone in the sharp travail of her soul, charged with sin, even when she is preparing for the world a Saviour, and likely, unless Heaven speedily interpose, to become an outcast, if not a martyr, thrown outside the circle of human courtesies and sympathies as a social leper. Like another heir of all the promises, she too is led as a lamb to the slaughter, a victim bound, and all but sacrificed, upon the altar of the public conscience. But Heaven did intervene, even as it stayed the knife of Abraham. An angel appears to Joseph, throwing around the suspected one the mantle of unsullied innocence, and assuring him that her explanation, though passing strange, was truth itself. And so the Lord did avenge His own elect, stilling the babble of unfriendly tongues, restoring to her all the lost confidences, together with a wealth of added hopes and prospective honours.

Not, however, out of Galilee must the Shiloh come, but out of Judah; and not Nazareth, but Bethlehem Ephratah is the designated place of His coming forth who shall be the Governor and Shepherd of "My people Israel." What means, then, this apparent divergence of the Providence from the Prophecy, the whole drift of the one being northward, while the other points steadily to the south? It is only a seeming divergence, the backward flash of the wheel that all the time is moving steadily, swiftly forward. The Prophecy and the Providence are but the two staves of the ark, moving in different but parallel lines, and bearing between them the Divine purpose. Already the line is laid that links Nazareth with Bethlehem, the line of descent we call lineage; and now we see Providence setting in motion another force, the Imperial Will, which, moving along this line, makes the purpose a realization. Nor was it the Imperial Will only; it was the Imperial Will acting through Jewish prejudices. These two forces, antagonistic, if not opposite, were the centrifugal and centripetal forces that kept the Divine Purpose moving in its appointed round and keeping Divine hours. Had the registration decreed by Cæsar been conducted after the Roman manner, Joseph and Mary would not have been required to go up to Bethlehem; but when, out of deference to Jewish prejudice, the registration was made in the Hebrew mode, this compelled them, both being descendants of David, to go up to their ancestral city. It has been thought by some that Mary possessed some inherited property in Bethlehem; and the narrative would suggest that there were other links that bound them to the city; for evidently they intended to make Bethlehem henceforth their place of residence, and they would have done so had not a Divine monition broken in upon their purpose (Matt. ii. 23).

And so they move southward, obeying the mandate of Cæsar, who now is simply the executor of the higher Will, the Will that moves silently but surely, back of all thrones, principalities, and powers. We will not attempt to gild the gold, by enlarging upon the story of the Nativity, and so robbing it of its sweet simplicity. The toilsome journey; its inhospitable ending; the stable and the manger; the angelic symphonies in the distance; the adoration of the shepherds--all form one sweet idyll, no word of which we can spare; and as the Church chants her Te Deum all down the ages this will not be one of its lowest strains:--

> "When Thou tookest upon Thee to deliver man
> Thou didst not abhor the Virgin's womb."

And so the Virgin becomes the Virgin Mother, graduating into motherhood amid the acclamations of the sky, and borne on to her exalted honours in the sweep of Imperial decrees.

After the Nativity she sinks back into a second--a far-off second--place, "for the greater glory doth dim the less;" and twice only does her voice break the silence of the thirty years. We hear it first in the Temple, as, in tones tremulous with anxiety and sorrow, she asks, "Son, why hast Thou thus dealt with us? Behold, Thy father and I sought Thee sorrowing." The whole incident is perplexing, and if we read it superficially, not staying to read between the lines, it certainly places the mother in anything but a favourable light. Let us observe, however, that there was no necessity that the mother should have made this pilgrimage, and evidently she had made it so that she might be near her precious charge. But now she strangely loses sight of Him, and goes even a day's journey without discovering her loss. How is this? Has she suddenly grown careless? or does she lose both herself and her charge in the excitements of the return journey? Thoughtfulness, as we have seen, was a characteristic feature of her life. Hers was the "harvest of the quiet eye," and her thoughts centred not on herself, but on her Divine Son; He was her Alpha and Omega, her first, her last, her only thought. It is altogether outside the range of possibilities that she now could be so negligent of her maternal duties, and so we are compelled to seek for our explanation elsewhere. May we not find it in this? The parents had left Jerusalem earlier in the day, arranging for the child Jesus to follow with another part of the same company, which, leaving later, would overtake them at their first camp. But Jesus not appearing when the second company starts, they imagine that He has gone on with the first company, and so proceed without Him. This seems the only probable solution of the difficulty; at any rate it makes plain and perfectly natural what else is most obscure and perplexing. Mary's mistake, however--and it was not her fault--opens to us a page in the sealed volume of the Divine Boyhood, letting us hear its solitary voice--"Wist ye not that I must be in My Father's house?"

We see the mother again at Cana, where she is an invited and honoured guest at the marriage, moving about among the servants with a certain quiet authority, and telling her Divine Son of the breakdown in the hospitalities: "They have no wine." We cannot now go into details, but evidently there was no distancing reserve between the mother and her Son. She goes to Him naturally; she speaks to Him freely and frankly, as any widow would speak to the son on whom she leaned. Nay, she seems to know, as by a sort of intuition, of the superhuman powers that are lying dormant in that quiet Son of hers, and she so correctly reads the horoscope of Heaven as to expect this will be the hour and the place of their manifestation. Perhaps her mind did not grasp the true Divinity of her Son--indeed, it could not have done so before the Resurrection--but that He is the Messiah she has no doubt, and so, strong in her confidence, she says to the servants, "Whatsoever He saith unto you, do it." And her faith must have been great indeed, when it required a "whatsoever" to measure it. Some have thought they could detect a tinge of impatience and a tone of rebuke in the reply of Jesus; and doubtless there is a little sharpness in our English rendering of it. It does sound to our ears somewhat unfilial and harsh. But to the Greeks the address "Woman" was both courteous and respectful, and Jesus Himself uses it in that last tender salute from the cross. Certainly, she did not take it as a rebuke, for one harsh word, like the touch on the sensitive plant, would have thrown her back into silence; whereas she goes off directly to the servants with her "whatsoever."

We get one more brief glimpse of her at Capernaum, as she and her other sons come out to Jesus to urge Him to desist from His long speaking. It is but a simple narrative, but it serves to throw a side-light on that home-life now removed to Capernaum. It shows us the thoughtful, loving mother, as, forgetful of herself and full of solicitude for Him, who, she fears, will tax Himself beyond His strength, she comes out to persuade Him home. But what is the meaning of that strange answer, and the significant gesture? "Mother," "brethren"? It is as if Jesus did not understand the words. They are something He has now outgrown, something He must now lay aside, as He gives Himself to the world at large. As there comes a time in the life of each when the mother is forsaken--left, that he may follow a higher call, and be himself a man--so Jesus now steps out into a world where Mary's heart, indeed, may still follow, but a world her mind may not enter. The earthly relation is henceforth to be overshadowed by the heavenly. The Son of Mary grows into the Son of man, belonging now to no special one, but to humanity at large, finding in all, even in us, who do the will of the Father in heaven, a brother, a sister, a mother. Not that Jesus forgets her. Oh, no! Even amid the agonies of the cross He thinks of her; He singles her out among the crowd, bespeaking for her a place--the place He Himself has filled--in the heart of His nearest earthly friend; and amid the prayer for His murderers, and the "Eloi, Eloi" of a terrible forsaking, He says to the Apostle of love, "Behold thy mother," and to her, "Behold thy son."

And so the Virgin Mother takes her place in the focal point of all the histories. Through no choice, no conceit or forwardness of her own, but by the grace of God and by an inherent fitness, she becomes the connecting-link between earth and heaven. And throwing, as she does, her unconscious shadow back within the Paradise Lost, and forward through the Gospels to the Paradise Regained, shall we not "magnify the Lord" with her? shall we not "magnify the Lord" for her, as, with all the generations, we "call her blessed"?

# CHAPTER V – THE ADORATION OF THE SHEPHERDS

*Luke ii. 8-21.*

The Gospel of St. Mark omits entirely the Nativity, passing at once to the words and miracles of His public ministry. St. John, too, dismisses the Advent and the earlier years of the Divine Life with one solitary phrase, how the Word, which in the beginning was with God and was God, "became flesh and dwelt among us" (i. 14). St. Luke, however, whose Gospel is the Gospel of the Humanity, lingers reverently over the Nativity, throwing a variety of side-lights upon the cradle of the Holy Child. Already has he shown how the Roman State prepared the cradle of the Infancy, and how Cæsar Augustus unconsciously wrought out the purpose of God, the breath of his imperial decree being but part of a higher inspiration; and now he proceeds to show how the shepherds of Judæa bring the greetings of the Hebrew world, the wave-sheaf of the ripening harvests of homage which yet will be laid, by Jew and Gentile alike, at the feet of Him who was Son of David and Son of man.

It is generally supposed that these anonymous shepherds were residents of Bethlehem, and tradition has fixed the exact spot where they were favoured with this Advent apocalypse, about a thousand paces from the modern village. It is a historic fact that there was a tower near that site, called Eder, or "the Tower of the Flock," around which were pastured the flocks destined for the Temple sacrifice; but the topography of ver. 8 is purposely vague. The expression "in that same country," written by one who both in years and in distance was far removed from the events recorded, would describe any circle within the radius of a few miles from Bethlehem as its centre, and the very vagueness of the expression seems to push back the scene of the Advent music to a farther distance than a thousand paces. And this view is confirmed by the language of the shepherds themselves, who, when the vision has faded, say one to another, "Let us now go even unto Bethlehem, and see this thing that is come to pass;" for they scarcely would have needed, or used, the adverbial "even" were they keeping their flocks so close up to the walls of the city. We may therefore infer, with some amount of probability, that whether the shepherds were residents of Bethlehem or not, when they kept watch over their flocks, it was not on the traditional site, but farther away over the hills. Indeed, it is difficult, and very often impossible, for us to fix the precise locality of these sacred scenes, these bright points of intersection, where Heaven's glories flash out against the dull carbon-points of earth; and the voices of tradition are at best but doubtful guesses. It would almost seem as if God Himself had wiped out these memories, hiding them away, as He hid the sepulchre of Moses, lest the world should pay them too great a homage, and lest we might think that one place lay nearer to heaven than another, when all places are equally distant, or rather equally near. It is enough to know that somewhere on these lonely hills came the vision of the angels, perhaps on the very spot where David was minding his sheep when Heaven summoned him to a higher task, passing him up among the kings.

While the shepherds were "watching the watches of the night over their flock," as the Evangelist expresses it, referring to the pastoral custom of dividing the night into watches, and keeping watch by turns, suddenly "an angel of the Lord stood by them, and the glory of the Lord shone round about them." When the angel appeared to Zacharias, and when Gabriel brought to Mary her evangel, we do not read of any supernatural portent, any celestial glory, attending them. Possibly because their appearances were in the broad daylight, when the glory would be masked, invisible; but now, in the dead of night, the angelic form is bright and luminous, throwing all around them a sort of heavenly halo, in which even the lustrous Syrian stars grow dim. Dazzled by the sudden burst of glory, the shepherds were awed by the vision, and stricken with a great fear, until the angel, borrowing the tones and accents of their own speech, addressed to them his message, the message he had been commissioned to bring: "Be not afraid; for behold, I bring you good tidings of great joy which shall be to all the people: for there is born to you this day in the city of David a Saviour, which is Christ the Lord." And then he gave them a sign by which they might recognize the Saviour Lord: "Ye shall find a babe wrapped in swaddling clothes, and lying in a manger."

From the indefinite wording of the narrative we should infer that the angel who brought the message to the shepherds was not Gabriel, who had before brought the good tidings to Mary. But whether or not the messenger was the same, the two messages are almost identical in structure and in thought, the only difference being the personal element of the equation, and the shifting of the time from the future to the present tense. Both strike the same key-note, the "Fear not" with which they seek to still the vibrations of the heart, that the Virgin and the shepherds may not have their vision blurred and tremulous through the agitation of the mind. Both make mention of the name of David, which name was the key-word which unlocked all Messianic hopes. Both speak of the Child as a Saviour--though Gabriel wraps up the title within the name, "Thou shalt call His name Jesus;" for, as St. Matthew explains it, "it is He that shall save His people from their sins." Both, too, speak of Him as the Messiah; for when the angel now calls Him the "Christ" it was the same "Anointed" one who, as Gabriel had said, "should reign over the house of Jacob for ever;" while in the last august title now given by the angel, "Lord," we may recognize the higher Divinity--that He is, in some unique, and to us incomprehensible sense, "the Son of the Most High" (i. 32). Such, then, is the triple crown the angel now bears to the cradle of the Holy Child. What He will be to the world is still but a prophecy; but as He, the Firstborn, is now brought into the world, God commands all the angels to worship Him (Heb. i. 6); and with united voice--though the antiphon sings back over a nine months silence--they salute the Child of Bethlehem as Saviour, Messiah, Lord. The one title sets up His throne facing the lower world, commanding the powers of darkness, and looking at the moral conditions of men; the second throws the shadow of His throne over the political relations of men, making it dominate all thrones; while the third title sets up His throne facing the heavens themselves, vesting Him with a supreme, a Divine authority.

No sooner was the message ended than suddenly there was with the angel a multitude of the heavenly host, praising God and saying--

*"Glory to God in the highest,
And on earth peace among men in whom He is well pleased."*

The Revised Version lacks the rhythmic qualities of the Authorized Version; and the wordy clause "among men in whom He is well pleased" seems but a poor substitute for the terse and clear "good-will toward men," which is an expression easy of utterance, and which seemed to have earned a prescriptive right to a place in our Advent music. The revised rendering, however, is certainly more in accord with the grammatical construction of the original, whose idiomatic form can scarcely be put into English, except in a way somewhat circuitous and involved. In both expressions the underlying thought is the same, representing man as the object of the Divine good-pleasure, that Divine "benevolence"--using the word in its etymological sense--which enfolds, in the germ, the Divine favour, compassion, mercy, and love. There is thus a triple parallelism running through the song, the "Glory to God in the highest" finding its corresponding terms in the "peace among (or to) men in whom He is well pleased on earth;" while altogether it forms one complete circle of praise, the "good-pleasure to man," the "peace on earth," the "glory to God" marking off its three segments. And so the song harmonizes with the message; indeed, it is that message in an altered shape; no longer walking in common prosaic ways, but winged now, it moves in its higher circles with measured beat, leaving a path from the cradle of the Infancy to the highest heavens all strewn with Glorias. And what is the triplicity of the song but another rendering of the three august titles of the message--Saviour, Messiah, Lord? the "Saviour" being the expression of the Divine good-pleasure; the "Messiah" telling of His reign upon earth who is Himself the Prince of peace; while the "Lord," which, as we have seen, corresponds with "the Son of the Most High," leads us up directly to the "heavenlies," to Him who commands and who deserves all doxologies.

But is this song only a song in some far-distant sky--a sweet memory indeed, but no experience? Is it not rather the original from which copies may be struck for our individual lives? There is for each of us an advent, if we will accept it; for what is regeneration but the beginning of the Divine life within our life, the advent of the Christ Himself? And let but that supreme hour come to us when place and room are made for Him who is at once the expression of the Divine favour and the incarnation of the Divine love, and the new era dawns, the reign of peace, the "peace of God," because the "peace with God, through our Lord Jesus Christ." Then will the heart throw off its Glorias, not in one burst of song, which subsides quickly into silence, but in one perpetual anthem, which ever becomes more loud and sweet as the day of its perfected redemption draweth nigh; for when the Divine displeasure is turned away, and a Divine peace or comfort takes its place, who can but say, "O Lord, I will praise Thee"?

Directly the angel-song had ceased, and the singers had disappeared in the deep silence whence they came, the shepherds, garnering up their scattered thoughts, said one to another (as if their hearts were speaking all at once and all in unison), "Let us now go even unto Bethlehem, and see this thing that is come to pass which the Lord hath made known unto us." The response was immediate. They do not shut out this heavenly truth by doubt and vain questioning; they do not keep it at a distance from them, as if it only indirectly and distantly concerned themselves, but yield themselves up to it entirely; and as they go hastily to Bethlehem, in the quick step and in the rapid beating of their heart, we can trace the vibrations of the angel-song. And why is this? Why is it that the message does not come upon them as a surprise? Why are these men ready with such a perfect acquiescence, their hearts leaping forward to meet and embrace this Gospel of the angels? We shall probably find our answer in the character of the men themselves. They pass into history unnamed; and after playing their brief part, they disappear, lost in the incense-cloud of their own praises. But evidently these shepherds were no mean, no common men. They were Hebrews, possibly of the royal line; at any rate they were Davids in their loftiness of thought, of hope and aspiration. They were devout, God-fearing men. Like their father Jacob, they too were citizens of two worlds; they could lead their flocks into green pastures, and mend the fold; or they could turn aside from flock and fold to wrestle with God's angels, and prevail. Heaven's revelations come to noble minds, as the loftiest peaks are always the first to hail the dawn. And can we suppose that Heaven would so honour them, lighting up the sky with an aureole of glory for their sole benefit, sending this multitude to sing to them a sweet chorale, if the men themselves had nothing heavenly about them, if their selfish, sordid mind could soar no higher than their flocks, and have no wider range than the markets for their wool?

> "Let but a flute
> Play 'neath the fine-mixed metal,
> Then shall the huge bell tremble, then the mass
> With myriad waves concurrent shall respond
> In low, soft unison."

But there must be the music hidden within, or there is no unison. And we may be sure of this, that the angel-song had passed by them as a cold night-wind, had not their hearts been tuned up by intense desire, until they struck responsive to the angel-voice. Though they knew it not, they had led their flock to the mount of God; and up the steps of sacred hopes and lofty aspirations they had climbed, until their lives had got within the circle of heavenly harmonies, and they were worthy to be the first apostles of the New Dispensation.

In our earthly modes of thinking we push the sacred and the secular far apart, as if they were two different worlds, or, at any rate, as opposite hemispheres of the same world, with but few points of contact between them. It is not so. The secular is the sacred on its under, its earthward side. It is a part of that great whole we call duty, and in our earthly callings, if they are but pure and honest, we may hear the echoes of a heavenly call. The temple of Worship and the temple of Work are not separated by indefinable spaces; they are contiguous, leaning upon each other, while they both front the same Divine purpose. Nor can it be simply a coincidence that Heaven's revelations should nearly always come to man in the moments of earthly toil, rather than in the hours of leisure or of so-called worship. It was from his shepherding the burning bush beckoned Moses aside; while Heaven's messenger found Gideon on the threshing-floor, and Elisha in the furrow. In the New Testament, too, in all the cases whose circumstances are recorded, the Divine call reached the disciples when engaged in their every-day task, sitting at the receipt of custom, and casting or mending their nets. The fact is significant. In the estimate of Heaven, instead of a discount being put upon the common tasks of life, those tasks are dignified and ennobled. They look towards heaven, and if the heart be only set in that direction they lead too up towards heaven. Our weeks are not unlike the sheet of Peter's vision; we take care to tie up the two ends, attaching them to heaven, and then we leave what we call the "week-days" bulging down earthward in purely secular fashion. But would not our weeks, and our whole life, swing on a higher and holier level, could we but recognize the fact that all days are the Lord's days, and did we but attach each day and each deed to heaven? Such is the truest, noblest life, that takes the "trivial rounds" as a part of its sacred duties, doing them all as unto the Lord. So, as we sanctify life's common things, they cease to be common, and the earthly becomes less earthly as we learn to see more of heaven in it. In the weaving of our life some of its threads stretch earthward, and some heavenward; but they cross and interlace, and together they form the warp and woof of one fabric, which should be, like the garment of the Master, without seam, woven from the top throughout. Happy is that life which, keeping an open eye over the flock, keeps too a heart open towards heaven, ready to listen to the angelic music, and ready to transfer its rhythm to their own hastening feet or their praising lips.

Our Evangelist tells us that they "came in haste" in search of the young Child, and we may almost detect that haste in the very accents of their speech. It is, "Let us now go across even to Bethlehem," allowing the prefix its proper meaning; as if their eager hearts could not stay to go round by the ordinary road, but like bees scenting a held of clover, they too must make their cross-country way to Bethlehem. Though the angel had not given explicit directions, the city of David was not so large but that they could easily discover the object of their search--the Child, as had been told them, wrapped in swaddling clothes and lying in a manger. It has been thought by some that the "inn" is a mistranslation, and that it really was the "guest-chamber" of some friend. It is true the word is rendered "guest-chamber" on the other two occasions of its use (Mark xiv. 14; Luke xxii. 11), but it also signified a public guest-house, as well as a private guest-chamber; and such evidently is its meaning here, for private hospitality, even had its "guest-chamber" been preoccupied, would certainly, under the circumstances, have offered something more human than a stable. That would not have been its only alternative.

It is an interesting coincidence, and one serving to link together the Old and the New Testament, that Jeremiah speaks of a certain geruth, or inn, as it may read, "which is by Bethlehem" (Jer. xli. 17). How it came into the possession of Chimham, who was a Gileadite, we are not told; but we are told that because of the kindness shown to David in his exile by Barzillai, his son Chimham received special marks of the royal favour, and was, in fact, treated almost as an adopted son (1 Kings ii. 7). What is certain is that the khan of Bethlehem bore, for successive generations, the name of Chimham; which fact is in itself evidence that Chimham was its builder, as the well of Jacob retained, through all the changes of inheritance, the name of the patriarch whose thought and gift it was. In all probability, therefore, the "inn" was built by Chimham, on that part of the paternal estate which David inherited; and as the khans of the East cling with remarkable tenacity to their original sites, it is probable, to say the least, that the "inn of Chimham" and the inn of Bethlehem, in which there was no room for the two late-comers from Nazareth, were, if not identical, at any rate related structures--so strangely does the cycle of history complete itself, and the Old merge into the New. And so, while Prophecy sings audibly and sweetly of the place which yet shall give birth to the Governor who shall rule over Israel, History puts up her silent hand, and salutes Beth-lehem Ephratah as by no means the least among the cities of Judah.

But not in the inn do the shepherds find the happy parents--the spring-tide of the unusual immigration had completely flooded that, leaving no standing-place for the son and daughter of David--but they find them in a stable, probably in some adjoining cave, the swaddled Child, as the angels had foretold, lying in the manger. Art has lingered reverently and long over this stable scene, hiding with exquisite draperies its baldness and meanness, and lighting up its darkness with wreaths of golden glory; but these splendours are apocryphal, existing only in the mind of the beholder; they are the luminous mist of an adoring love. What the shepherds do find is an extemporized apartment, mean in the extreme; two strangers fresh from Nazareth, both young and both poor; and a new-born infant asleep in the manger, with a group of sympathizing spectators, who have brought, in the emergency, all kinds of proffered helps. It seems a strange ending for an angel-song, a far drop from the superhuman to the subhuman. Will it shake the faith of these apostle-shepherds? Will it shatter their bright hope? And chagrined that their auroral dream should have so poor a realization, will they return to their flocks with heavy hearts and sad? Not they. They prostrate themselves before the Infant Presence, repeating over and over the heavenly words the angels had spoken unto them concerning the Child, and while Mary announces the name as "Jesus," they salute Him, as the angels had greeted Him before, as Saviour, Messiah, Lord; thus putting on the head of the Child Jesus that triple crown, symbol of a supremacy which knows no limit either in space or time. It was the Te Deum of a redeemed humanity, which succeeding years have only made more deep, more full, and which in ever-rising tones will yet grow into the Alleluias of the heavens. Saviour, Messiah, Lord! these titles struck upon Mary's ear not with surprise, for she has grown accustomed to surprises now, but with a thrill of wonder. She could not yet spell out all their deep meaning, and so she pondered "them in her heart," hiding them away in her maternal soul, that their deep secrets might ripen and blossom in the summer of the after-years.

The shepherds appear no more in the Gospel story. We see them returning to their task "glorifying and praising God for all the things that they had heard and seen," and then the mantle of a deep silence falls upon them. As a lark, rising heavenward, loses itself from our sight, becoming a sweet song in the sky, so these anonymous shepherds, these first disciples of the Lord, having laid their tribute at His feet--in the name of humanity saluting the Christ who was to be--now pass out of our sight, leaving for us the example of their heavenward look and their simple faith, and leaving, too, their Glorias, which in multiplied reverberations fill all lands and all times, the earthly prelude of the New, the eternal Song.

## CHAPTER VI – THE VOICE IN THE WILDERNESS

When the Old Testament closed, prophecy had thrown upon the screen of the future the shadows of two persons, cast in heavenly light. Sketched in outline rather than in detail, still their personalities were sufficiently distinct as to attract the gaze and hopes of the intervening centuries; while their differing, though related missions were clearly recognized. One was the Coming One, who should bring the "consolation" of Israel, and who should Himself be that Consolation; and gathering into one august title all such glittering epithets as Star, Shiloh, and Emmanuel, prophecy reverently saluted Him as "the Lord," paying Him prospective homage and adoration. The other was to be the herald of another Dispensation, proclaiming the new kingdom and the new King, running before the royal chariot, even as Elijah ran before Ahab to the ivory palace at Jezreel, his voice then dying away in silence, as he himself passes out of sight behind the throne. Such were the two figures that prophecy, in a series of dissolving views, had thrown forward from the Old into the New Testament; and such was the signal honour accorded to the Baptist, that while many of the Old Testament characters appear as reflections in the New, his is the only human shadow thrown back from the New into the Old.

The forerunner thus had a virtual existence long before the time of the Advent. Known by his synonym of Elias, the prophesied, he became as a real presence, moving here and there among their thoughts and dreams, and lighting up their long night with the beacon-fires of new and bright hopes. His voice seemed familiar, even though it came to them in far-distant echoes, and the listening centuries had caught exactly both its accent and its message. And so the preparer of the way found his own path prepared; for John's path and "the way of the Lord" were the same; it was the way of obedience and of sacrifice. The two lives were thus thrown into conjunction from the first, the lesser light revolving around the Greater, as they fulfil their separate courses--separate indeed, as far as the human must ever be separated from the Divine, yet most closely related.

Living thus through the pre-Advent centuries, both in the Divine purpose and in the thoughts and hopes of men, so early designated to his heraldic office, "My messenger," in a singular sense, as no other of mortals could ever be, it is no matter of apology, or even of surprise, that his birth should be attended by so much of the supernatural. The Divine designation seems to imply, almost to demand, a Divine declaration; and in the birth-story of the Baptist the flashes of the supernatural, such as the angelic announcement and the miraculous conception, come with a simple naturalness. The prelude is in perfect symphony with the song. St. Luke is the only Evangelist who gives us the birth-story. The other three speak only of his mission, introducing him to us abruptly, as, like another Moses, he comes down from his new Sinai with the tables of the law in his hands and the strange light upon his face. St. Luke takes us back to the infancy, that we may see the beginnings of things, the Divine purpose enwrapped in swaddling clothes, as it once was set adrift in a rush-plaited ark. Before the message he puts the man, and before the man he puts the child--for is not the child a prophecy or invoice of the man?--while all around the child he puts the environment of home, showing us the subtle, powerful influences that touched and shaped the young prophet-life. As a plant carries up into its outmost leaves the ingredients of the rock around which its fibres cling, so each upspringing life--even the life of a prophet--carries into its farthest reaches the unconscious influence of its home associations. And so St. Luke sketches for us that quiet home in the hill-country, whose windows opened and whose doors turned toward Jerusalem, the "city of the great" and invisible "King." He shows us Zacharias and Elisabeth, true saints of God, devout of heart and blameless of life, down into whose placid lives an angel came, rippling them with the excitements of new promises and hopes. Where could the first meridian of the New Dispensation run better than through the home of these seers of things unseen, these watchers for the dawn? Where could be so fitting a receptacle for the Divine purpose, where it could so soon and so well ripen? Had not God elected them to this high honour, and Himself prepared them for it? Had He not purposely kept back all earlier, lower shoots, that their whole growth should be upward, one reaching out towards heaven, like the palm, its fruit clustering around its outmost branches? We can easily imagine what intense emotion the message of the angel would produce, and that Zacharias would not so much miss the intercourse of human speech now that God's thoughts were audible in his soul. What loving preparation would Elisabeth make for this child of hers, who was to be "great in the sight of the Lord"! what music she would strike out from its name, "John" (the Grace of Jehovah), the name which was both the sesame and symbol of the New Dispensation! How her eager heart would outrun the slow months, as she threw herself forward in anticipation among the joys of maternity, a motherhood so exalted! And why did she hide herself for the five months, but that she might prepare herself for her great mission? that in her seclusion she might hear more distinctly the voices that spake to her from above, or that in the silence she might hear her own heart sing?

But neither the eagerness of Elisabeth nor the dumbness of Zacharias is allowed to hasten the Divine purpose. That purpose, like the cloud of old, accommodates itself to human conditions, the slow processions of the humanities; and not until the time is "full" does the hope become a realization, and the infant voice utter its first cry. And now is gathered the first congregation of the new era. It is but a family gathering, as the neighbours and relatives come together for the circumcising of the child--which rite was always performed on the corresponding day of the week after its birth; but it is significant as being the first of those ever-widening circles that moving outwards from its central impulse, spread rapidly over the land, as they are now rapidly spreading over all lands. Zacharias, of course, was present; but mute and deaf, he could only sit apart, a silent spectator. Elisabeth, as we may gather from various references and hints, was of modest and retiring disposition, fond of putting herself in the shade, of standing behind; and so now the conduct of the ceremony seems to have fallen into the hands of some of the relatives. Presuming that the general custom will be observed, that the first-born child will take the name of the father, they proceed to name it "Zacharias." This, however, Elisabeth cannot allow, and with an emphatic negative, she says, "Not so; but he shall be called John." Persistent still in their own course, and not satisfied with the mother's affirmation, the friends turn to the aged and mute priest, and by signs ask how they shall name the child (and had Zacharias heard the conversation, he certainly would not have waited for their question, but would have spoken or written at once); and Zacharias, calling for the writing-table, which doubtless had been his close companion, giving him his only touch of the outer world for the still nine months, wrote, "His name is John." Ah, they are too late! the child was named even long before its birth, named, too, within the Holy Place of the Temple, and by an angel of God. "John" and "Jesus," those two names, since the visit of the Virgin, have been like two bells of gold, throwing waves of music across heart and home, ringing their welcome to "the Christ who is to be," the Christ who is now so near. "His name is John;" and with that brief stroke of his pen Zacharias half rebukes these intrusions and interferences of the relatives, and at the same time makes avowal of his own faith. And as he wrote the name "John," his present obedience making atonement for a past unbelief, instantly the paralyzed tongue was loosed, and he spake, blessing God, throwing the name of his child into a psalm; for what is the Benedictus of Zacharias but "John" written large and full, one sweet and loud magnifying of "the Grace and Favour of Jehovah"?

It is only a natural supposition that when the inspiration of the song had passed away, Zacharias' speech would begin just where it was broken off, and that he would narrate to the guests the strange vision of the Temple, with the angel's prophecy concerning the child. And as the guests depart to their own homes, each one carries the story of this new apocalypse, as he goes to spread the evangel, and to wake among the neighbouring hills the echoes of Zacharias' song. No wonder that fear came upon all that dwelt round about, and that they who pondered these things in their hearts should ask, "What then shall this child be?"

And here the narrative of the childhood suddenly ends, for with two brief sentences our Evangelist dismisses the thirty succeeding years. He tells us that "the hand of the Lord was with the child," doubtless arranging its circumstances, giving it opportunities, preparing it for the rugged manhood and the rugged mission which should follow in due course; and that "the child grew, and waxed strong in spirit," the very same expression he afterwards uses in reference to the Holy Child, an expression we can best interpret by the angel's prophecy, "He shall be filled with the Holy Ghost even from his mother's womb." His native strength of spirit was made doubly strong by the touch of the Divine Spirit, as the iron, coming from its baptism of fire, is hardened and tempered into steel. And so we see that in the Divine economy even a consecrated childhood is a possible experience; and that it is comparatively infrequent is owing rather to our warped views, which possibly may need some readjustment, than to the Divine purpose and provision. Is the child born into the Divine displeasure, branded from its birth with the mark of Cain? Is it not rather born into the Divine mercy, and all enswathed in the abundance of Divine love? True, it is born of a sinful race, with tendencies to self-will which may lead it astray; but it is just as true that it is born within the covenant of grace; that around its earliest and most helpless years is thrown the ægis of Christ's atonement; and that these innate tendencies are held in check and neutralized by what is called "prevenient grace." In the struggle for that child-life are the powers of darkness the first in the field, outmarching and out-manoeuvring the powers of light? Why, the very thought is half-libellous. Heaven's touch is upon the child from the first. Ignore it as we may, deny it as some will, yet back in life's earliest dawn the Divine Spirit is brooding over the unformed world, parting its firmaments of right and wrong, and fashioning a new Paradise. Is evil the inevitable? Must each life taste the forbidden fruit before it can attain to a knowledge of the good? In other words, is sin a great though dire necessity? If a necessity, then it is no longer sin, and we must seek for another and more appropriate name. No; childhood is Christ's purchased and peculiar possession; and the best type of religious experience is that which is marked by no rapid transitions, which breaks upon the soul softly and sweetly as a dawn, its beginnings imperceptible, and so unremembered. So not without meaning is it that right at the gate of the New Dispensation we find the cradle of a consecrated childhood. Placed there by the gate, so that all may see it, and placed in the light, so that all may read it, the childhood of the Baptist tells us what our childhood might oftener be, if only its earthly guardians--whose hands are so powerful to impress and mould the plastic soul--were, like Zacharias and Elisabeth, themselves prayerful, blameless, and devout.

Now the scene shifts; for we read he "was in the deserts till the day of his showing unto Israel." From the fact that this clause is intimately connected with the preceding, "and the child grew and waxed strong in spirit"--the two clauses having but one subject--some have supposed that John was but a child when he turned away from the parental roof and sought the wilderness. But this does not follow. The two parts of the sentence are only separated by a comma, but that pause may bridge over a chasm wide enough for the flow of numerous years, and between the childhood and the wilderness the narrative would almost compel us to put a considerable space. As his physical development was, in mode and proportion, purely human, with no hint of anything unnatural or even supernatural, so we may suppose was his mental and spiritual development. The voice must become articulate; it must play upon the alphabet, and turn sound into speech. It must learn, that it may think; it must study, that it may know. And so the human teacher is indispensable. Children reared of wolves may learn to bark, but, in spite of mythology, they will not build cities and found empires. And where could the child find better instructors than in his own parents, whose quiet lives had been passed in an atmosphere of prayer, and to whom the very jots and tittles of the law were familiar and dear? Indeed, we can scarcely suppose that after having prepared Zacharias and Elisabeth for their great mission, working what is something like a miracle, that she and no one else shall be the mother of the forerunner, the child should then be torn away from its natural guardians before the processes of its education are complete. It is true they were both "well stricken in years," but that phrase would cover any period from threescore years and upwards, and to that threescore the usual longevity of the Temple ministrants would easily allow another twenty years to be added. May we not, then, suppose that the child-Baptist studied and played under the parental roof, the bright focus to which their hopes, and thoughts, and prayers converged; that here, too, he spent his boyhood and youth, preparing for that priestly office to which his lineage entitled and designated him? for why should not the "messenger of the Lord" be priest as well? We have no further mention of Zacharias and Elisabeth, but it is not improbable that their death was the occasion of John's retirement to the deserts, now a young man, perhaps, of twenty years.

According to custom, John now should have been introduced and consecrated to the priesthood, twenty years being the general age of the initiates; but in obedience to a higher call, John renounces the priesthood, and breaks with the Temple at once and for ever. Retiring to the deserts, which, wild and gloomy, stretch westward from the Dead Sea, and assuming the old prophet garb--a loose dress of camel's hair, bound with a thong of leather--the student becomes the recluse. Inhabiting some mountain cave, tasting only the coarse fare that nature offered--locusts and wild honey--the new Elias has come and has found his Cherith; and here, withdrawn far from "the madding crowd" and the incessant babble of human talk, with no companions save the wild beasts and the bright constellations of that Syrian sky, as they wheel round in their nightly dance, the lonely man opens his heart to God's great thoughts and purposes, and by constant prayer keeps his clear, trumpet voice in drill. Evidently, John had seen enough of so-called "society," with its cold conventionalities and hypocrisies; his keen eye had seen only too easily the hollowness and corruption that lay beneath the outer gloss and varnish--the thin veneer that but half concealed the worminess and rottenness that lay beneath. John goes out into the desert like another scapegoat, bearing deep within his heart the sins of his nation--sins, alas, which are yet unrepented of and unforgiven! It was doubtless thoughts like these, and the constant brooding upon them, which gave to the Baptist the touch of melancholy that we can detect both in his features and his speech. Austere in person, with a wail in his voice like the sighing of the wind, or charged at times with suppressed thunders, the Baptist reminds us of the Peri, who

"At the gate
Of Eden stood disconsolate."

Sin had become to John an awful fact. He could see nothing else. The fragments of the law's broken tables strewed the land, even the courts of the Temple itself, and men were everywhere tripping against them and falling. But John did see something else; it was the day of the Lord, now very near, the day that should come scathing and burning "as a furnace," unless, meanwhile, Israel should repent. So the prophet mused, and as he mused the fire burned within his soul, even the fire of the Refiner, the fire of God.

Our Evangelist characterizes the opening of John's ministry with an official word. He calls it a "showing," a "manifestation," putting upon the very word the stamp and sanction of a Divine appointment. He is careful, too, to mark the time, so giving the Gospel story its place among the chronologies of the world; which he does in a most elaborate way. He first reads the time on the horoscope of the Empire, whose swinging pendulum was a rising or a falling throne; and he states that it was "the fifteenth year of the reign of Tiberius Cæsar," counting the two years of his joint rule with Augustus. Then, as if that were not enough, he notes the hour as indicated on the four quarters of the Hebrew commonwealth, the hour when Pilate, Herod, Philip, and Lysanias were in conjunction, ruling in their divided heavens. Then, as if that even were not enough, he marks the ecclesiastical hour as indicated by the marble time-piece of the Temple; it was when Annas and Caiaphas held jointly the high priesthood. What is the meaning of this elaborate mechanism, wheels within wheels? Is it because the hour is so important, that it needs the hands of an emperor, a governor, three tetrarchs, and two high priests to point it? Ewald is doubtless right in saying that St. Luke, as the historian, wished "to frame the Gospel history into the great history of the world" by giving precise dates; but if that were the Evangelist's main reason, such an accumulation of time-evidence were scarcely necessary; for what do the subsequent statements add to the precision of the first--"In the fifteenth year of Tiberius"? We must, then, seek for the Evangelist's meaning elsewhere. Among the oldest of the Hebrew prophecies concerning the Messiah was that of Jacob. Closing his life, as Moses did afterwards, with a wonderful vision, he looked down on the far-off years, and speaking of the coming "Seed," he said, "The sceptre shall not depart from Judah, nor a lawgiver from between his feet, until Shiloh come" (Gen. xlix. 10). Might not this prophecy have been in the thought of the Evangelist when he stayed so much longer than his wont to note times and seasons? Why does he mention Herod and Pilate, Philip and Lysanias, but to show how the sceptre has, alas, departed from Judah, and the lawgiver from between his feet, and how the chosen land is torn to pieces by the Roman eagles? And why does he name Annas and Caiaphas, but to show how the same disintegrating forces are at work even within the Temple, when the rightful high priest can be set aside and superseded by the nominee of a foreign and a Pagan power? Verily "the glory has departed from Israel;" and if St. Luke introduces foreign emperors, tetrarchs, and governors, it is that they may ring a muffled peal over the grave of a dead nation, a funeral knell, which, however, shall be the signal for the coming of the Shiloh, and the gathering of the people unto Him.

Such were the times--times of disorganization, disorder, and almost despair--when the word of God came unto John in the wilderness. It came "upon" him, as it literally reads, probably in one of those wonderful theophanies, as when God spake to Moses from the flaming bush, or as when He appeared to Elijah upon Horeb, sending him back to an unfinished task. John obeyed. Emerging from his wilderness retreat, clad in his strange attire, spare in build, his features sharp and worn with fasting, his long, dishevelled hair telling of his Nazarite vow, he moves down to the Jordan like an apparition. His appearance is everywhere hailed with mingled curiosity and delight. Crowds come in ever-increasing numbers, not one class only, but all classes--priests, soldiers, officials, people--until it seemed as if the cities had emptied themselves into the Jordan valley. And what went they "out for to see"? "A reed shaken with the wind"? A prophesier of smooth things? A preacher of revolt against tyranny? Nay; John was no wind-shaken reed, he was rather the heavenly wind itself, swaying the multitudes at will, and bending hearts and consciences into penitence and prayer. John was no preacher of revolt against the powers that be; in his mind, Israel had revolted more and more, and he must bring them back to their allegiance, or himself die in the attempt. John was no preacher of smooth things; there was not even the charm of variety about his speech. The one burden of his message was, "Repent: for the kingdom of heaven is at hand." But the effect was marvellous. The lone voice from the wilderness swept over the land like the breath of God. Borne forwards on a thousand lips, it echoed through the cities and penetrated into remotest places. Judæa, Samaria, and even distant Galilee felt the quiver of the strange voice, and even from the shore of the Northern Sea men came to sit at the feet of the new teacher, and to call themselves John's disciples. So widespread and so deep was the movement, it sent its ripples even within the royal palace, awaking the curiosity, and perhaps the conscience, of Herod himself. It was a genuine revival of religion, such as Judæa had not witnessed since the days of Ezra, the awaking of the national conscience and of the national hope.

Perhaps it would be difficult, by any analysis of ours, to discover or to define the secret of

John's success. It was the resultant, not of one force, but of many. For instance, the hour was favourable. It was the Sabbatic year, when field-work was in the main suspended, and men everywhere had leisure mind and hand lying, as it were, fallow. Then, too, the very dress of the Baptist would not be without its influence, especially on a mind so sensitive to form and colour as the Hebrew mind was. Dress to them was a form of duty. They were accustomed to weave into their tassels sacred symbols, so making the external speak of the eternal. Their hands played on the parti-coloured threads most faithfully and sacredly; for were not these the chords of Divine harmonies? But here is one who discards both the priestly and the civilian dress, and who wears, instead, the rough camel's hair robe of the old prophets. The very dress would thus appeal most powerfully to their imagination, carrying back their thoughts to the time of the Theocracy, when Jehovah was not silent as now, and when Heaven was so near, speaking by some Samuel or Elijah. Are those days returning? they would ask. Is this the Elias who was to come and restore all things? Surely it must be. And in the rustle of the Baptist's robe they heard the rustle of Elijah's mantle, dropping a second time by these Jordan banks. Then, too, there was the personal charm of the man. John was young, if years are our reckoning, for he counted but thirty; but in his case the verve and energy of youth were blended with the discretion and saintliness of age. What was the world to him, its fame, its luxury and wealth? They were only the dust he shook from his feet, as his spirit sighed for and soared after Heaven's better things. He asks nothing of earth but her plainest fare, a couch of grass, and by-and-by a grave. Then, too, there was a positiveness about the man, that would naturally attract, in a drifting, shifting, vacillating age. The strong will is magnetic; the weaker wills follow and cluster round it, as swarming bees cluster around their queen. And John was intensely positive. His speech was clear-cut and incisive, with a tremendous earnestness in it, as if a "Thus saith the Lord" were at his heart. John's mood was not the subjunctive, where his words could eddy among the "mays" and "mights;" it was plainly the indicative, or better still, the imperative. He spoke as one who believed, and who intensely felt what he believed. Then, too, there was a certain nobleness about his courage. He knew no rank, no party; he was superior to all. He feared God too much to have any fear of man. He spake no word for the sake of pleasing, and he kept back no word--even the hot rebuke--for fear of offending. Truth to him was more than titles, and right was the only royalty. How he painted the Pharisees--those shiny, slimy men, with creeping, sinuous ways--with that dark epithet "brood of vipers"! With what a fearless courage he denounced the incest of Herod! He will not level down Sinai, accommodating it to royal passions! Not he. "It is not lawful for thee to have her"--such were his words, that rolled in upon Herod's conscience like a peal of Sinai's thunder, telling him that law was law, that right was more than might, and purity more than power. Then, too, there was something about his message that was attractive. That word "the kingdom of heaven" struck upon the national heart like a bell, and set it vibrating with new hopes, and awaking all kinds of beautiful dreams of recovered pre-eminence and power.

But while all these were auxiliaries, factors, and co-efficients in the problem of the Baptist's success, they are not sufficient in themselves to account for that success. It is not difficult for a man of superior mental attainment, and of strong individuality, to attract a following, especially if that following be in the direction of self-interest. The emotions and passions of humanity lie near the surface; they can be easily swept into a storm by the strong or by the pathetic voice. But to reach the conscience, to lift up the veil, and to pass within to that Most Holy of the human soul is what man, unaided, cannot do. Only the Divine Voice can break those deep silences of the heart; or if the human voice is used the power is not in the words of human speech--those words, even the best, are but the dead wires along which the Divine Voice moves--it is the power of God.

> "Some men live near to God, as my right arm
> Is near to me; and then they walk about
> Mailed in full proof of faith, and bear a charm
> That mocks at fear, and bars the door on doubt,
> And dares the impossible."

Just such a man was the Baptist. He was a "man of God." He lived, and moved, and had his being in God. Self to him was an extinct passion. Envy, pride, ambition, jealousy, these were unknown tongues; his pure soul understood not their meaning. Like his great prototype, "the Spirit of the Lord God" was upon him. His life was one conscious inspiration; and John himself had been baptized with the baptism of which he spoke, but which he himself could not give, the baptism of the Holy Ghost and of fire. This only will account for the wonderful effects produced by his preaching. John, in his own experience, had antedated Pentecost, receiving the "power from on high," and as he spoke it was with a tongue of fire, a voice in whose accent and tone the people could detect the deeper Voice of God.

But if John could not baptize with the higher baptism, usurping the functions of the One coming after, he could, and he did, institute a lower, symbolic baptism of water, that thus the visible might lead up to the invisible. In what mode John's baptism was administered we cannot tell, nor is it material that we should know. We do know, however, that the baptism of the Spirit--and in John's mind the two were closely related--was constantly referred to in Scripture as an effusion, a "pouring out," a sprinkling, and never once as an immersion. And what was the "baptism of fire" to the mind of John? Was it not that which the prophet Isaiah had experienced, when the angel touched his lips with the live coal taken from the altar, pronouncing over him the great absolution, "Lo, this hath touched thy lips; and thine iniquity is taken away, and thy sin purged" (Isa. vi. 7)? At best, the baptism of water is but a shadow of the better thing, the outward symbol of an inward grace. We need not quarrel about modes and forms. Scripture has purposely left them indeterminate, so that we need not wrangle about them. There is no need that we exalt the shadow, levelling it up to the substance; and still less should we level it down, turning it into a playground for the schools.

Thus far the lives of Jesus and John have lain apart. One growing up in the hill-country of Galilee, the other in the hill-country of Judæa, and then in the isolation of the wilderness, they have never looked in each other's face, though they have doubtless heard often of each other's mission. They meet at last. John had been constantly telling of One who was coming after--"after," indeed, in order of time, but "before," infinitely before, in pre-eminence and authority. Mightier than he, He was the Lord. John would deem it an honour to kneel down before so august a Master, to untie and bear away His shoes; for in such a Presence servility was both becoming and ennobling. With such words as these the crier in the wilderness had been transferring the people's thought from himself, and setting their hearts listening for the Coming One, so preparing and broadening His way. Suddenly, in one of the pauses of his ministrations, a Stranger presents Himself, and asks that the rite of baptism may be administered to Him. There is nothing peculiar about His dress; He is younger than the Baptist--much younger, apparently, for the rough, ascetic life has prematurely aged him--but such is the grace and dignity of His person, such the mingled "strength and beauty" of His manhood, that even John, who never quailed in the presence of mortal before, is awed and abashed now. Discerning the innate royalty of the Stranger, and receiving a monition from the Higher World, with which he kept up close correspondence, the Baptist is assured that it is He, the Lord and Christ. Immediately his whole manner changes. The voice that has swept over the land like a whirlwind, now is hushed, subdued, speaking softly, deferentially, reverentially. Here is a Presence in which his imperatives all melt away and disappear, a Will that is infinitely higher than his own, a Person for whom his baptism is out of place. John is perplexed; he hesitates, he demurs. "I have need to be baptized of Thee, and comest Thou to me?" and John, Elias-like, would fain have wrapped his mantle around his face, burying out of sight his little "me," in the presence of the Lord. But Jesus said, "Suffer it now: for thus it becometh us to fulfil all righteousness" (Matt. iii. 15).

The baptism of Jesus was evidently a new kind of baptism, one in which the usual formulas were strangely out of place; and the question naturally arises, Why should Jesus submit to, and even ask for, a baptism that was so associated with repentance and sin? Could there be any place for repentance, any room for confession, in the Sinless One? John felt the anomaly, and so shrank from administering the rite, till the reply of Jesus put His baptism on different ground--ground altogether clear of any personal demerit. Jesus asked for baptism, not for the washing away of sin, but that He might "fulfil all righteousness." He was baptized, not for His own sake, but for the world's sake. Coming to redeem humanity, He would identify Himself with that humanity, even the sinful humanity that it was. Son of God, He would become a true Son of man, that through His redemption all other sons of men might become true sons of God. Bearing the sins of many, taking away the sin of the world, that heavy burden lay at His heart from the first; He could not lay it down until He left it nailed to His cross. Himself knowing no sin, He yet becomes the Sin-offering, and is "numbered among the transgressors." And as Jesus went to the cross and into the grave mediatorially, as Humanity's Son, so Jesus now passes into the baptismal waters mediatorially, repenting for that world whose heart is still hard, and whose eyes are dry of godly tears, and confessing the sin which He in love has made His own, the "sin of the world," the sin He has come to make atonement for and to bear away.

Such is the meaning of the Jordan baptism, in which Jesus puts the stamp of Divinity upon John's mission, while John bears witness to the sinlessness of Jesus. But a Higher Witness came than even that of John; for no sooner was the rite administered, and the river-bank regained, than the heavens were opened, and the Spirit of God, in the form of a fiery dove, descended and alighted on the head of Jesus; while a Voice out of the Unseen proclaimed, "This is My beloved Son, in whom I am well pleased." And so the Son of man receives the heavenly, as well as the earthly baptism. Baptized with water, He is now baptized with the Holy Ghost and with fire, anointed with the unction of the Holy One. But why should the Holy Spirit descend upon Jesus in the form of a dove, and afterwards upon the disciples in the form of cloven tongues of fire? We can understand the symbolism of the cloven tongues; for was not their mission to preach and teach, spreading and establishing the kingdom by a consecrated speech--the Divine word carried forward by the human voice? What, then, is the meaning of the dove-form? Does it refer to the dove of the Old Dispensation, which bearing the olive-leaf in its mouth, preached its Gospel to the dwellers in the ark, telling of the abatement of the angry waters, and of a salvation that was near? And was not Jesus a heavenly Dove, bearing to the world the olive-branch of reconciliation and of peace, proclaiming the fuller, wider Gospel of mercy and of love? The supposition, at any rate, is a possible one, while the words of Jesus would almost make it a probable one; for speaking of this same baptism of the Spirit, He says--and in His words we can hear the beat and whir of dove-wings--"He anointed me to preach good tidings to the poor: He hath sent me to proclaim release to the captives, ... to set at liberty them that are bruised" (iv. 18).

The interview between Jesus and John was but brief, and in all probability final. They spend the following night near to each other, but apart. The day after, John sees Jesus walking, but the narrative would imply that they did not meet. John only points to Him and says, "Behold the Lamb of God, which taketh away the sin of the world;" and they part, each to follow his separate path, and to accomplish his separate mission.

"The Lamb of God, which taketh away the sin of the world." Such was John's testimony to Jesus, in the moment of his clearest illumination. He saw in Jesus, not as one learned writer would have us suppose, the sheep of David's pastoral, its life encircled with green pastures and still waters--not this, but a lamb, "the Lamb of God," the Paschal Lamb, led all uncomplaining to the slaughter, and by its death bearing away sin--not either the sin of a year or the sin of a race, but "the sin of the world." Never had prophet so prophesied before; never had mortal eye seen so clearly and so deeply into God's great mystery of mercy. How, then, can we explain that mood of disappointment and of doubt which afterwards fell upon John? What does it mean that from his prison he should send two of his disciples to Jesus with the strange question, "Art Thou He that cometh, or look we for another?" (vii. 19). John is evidently disappointed--yes, and dejected too; and the Elias still, Herod's prison is to him the juniper of the desert. He thought the Christ would be one like unto himself, crying in the wilderness, but with a louder voice and more penetrating accent. He would be some ardent Reformer, with axe in hand, or fan, and with baptism of fire. But lo, Jesus comes so different from his thought--with no axe in hand that he can see, with no baptism of fire that he can hear of, a Sower rather than a Winnower, scattering thoughts, principles, beatitudes, and parables, telling not so much of "the wrath to come" as of the love that is already come, if men will but repent and receive it--that John is fairly perplexed, and actually sends to Jesus for some word that shall be a solvent for his doubts. It only shows how this Elias, too, was a man of like passions with ourselves, and that even prophets' eyes were sometimes dim, reading God's purposes with a blurred vision. Jesus returns a singular answer. He says neither Yes nor No; but He goes out and works His accustomed miracles, and then dismisses the two disciples with the message, "Go your way, and tell John what things ye have seen and heard; how that the blind see, the lame walk, the lepers are cleansed, the deaf hear, the dead are raised, to the poor the Gospel is preached. And blessed is he, whosoever shall not be offended in Me." These words are in part a quotation from John's favourite prophet, Isaiah, who emphasized as no other prophet did the evangelistic character of Christ's mission--which characteristic John seems to have overlooked. In his thought the Christ was Judge, the great Refiner, sifting the base from the pure, and casting it into some Gehenna of burnings. But Jesus reminds John that mercy is before and above judgment; that He has come, "not to condemn the world," but to save it, and to save it, not by reiterations of the law, but by a manifestation of love. Ebal and Sinai have had their word; now Gerizim and Calvary must speak.

And so this greatest of the prophets was but human, and therefore fallible. He saw the Christ, no longer afar off, but near--yea, present; but he saw in part, and he prophesied in part. He did not see the whole Christ, or grasp the full purport of His mission. He stood on the threshold of the kingdom; but the least of those who should pass within that kingdom should stand on a higher vantage-ground, and so be greater than he. Indeed, it seems scarcely possible that John could have fully understood Jesus; the two were so entirely different. In dress, in address, in mode of life, in thought the two were exact opposites. John occupies the border-region between the Old and the New; and though his life appears in the New, he himself belongs rather to the Old Dispensation. His accent is Mosaic, his message a tritonomy, a third giving of the law. When asked the all-important question, "What shall we do?" John laid stress on works of charity, and by his metaphor of the two coats he showed that men should endeavour to equalize their mercies. And when publicans and soldiers ask the same question John gives a sort of transcript of the old tables, striking the negatives of duty: "Extort no more than that which is appointed you;" "Do violence to no man." Jesus would have answered in the simple positive that covered all classes and all cases alike: "Thou shalt love thy neighbour as thyself." But such was the difference between the Old and the New: the one said, "Do, and thou shalt live;" the other said, "Live, and thou shalt do." The voice of John awoke the conscience, but he could not give it rest. He was the preparer of the way; Jesus was the Way, as He was the Truth and the Life. John was the Voice; Jesus was the Word. John must "decrease" and disappear; Jesus must "increase," filling all times and all climes with His glorious, abiding presence.

But the mission of John is drawing to a close, and dark clouds are gathering in the west. The popular idol still, a hostile current has set against him. The Pharisees, unforgetting and unforgiving, are deadly bitter, creeping across his path, and hissing out their "Devil;" while Herod, who in his better moods had invited the Baptist to his palace, now casts him into prison. He will silence the voice he has failed to bribe, the voice that beat against the chambers of his revelry, like a strange midnight gust, and that set him trembling like an aspen. We need not linger over the last sad tragedy--how the royal birthday was kept, with a banquet to the State officials; how the courtesan daughter of Herodias came in and danced before the guests; and how the half-drunken Herod swore a rash oath, that he would give her anything she might ask, up to the half of his kingdom. Herodias knew well what wine and passion would do for Herod. She even guessed his promise beforehand, and had given full directions to her daughter; and soon as the rash oath had fallen from his lips-- before he could recall or change his words--sharp and quick the request is made, "Give me here John Baptist's head in a charger." There is a momentary conflict, and Herod gives the fearful word. The head of John is brought into the banquet-hall before the assembled guests--the long flowing locks, the eyes that even in death seemed to sparkle with the fire of God; the lips sacred to purity and truth, the lips that could not gloss a sin, even the sin of a Herod. Yes; it is there, the head of John the Baptist. The courtiers see it, and smile; Herod sees it, but does not smile. That face haunts him; he never forgets it. The dead prophet lives still, and becomes to Herod another conscience.

"And she brought it to her mother. And his disciples came, and took up the corpse, and buried him; and they went and told Jesus" (Matt. xiv. 11, 12). Such is the finis to a consecrated life, and such the work achieved by one man, in a ministry that was only counted by months. Shall not this be his epitaph, recording his faithfulness and zeal, and at the same time rebuking our aimlessness and sloth?--

> *"He liveth long who liveth well;*
> *All other life is short and vain:*
> *He liveth longest who can tell*
> *Of living most for heavenly gain."*

## CHAPTER VII - THE TEMPTATION

The waters of the Jordan do not more effectually divide the Holy Land than they bisect the Holy Life. The thirty years of Nazareth were quiet enough, amid the seclusions of nature and the attractions of home; but the double baptism by the Jordan now remits that sweet idyll to the past. The I AM of the New Testament moves forward from the passive to the active voice; the long peace is exchanged for the conflict whose consummation will be the Divine Passion.

The subject of our Lord's temptation is mysterious, and therefore difficult. Lying in part within the domain of human consciousness and experience, it stretches far beyond our sight, throwing its dark projections into the realm of spirit, that realm, "dusk with horrid shade," which Reason may not traverse, and which Revelation itself has not illumined, save by occasional lines of light, thrown into, rather than across it. We cannot, perhaps, hope to have a perfect understanding of it, for in a subject so wide and deep there is room for the play of many hypotheses; but inspiration would not have recorded the event so minutely had it not a direct bearing upon the whole of the Divine Life, and were it not full of pregnant lessons for all times. To Him who suffered within it, it was a wilderness indeed; but to us "the wilderness and the solitary place" have become "glad, and the desert ... blossoms as the rose." Let us, then, seek the wilderness reverently yet hopefully, and in doing so let us carry in our minds these two guiding thoughts--they will prove a silken thread for the labyrinth--first, that Jesus was tempted as man; and second, that Jesus was tempted as the Son of man.

Jesus was tempted as man. It is true that in His Person the human and the Divine natures were in some mysterious way united; that in His flesh was the great mystery, the manifestation of God; but now we must regard Him as divested of these dignities and Divinities. They are laid aside, with all other pre-mundane glories; and whatever His miraculous power, for the present it is as if it were not. Jesus takes with Him into the wilderness our manhood, a perfect humanity of flesh and blood, of bone and nerve; no Docetic shadow, but a real body, "made in all things like unto His brethren;" and He goes into the wilderness, to be tempted, not in some unearthly way, as one spirit might be tempted of another, but to be "tempted in all points like as we are," in a fashion perfectly human. Then, too, Jesus was tempted as the Son of man, not only as the perfect Man, but as the representative Man. As the first Adam, by disobedience, fell, and fallen, was driven forth into the wilderness, so the second Adam comes to take the place of the first. Tracking the steps of the first Adam, He too goes out into the wilderness, that He may spoil the spoiler, and that by His perfect obedience He may lead a fallen but redeemed humanity back again to Paradise, reversing the whole drift of the Fall, and turning it into a "rising again for many." And so Jesus goes, as the Representative Man, to do battle for humanity, and to receive in His own Person, not one form of temptation, as the first Adam did, but every form that malignant Evil can devise, or that humanity can know. Bearing these two facts in mind, we will consider--(1) the circumstances of the Temptation, and (2) the nature of the temptation.

1. The circumstances of the Temptation. "And Jesus, full of the Holy Spirit, returned from the Jordan, and was led by the Spirit in the wilderness." The Temptation, then, occurred immediately after the twofold baptism; or, as St. Mark expresses it, using his characteristic word, "And straightway the Spirit driveth Him forth into the wilderness" (Mark i. 12). Evidently there is some connection between the Jordan and the wilderness, and there were Divine reasons why the test should be placed directly after the baptism. Those Jordan waters were the inauguration for His mission--a kind of Beautiful Gate, leading up to the different courts and courses of His public ministry, and then up to the altar of sacrifice. The baptism of the Spirit was His anointing for that ministry, and borrowing our light from the after Pentecostal days, His enduement of power for that ministry. The Divine purpose, which had been gradually shaping itself to His mind, now opens in one vivid revelation. The veil of mist in which that purpose had been enwrapped is swept away by the Spirit's breath, disclosing to His view the path redeeming Love must take, even the way of the cross. It is probable, too, that He received at the same time, if not the enduement, at least the consciousness of miraculous power; for St. John, with one stroke of his pen, brushes away those glossy webs that later tradition has spun, the miracles of the Childhood. The Scriptures do not represent Jesus as any prodigy. His childhood, youth, and manhood were like the corresponding phases of other lives; and the Gospels certainly put no aureole about His head--that was the

afterglow of traditional fancy. Now, however, as He leaves the wilderness, He goes to open His mission at Cana, where He works His first miracle, turning, by a look, the water into wine. The whole Temptation, as we shall see, was one prolonged attack upon His miraculous power, seeking to divert it into unlawful channels; which makes it more than probable that this power was first consciously received at the baptism--the second baptism of fire; it was a part of the anointing of the Lord He then experienced.

We read that Jesus now was "full of the Holy Spirit." It is an expression not infrequent in the pages of the New Testament, for we have already met with it in connection with Zacharias and Elisabeth; and St. Luke makes use of it several times in his later treatise on the "Acts." In these cases, however, it generally marked some special and sudden illumination or inspiration, which was more or less temporary, the inspiration passing away when its purpose was served. But whether this "filling of the Spirit" was temporary, or permanent, as in the case of Stephen and Barnabas, the expression always marked the highest elevation of human life, when the human spirit was in entire subordination to the Divine. To Jesus, now, the Holy Spirit is given without measure; and we, who in our far-off experiences can recall moments of Divine baptisms, when our spirits seemed for the time to be caught up into Paradise, hearing voices and beholding visions we might not utter, even we may understand in part--though but in part--what must have been the emotions and ecstasies of that memorable hour by the Jordan. How much the opened heavens would mean to Him, to whom they had been so long and strangely closed! How the Voice that declared His heavenly Sonship, "This is My beloved Son," must have sent its vibrations quivering through soul and spirit, almost causing the tabernacle of His flesh to tremble with the new excitements! Mysterious though it may seem to us, who ask impotently, How can these things be? yet unless we strip the heavenly baptism of all reality, reducing it to a mere play of words, we must suppose that Jesus, who now becomes Jesus Christ, was henceforth more directly and completely than before under the conscious inspiration of the Holy Spirit. What was an atmosphere enswathing the young life, bringing to that life its treasures of grace, beauty, and strength, now becomes a breath, or rather a rushing wind, of God, carrying that life forward upon its mission and upward to its goal. And so we read, He "was led by the Spirit in the wilderness." The verb generally implies pressure, constraint; it is the enforced leading of the weaker by the stronger. In this case, however, the pressure was not upon a resisting, but a yielding medium. The will of Jesus swung round instantly and easily, moving like a vane only in the direction of the Higher Will. The narrative would imply that His own thought and purpose had been to return to Galilee; but the Divine Spirit moves upon Him with such clearness and force--"driveth" is St. Mark's expressive word--that He yields Himself up to the higher impulse, and allows Himself to be carried, not exactly as the heath is swept before the wind, but in a passive-active way, into the wilderness. The wilderness was thus a Divine interjection, thrown across the path of the Son of God and Son of man.

Where it was is a point of no great moment. That it was in the Desert of Sinai, as some suppose, is most unlikely. Jesus did not so venerate places; nor was it like Him to make distant excursions to put Himself in the track of Moses or Elijah. He beckons them to Him. He does not go to them, not even to make historical repetitions. There is no reason why we may not accept the traditional site of the Quarantania, the wild, mountainous region, intersected by deep, dark gorges, that sweeps westward from Jericho. It is enough to know that it was a wilderness indeed, a wildness, unsoftened by the touch of human strength or skill; a still, vacant solitude, where only the "wild beasts," preying upon each other, or prowling outward to the fringe of civilization, could survive.

In the narrative of the Transfiguration we read that Moses and Elias appeared on the holy mount "talking with Jesus;" and that these two only, of all departed saints, should be allowed that privilege--the one representing the Law, and the other the Prophets--shows that there was some intimate connection between their several missions. At any rate, we know that the emancipator and the regenerator of Israel were specially commissioned to bear Heaven's salutation to the Redeemer. It would be an interesting study, did it lie within the scope of our subject, to trace out the many resemblances between the three. We may, however, notice how in the three lives the same prolonged fast occurs, in each case covering the same period of forty days; for though the expression of St. Matthew would not of necessity imply a total abstention from food, the more concise statement of St. Luke removes all doubt, for we read, "He did eat nothing in those days." Why there should be this fast is more difficult to answer, and our so-called reasons can be only guesses. We know, however, that the flesh and the spirit, though closely associated, have but few things in common. Like the centripetal and the centrifugal forces in nature, their tendencies and propulsions are in different and opposite directions. The one looks earthward, the other heavenward. Let the flesh prevail, and the life gravitates downwards, the sensual takes the place of the spiritual. Let the flesh be placed under restraint and control, taught its subordinate position, and there is a general uplift to the life, the untrammelled spirit moving upwards toward heaven and

God. And so in the Scriptures we find the duty of fasting prescribed; and though the Rabbis have treated it in an ad absurdum fashion, bringing it into disrepute, still the duty has not ceased, though the practice may be well-nigh obsolete. And so we find in Apostolic days that prayer was often joined to fasting, especially when a question of importance was under consideration. The hours of fasting, too, as we may learn from the cases of the centurion and of Peter, were the perihelion of the Christian life, when it swung up in its nearest approaches to heaven, getting amid the circles of the angels and of celestial visions. Possibly in the case before us there was such an absorption of spirit, such rapture (using the word in its etymological, rather than in its derived meaning), that the claims of the body were utterly forgotten, and its ordinary functions were temporarily suspended; for to the spirit caught up into Paradise it matters little whether in the body or out of it.

Then, too, the fast was closely related to the temptation; it was the preparation for it. If Jesus is tempted as the Son of man, it must be our humanity, not at its strongest, but at its weakest. It must be under conditions so hard, no other man could have them harder. As an athlete, before the contest, trains up his body, bringing each muscle and nerve to its very best, so Jesus, before meeting the great adversary in single combat, trains down His body, reducing its physical strength, until it touches the lowest point of human weakness. And so, fighting the battle of humanity, He gives the adversary every advantage. He allows him choice of place, of time, of weapons and conditions, so that His victory may be more complete. Alone in the wild, dreary solitude, cut off from all human sympathies, weak and emaciated with the long fast, the Second Adam waits the attack of the tempter, who found the first Adam too easy a prey.

2. The nature of the Temptation. In what form the tempter came to Him, or whether he came in any form at all, we cannot tell. Scripture observes a prudent silence, a silence which has been made the occasion of much speculative and random speech on the part of its would-be interpreters. It will serve no good purpose even to enumerate the different forms the tempter is said to have assumed; for what need can there be for any incarnation of the evil spirit? and why clamour for the supernatural when the natural will suffice? If Jesus was tempted "as we are," will not our experiences throw the truest light on His? We see no shape. The evil one confronts us; he presents thoughts to our minds; he injects some proud or evil imagination; but he himself is masked, unseen, even when we are distinctly conscious of his presence. Just so we may suppose the tempter came to Him. Recalling the declaration made at the baptism, the announcement of His Divine Sonship, the devil says, "If" (or rather "Since," for the tempter is too wary to suggest a doubt as to His relationship with God) "Thou art the Son of God, command this stone that it become bread." It is as if he said, "You are a-hungered, exhausted, Your strength worn away by Your long fast. This desert, as You see, is wild and sterile; it can offer You nothing with which to supply Your physical wants; but You have the remedy in Your own hands. The heavenly Voice proclaimed You as God's Son--nay, His beloved Son. You were invested, too, not simply with Divine dignities, but with Divine powers, with authority, supreme and absolute, over all creatures. Make use now of this newly given power. Speak in these newly learned tones of Divine authority, and command this stone that it become bread." Such was the thought suddenly suggested to the mind of Jesus, and which would have found a ready response from the shrinking flesh, had it been allowed to speak. And was not the thought fair and reasonable, to our thinking, all innocent of wrong? Suppose Jesus should command the stone into bread, is it any more marvellous than commanding the water into wine? Is not all bread stone, dead earth transformed by the touch of life? If Jesus can make use of His miraculous power for the benefit of others, why should He not use it in the emergencies of His own life? The thought seemed reasonable and specious enough; and at first glance we do not see how the wings of this dove are tipped, not with silver, but with soot from the "pots." But stop. What does this thought of Satan mean? Is it as guileless and guiltless as it seems? Not quite; for it means that Jesus shall be no longer the Son of man. Hitherto His life has been a purely human life. "Made in all things like unto His brethren," from His helpless infancy, through the gleefulness of childhood, the discipline of youth, and the toil of manhood, His life has been nourished from purely human sources. His "brooks in the way" have been no secret springs, flowing for Himself alone; they have been the common brooks, open and free to all, and where any other child of man might drink. But now Satan tempts Him to break with the past, to throw up His Son-of-manhood, and to fall back upon His miraculous power in this, and so in every other emergency of life. Had Satan succeeded, and had Jesus wrought this miracle for Himself, putting around His human nature the shield of His Divinity, then Jesus would have ceased to be man. He would have forsaken the plane of human life for celestial altitudes, with a wide gulf--and oh, how wide!--between Himself and those He had come to redeem. And let the perfect humanity go, and the redemption goes with it; for if Jesus, just by an appeal to His miraculous power, can surmount every difficulty, escape any danger, then you leave no room for the Passion, and no ground on which the cross may rest.

Again, the suggestion of Satan was a temptation to distrust. The emphasis lay upon the title, "Son of God." "The Voice proclaimed You, in a peculiar sense, the beloved Son of God; but where have been the marks of that special love? Where are the honours, the heritage of joy, the Son should have? Instead of that, He gives You a wilderness of solitude and privation; and He who rained manna upon Israel, and who sent an angel to prepare a cake for Elias, leaves You to pine and hunger. Why wait longer for help which has already tarried too long? Act now for Yourself. Your resources are ample; use them in commanding this stone into bread." Such was the drift of the tempter's words; it was to make Jesus doubt the Father's love and care, to lead Him to act, not in opposition to, but independently of, the Father's will. It was an artful endeavour to throw the will of Jesus out of gear with the Higher Will, and to set it revolving around its own self-centre. It was, in reality, the same temptation, in a slightly altered form, which had been only too successful with the first Adam.

The thought, however, was no sooner suggested than it was rejected; for Jesus had a wonderful power of reading thought, of looking into its very heart; and He meets the evil suggestion, not with an answer of His own, but with a singularly apt quotation from the Old Testament: "It is written, Man shall not live by bread alone." The reference is to a parallel experience in the history of Israel, a narrative from which doubtless Jesus had drawn both strength and solace during His prolonged desert fast. Had not the Divine Voice adopted Israel to a special relationship and privilege, announcing within the palace of Pharaoh, "Israel is My Son, My firstborn"? (Exod. iv. 22). And yet had not God led Israel for forty years through the desert, suffering him to hunger, that He might humble and prove him, and show him that men are

*"Better than sheep and goats,
That nourish a blind life within the brain;"*

that man has a nature, a life, that cannot live on bread, but--as St. Matthew completes the quotation--"by every word that proceedeth out of the mouth of God"? Some have supposed that by "bread alone" Jesus refers to the manifold provision God has made for man's physical sustenance; that He is not limited to one course, but that He can just as easily supply flesh, or manna, or a thousand things besides. But evidently such is not the meaning of Jesus. It was not His wont to speak in such literal, commonplace ways. His thought moved in higher circles than His speech, and we must look upward through the letter to find the higher spirit. "I have meat to eat that ye know not of," said Jesus to His disciples; and when He caught the undertone of their literalistic questions He explained His meaning in words that will interpret His answer to the tempter: "My meat is to do the will of Him that sent Me." So now it is as if He said, "The Will of God is My meat. That Will brought Me hither; that Will detains Me here. Nay, that Will commands Me to fast and hunger, and so abstinence from food is itself My food. I do not fear. This wilderness is but the stone-paved court of My Father's house, whose many chambers are filled with treasures, 'bread enough and to spare,' and can I perish with hunger? I wait His time; I accept His will; nor will I taste of bread that is not of His sending."

The tempter was foiled. The specious temptation fell upon the mind of Jesus like a spark in the sea, to be quenched, instantly and utterly; and though Satan found a powerful lever in the pinch of the terrible hunger--one of the sorest pains our human nature can feel--yet even then he could not wrench the will of Jesus from the will of God. The first Adam doubted, and then disobeyed; the Second Adam rests in God's will and word; and like the limpet on the rocks, washed by angry waves, the pressure of the outward storm only unites His will more firmly to the Father's; nor does it for one moment break in upon that rest of soul. And Jesus never did make use of His miraculous power solely for His own benefit. He would live as a man among men, feeling--probably more intensely than we do--all the weaknesses and pains of humanity, that He might be more truly the Son of man, the sympathizing High Priest, the perfect Saviour. He became in all points--sin excepted--one with us, so that we might become one with Him, sharing with Him the Father's love on earth, and then sharing His heavenly joys.

Baffled, but not confessing himself beaten, the tempter returns to the charge. St. Luke here inverts the order of St. Matthew, giving as the second temptation what St. Matthew places last. We prefer the order of St. Luke, not only because in general he is more observant of chronology, but because there is in the three temptations what we might call a certain seriality, which demands the second place for the mountain temptation. It is not necessary that we put a literal stress upon the narrative, supposing that Jesus was transported bodily to the "exceeding high mountain." Not only has such a supposition an air of the incredulous about it, but it is set aside by the terms of the narrative itself; for the expression he "showed Him all the kingdoms of the world in a moment of time" cannot be forced into a literalistic mould. It is easier and more natural to suppose that this and the succeeding temptation were presented only to the spirit of Jesus, without any physical accessories; for after all, it is not the eye that sees, but the soul. The bodily eye had not seen the "great sheet let down from heaven," but it was a real vision, nevertheless, leading to very practical results--the readjustment of Peter's views of duty, and the opening of the door of grace and privilege to the Gentiles. It was but a mental picture, as the "man of Macedonia" appeared to Paul, but the vision was intensely real--more real, if that were possible, than the leagues of intervening sea; and louder to him than all the voices of the deep--of winds, and waves, and storm--was the voice, "Come over and help us," the cry which only the ear of the soul had heard. It was in a similar manner, probably, that the second temptation was presented to Jesus.

He finds Himself upon a lofty eminence, when suddenly, "in a moment of time," as St. Luke expresses it, the world lies unveiled at His feet. Here are fields white with ripened harvests, vineyards red with clustering grapes, groves of olives shimmering in the sunlight like frosted silver, rivers threading their way through a sea of green; here are cities on cities innumerable, quivering with the tread of uncounted millions, streets set with statues, and adorned with temples, palaces, and parks; here are the flagged Roman roads, all pointing to the world's great centre, thronged with chariots and horsemen, the legions of war, and the caravans of trade. Beyond are seas where a thousand ships are skimming over the blue; while still beyond, all environed with temples, is the palace of the Cæsars, the marble pivot around which the world revolves.

Such was the splendid scene set before the mind of Jesus. "All this is mine," said Satan, speaking a half-truth which is often but a whole lie; for he was indeed the "prince of the power of the air," ruling, however, not in absolute kingship, but as a pretender, a usurper; "and I give it to whom I will. Only worship me (or rather, 'do homage to me as Your superior'), and all shall be thine." Amplified, the temptation was this: "You are the Son of God, the Messiah-King, but a King without a retinue, without a throne. I know well all the devious, somewhat slippery ways to royalty; and if You will but assent to my plan, and work on my lines, I can assure You of a throne that is higher, and of a realm that is vaster, than that of Cæsar. To begin with: You have powers not given to other mortals, miraculous powers. You can command nature as easily as You can obey her. Trade with these at first, freely. Startle men with prodigies, and so create a name and gain a following. Then when that is sufficiently large set up the standard of revolt. The priesthood and the people will flock to it; Pharisees and Sadducees, giving up their paper-chases after phantoms, shadows, will forget their strife in the peace of a common war, and before a united people. Rome's legions must retire. Then, pushing out Your borders, and avoiding reverse and disaster by a continual appeal to Your miraculous powers, one after another You will make the neighbouring nations dependent and tributary. So, little by little, You will hem in the might of Rome, until by one desperate struggle You will vanquish the Empire. The lines of history will then be all reversed. Jerusalem will become the mistress, the capital of the world; along all these roads swift messengers shall carry Your decrees; Your word shall be law, and Your will over all human wills shall be supreme."

Such was the meaning of the second temptation. It was the chord of ambition Satan sought to strike, a chord whose vibrations are so powerful in the human heart, often drowning or deafening other and sweeter voices. He put before Jesus the highest possible goal, that of universal empire, and showed how that goal was comparatively easy of attainment, if Jesus would only follow his directions and work on his plans. The objective point at which the tempter aimed was, as in the first temptation, to shift Jesus from the Divine purpose, to detach His will from the Father's will, and to induce Him to set up a sort of independence. The life of Jesus, instead of moving on steadily around its Divine centre, striking in with absolute precision to the beat of the Divine purpose, should revolve only around the centre of its narrower self, exchanging its grander, heavenlier sweep for certain intermittent, eccentric motions of its own. If Satan could not prevent the founding of "the kingdom," he would, if it were possible, change its character. It should not be the kingdom of heaven, but a kingdom of earth, pure and simple, under earthly conditions and earthly laws. Might should take the place of right, and force the place of love. He would set Jesus after gaining the whole world, that so He might forget that His mission was to save it. Instead of a Saviour, they should have a Sovereign, decked with this world's glory and the pomps of earthly empire.

It is easy to see that if Jesus had been merely man the temptation would have been most subtle and most powerful; for how many of the sons of men, alas, have been led astray from the Divine purpose with a far less bait than a whole world! A momentary pleasure, a handful of glittering dust the more, some dream of place or fame--these are more than enough to tempt men to break with God. But while Jesus was man, the Perfect Man, He was more. The Holy Spirit was now given to Him without measure. From the beginning His will had been subordinate to the Father's, growing up within it and configuring itself to it, even as the ductile metal receives the shape of the mould. The Divine purpose, too, had now been revealed to Him in the vivid enlightenment of the Baptism; for the shadow of the cross was thrown back over His life, at any rate as far as the Jordan. And so the second temptation fell harmless as the first. The chord of ambition Satan sought to strike was not found in the pure soul of Jesus, and all these visions of victory and empire awoke no response in His heart, any more than the flower-wreaths laid upon the breast of the dead can quicken the beat of the now silent heart.

The answer of Jesus was prompt and decisive. Not deigning to use any words of His own, or to hold any parley, even the shortest, He meets the word of the tempter with a Divine word: "It is written, Thou shalt worship the Lord thy God, and Him only shalt thou serve." The tempting thought is something foreign to the mind of Jesus, something unwelcome, repulsive, and it is rejected instantly. Instead of allowing Himself to be diverted from the Divine purpose, His will detached from the Father's will, He turns to that will and word at once. It is His refuge, His home. The thought of Jesus cannot pass beyond the circle of that will, any more than a dove can pass beyond the over-arching sky. He sees the Throne that is above all thrones, and gazing upon that, worshipping only the Great King, who is over all and in all, the thrones and crowns of earthly dominion are but as motes of the air. The victory was complete. Quickly as it came, the splendid vision conjured up by the tempter disappeared, and Jesus turned away from the path of earthly glory, where power without measure and honours without number awaited Him, to tread the solitary, lowly path of submission and of sacrifice, the path that had a crucifixion, and not a coronation, as its goal.

Twice baffled, the enemy comes once again to the charge, completing the series with the pinnacle temptation, to which St. Luke naturally, and as we think rightly, gives the third place. It follows the other two in orderly sequence, and it cannot well be placed second, as in St. Matthew, without a certain overlapping of thought. If we must adhere to the literalistic interpretation, and suppose Jesus led up to Jerusalem bodily, then, perhaps, St. Matthew's order would be more natural, as that would not necessitate a return to the wilderness. But that is an interpretation to which we are not bound. Neither the words of the narrative nor the conditions of the temptation require it; and when art represents Jesus as flying with the tempter through the air it is a representation both grotesque and gratuitous. Thus far, in his temptations, Satan has been foiled by the faith of Jesus, the implicit trust He reposed in the Father; but if he cannot break in upon that trust, causing it to doubt or disobey, may he not push the virtue too far, goading Him "to sin in loving virtue"? If the mind and heart of Jesus are so grooved in with the lines of the Divine will that he cannot throw them off the metals, or make them reverse their wheels, perhaps he may push them forward so fast and so far as to bring about the collision he seeks--the clash of the two wills. It is the only chance left him, a forlorn hope, it is true, but still a hope, and Satan moves forward, if perchance he may realize it.

As in the second temptation, the wilderness fades out of sight. Suddenly Jesus finds Himself standing on the pinnacle of the Temple, probably the eastern corner of the royal portico. On the one side, deep below, were the Temple courts, crowded with throngs of worshippers; on the other lay the gorge of the Kedron, a giddy depth, which made the eye of the down looker to swim, and the brain to reel. "If (or rather 'Since') said Satan, Thou art the Son of God, cast Thyself down from hence; for it is written, He shall give His angels charge concerning Thee, to guard Thee; on their hands they shall bear Thee up, lest haply Thou dash Thy foot against a stone." It is as if he said, "You are the Son of God, in a special, favoured sense. You are set in title and authority above the angels; they are Your ministering servants; and You reciprocate the trust Heaven reposes in You. The will of God is more to You than life itself; the word of God outweighs with You thrones and empires. And You do well. Continue thus, and no harm can overtake You. And just to show how absolute is Your faith in God, cast Yourself down from this height. You need not fear, for You will but throw Yourself upon the word of God; and You have only to speak, and unseen angels will crowd the air, bearing You up in their hands. Cast Yourself down, and so test and attest Your faith in God; and doing so You will give to these multitudes indubitable proof of Your Sonship and Messiahship." Such was the argument, specious, but fallacious, of the tempter. Misquoting Scripture by omitting its qualifying clause, distorting the truth into a dangerous error, he sought to impale his Victim on the horn of a dilemma. But Jesus was on the alert. He recognized at once the seductive thought, though, Jacob-like, it had come robed in the assumed dress of Scripture. Is not obedience as sacred as trust? Is not obedience the life, the soul of trust, without which the trust itself is but a semblance, a decaying, corrupt thing? But Satan asks Him to disobey, to set Himself above the laws by which the world is governed. Instead of His will being entirely subordinate, conforming itself in all things to the Divine will, if He should cast Himself down from this pinnacle it would be putting pressure upon that Divine will, forcing it to repeal its own physical laws, or at any rate to suspend their action for a time. And what would that be but insubordination, no longer faith, due presumption, a tempting, and not a trusting God? The Divine promises are not cheques made payable to "bearer," regardless of character, place, or time, and to be realized by any one who may happen to possess himself of them, anywhere. They are cheques drawn out to "order," crossed cheques, too, negotiated only as the conditions of character and time are fulfilled. The Divine protection and guardianship are indeed assured to every child of God, but only as he "dwelleth in the secret place of the Most High, as he abides under the shadow of the Almighty;" in other words, so long as "thy ways" are "His ways." Step out from that pavilion of the Most High, and you step from under the bright bow of promise. Put yourself above, or put yourself out of, the Divine order of things, and the very promise becomes a threatening, and the cloud that else would protect and guide becomes a cloud full of suppressed thunders, and flashing in vivid lightnings its thousand swords of flame. Faith and fidelity are thus inseparable. The one is the calyx, the other the involved corolla; and as they open outwards into the perfect flower they turn towards the Divine will, configuring themselves in all things to that will.

    A third time Jesus replied to the tempter in words of Old Testament Scripture, and a third time, too, from the same book of Deuteronomy. It will be observed, however, that the terms of His reply are slightly altered. He no longer uses the "It is written," since Satan himself has borrowed that word, but substitutes another: "It is said, Thou shalt not tempt the Lord thy God." It has been thought by some that Jesus used the quotation in an accommodated sense, referring the "Thou" to the tempter himself, and so making "the Lord thy God" an attestation of His own Divinity. But such an interpretation is forced and unnatural. Jesus would not be likely to hide the deep secret from His own disciples, and announce it for the first time to the ears of the seducer. It is an impossible supposition. Besides, too, it was as man that Jesus was tempted. Only on the side of His humanity could the enemy approach Him, and for Jesus now to take refuge in His Divinity would strip the temptation of all its meaning, making it a mere acting. But Jesus does not so throw up humanity, or which is the same thing, take Himself out of it, and when He says, "Thou shalt not tempt the Lord thy God" He includes Himself in the "thou." Son though He is, He must put Himself under the law that prescribes the relations of man towards God. He must learn obedience as other sons of men. He must submit, that He may serve, not seeking to impose His will upon the Father's will, even by way of suggestion, much less by way of demand, but waiting upon that will in an absolute self-surrender and instant acquiescence. Moses must not command the cloud; all that he is permitted to do is to observe it and follow. To go before God is to go without God, and to go without Him is to go against Him; and as to the angels bearing Him up in their hands, that depends altogether upon the path and the errand. Let it be the Divinely ordered path, and the unseen convoys of heaven will attend, a sleepless, invincible guard; but let it be some self-chosen path, some forbidden way, and the angel's sword will flash its warning, and send the foot of the unfaithful servant crushing against the wall.

    And so the third temptation failed, as did the other two. With but a little tension, Satan had made the will of the first Adam to strike a discordant note, throwing it out of all harmony with the Higher Will; but by no pressure, no enticements, can he influence the Second Adam. His will vibrates in a perfect consonance with the Father's, even under the terrible pressure of hunger, and the more terrible pressure, the fearful impact of evil.

    So Satan completed, and so Jesus resisted, "every temptation"--that is, every form of temptation. In the first, Jesus was tempted on the side of His physical nature; in the second the attack was on the side of His intellectual nature, looking out on His political life; while in the third the assault was on the side of His spiritual life. In the first He is tempted as the Man, in the second as the Messiah, and in the third as the Divine Son. In the first temptation He is asked to make use of His newly received miraculous power over nature--passive, unthinking nature; in the second He is asked to throw it over the "world", which in this case is a synonym for humankind; while in the third He is asked to widen the realm of His authority, and to command the angels, nay, God Himself. So the three temptations are really one, though the fields of battle lie in three several planes. And the aim was one. It was to create a divergence between the two wills, and to set the Son in a sort of antagonism to the Father, which would have been another Absalom revolt, a Divine mutiny it is impossible for us even to conceive.

    St. Luke omits in his narrative the ministry of angels mentioned by the other two Synoptists, a sweet postlude we should have missed much, had it been wanting; but he gives us instead the retreat of the adversary: "He departed from Him for a season." How long a season it was we do not know, but a brief one it must have been, for again and again in the story of the Gospels we see the dark shadow of the evil one; while in Gethsemane the "prince of this world" cometh, but to find "nothing in Me." And what was the horror of great darkness, that strange eclipse of soul Jesus suffered upon Calvary, but the same fearful presence, intercepting for a time even the Father's smile, and throwing upon the pure and patient Sufferer a strip of the outer darkness itself?

    The test was over. Tried in the fires of a persistent assault, the faith and obedience of Jesus were found perfect. The shafts of the tempter had recoiled upon himself, leaving all stainless and scatheless the pure soul of Jesus. The Son of man had conquered, that all other sons of men may learn the secret of constant and complete victory; how faith overcomes, putting to flight "the armies

*Henry Burton*

of the aliens," and making even the weakest child of God "more than conqueror." And from the wilderness, where innocence has ripened into virtue, Jesus passes up, like another Moses, "in the power of the Spirit," to challenge the world's magicians, to baffle their sleight of hand and skill of speech, and to proclaim to redeemed humanity a new Exodus, a life-long Jubilee.

# CHAPTER VIII - THE GOSPEL OF THE JUBILEE

Immediately after the Temptation Jesus returned, "in the power of the Spirit," and with all the added strength of His recent victories, to Galilee. Into what parts of Galilee He came, our Evangelist does not say; but omitting the visit to Cana, and dismissing the first Galilean tour with a sentence--how "He taught in their synagogues, being glorified of all"--St. Luke goes on to record in detail the visit of Jesus to Nazareth, and His rejection by His townsmen. In putting this narrative in the forefront of his Gospel is St. Luke committing a chronological error? or is he, as some suppose, purposely antedating the Nazareth story, that it may stand as a frontispiece to his Gospel, or that it may serve as a key for the after-music? This is the view held by most of our expositors and harmonists, but, as it appears to us, on insufficient grounds; the balance of probability is against it. It is true that St. Matthew and St. Mark record a visit to Nazareth which evidently occurred at a later period of His ministry. It is true also that between their narratives and this of St. Luke there are some striking resemblances, such as the teaching in the synagogue the astonishment of His hearers, their reference to His parentage, and then the reply of Jesus as to a prophet receiving scant honour in his own country--resemblances which would seem to indicate that the two narratives were in reality one. But still it is possible to push these resemblances too far, reading out from them what we have first read into them. Let us for the moment suppose that Jesus made two visits to Nazareth; and is not such a supposition both reasonable and natural? It is not necessary that the first rejection should be a final rejection, for did not the Jews seek again and again to kill Him, before the cross saw their dire purpose realized? Remaining for so long in Galilee, would it not be a most natural wish on the part of Jesus to see the home of His boyhood once again, and to give to His townspeople one parting word before taking His farewell of Galilee? And suppose He did, what then? Would He not naturally go to the synagogue--as was His custom in every place--and speak? And would they not listen with the same astonishment, and then harp on the very same questions as to His parentage and brotherhood--questions that would have their readiest and fittest answer in the same familiar proverb? Instead, then, of these resemblances identifying the two narratives, and proving that St. Luke's story is but an amplification of the narratives of the other Synoptists, the resemblances themselves are what we might naturally expect in our supposition of a second visit. But if there are certain coincidences between the two narratives, there are marked differences, which make it extremely improbable that the Synoptists are recording one event. In the visit recorded by St. Luke there were no miracles wrought; while St. Matthew and St. Mark tell us that He could not do many mighty works there, because of their unbelief, but that He "laid His hands on a few sick folk, and healed them." In the narrative by St. Mark we read that His disciples were with Him while St. Luke makes no mention of His disciples; but St. Luke does mention the tragic ending of the visit, the attempt of the men of Nazareth to hurl Him down from a lofty cliff, an incident St. Matthew and St. Mark omit altogether. But can we suppose the men of Nazareth would have attempted this, had the strong body-guard of disciples been with Jesus? Would they be likely to stand by, timidly acquiescent? Would not Peter's sword have flashed instantly from its scabbard, in defence of Him whom he served and dearly loved? That St. Matthew and St. Mark should make no reference to this scene of violence, had it occurred at the visit they record, is strange and unaccountable; and the omission is certainly an indication, if not a proof, that the Synoptists are describing two separate visits to Nazareth--the one, as narrated by St. Luke, at the commencement of His ministry; and the other at a later date, probably towards its close. And with this view the substance of the Nazareth address perfectly accords. The whole address has the ring of an inaugural message; it is the voice of an opening spring, and not of a waning summer. "This day is this Scripture fulfilled in your ears" is the blast of the silver trumpet announcing the beginning of the Messianic year, the year of a truer, wider Jubilee.

It seems to us, therefore, that the chronology of St. Luke is perfectly correct, as he places in the forefront of his Gospel the earlier visit to Nazareth, and the violent treatment Jesus there received. At the second visit there was still a widespread unbelief, which caused Jesus to marvel; but there was no attempt at violence, for His disciples were with Him now, while the report of His Judæan ministry, which had gone before Him, and the miracles He wrought in their presence, had softened down even Nazareth prejudices and asperities. The events of the first Galilean tour were probably in the following order. Jesus, with His five disciples, goes to Cana, invited guests at the marriage, and here He opens His miraculous commission, by turning the water into wine. From Cana they proceed to Capernaum, where they remain for a short time, Jesus preaching in their synagogue, and probably continuing His miraculous works. Leaving His disciples behind at Capernaum--for between the preliminary call by the Jordan and the final call by the lake the fisher-disciples get back to their old occupations for a while--Jesus goes up to Nazareth, with His mother and His brethren. Thence, after His violent rejection, He returns to Capernaum, where He calls His disciples from their boats and receipt of custom, probably completing the sacred number before setting out on His journey southward to Jerusalem. If this harmony be correct--and the weight of probability seems to be in its favour--then the address at Nazareth, which is the subject for our consideration now, would be the first recorded utterance of Jesus; for thus far Cana gives us one startling miracle, while in Capernaum we find the report of His acts, rather than the echoes of His words. And that St. Luke alone should give us this incident, recording it in such a graphic manner, would almost imply that he had received the account from an eye-witness, probably--if we may gather anything from the Nazarene tone of St. Luke's earlier pages--from some member of the Holy Family.

Jesus has now fairly embarked upon His Messianic mission, and He begins that mission, as prophecy had long foretold He should, in Galilee of the Gentiles. The rumour of His wonderful deeds at Cana and Capernaum had already preceded Him thither, when Jesus came once again to the home of His childhood and youth. Going, as had been His custom from boyhood, into the synagogue on the Sabbath day (St. Luke is writing for Gentiles who are unversed in Jewish customs), Jesus stood up to read. "The Megilloth," or Book of the Prophets, having been handed to Him, He unrolled the book, and read the passage in Isaiah (lxi. 1) to which His mind had been Divinely directed, or which He had purposely chosen:--

*"The Spirit of the Lord is upon Me,*
*Because He anointed Me to preach good tidings to the poor,*
*He hath sent Me to proclaim release to the captives,*
*And recovering of sight to the blind,*
*To set at liberty them that are bruised,*
*To proclaim the acceptable year of the Lord."*

Then closing, or rolling up, the book, and handing it back to the attendant, Jesus sat down, and began His discourse. The Evangelist does not record any of the former part of the discourse, but simply gives us the effect produced, in the riveted gaze and the rising astonishment of His auditors, as they caught up eagerly His sweet and gracious words. Doubtless, He would explain the words of the prophet, first in their literal, and then in their prophetic sense; and so far He carried the hearts of His hearers with Him, for who could speak of their Messianic hopes without awaking sweet music in the Hebrew heart? But directly Jesus applies the passage to Himself, and says, "This day is this Scripture fulfilled in your ears," the fashion of their countenance alters; the Divine emphasis He puts upon the Me curdles in their heart, turning their pleasure and wonder into incredulity, envy, and a perfect frenzy of rage. The primary reference of the prophecy seems to have been to the return of Israel from captivity. It was a political Jubilee he proclaimed, when Zion should have a "garland for ashes," when the captive should be free, and aliens should be their servants. But the flowers of Scripture are mostly double; its pictures and parables have often a nearer meaning, and another more remote, or a spiritual, involved in the literal sense. That it was so here is evident, for Jesus takes this Scripture--which we might call a Babylonish garment, woven out of the Exile--and wraps it around Himself, as if it belonged to Himself alone, and were so intended from the very first. His touch thus invests it with a new significance; and making this Scripture a vestment for Himself, Jesus, so to speak, shakes out its narrower folds, and gives it a wider, an eternal meaning. But why should Jesus select this passage above all others? Were not the Old Testament Scriptures full of types, and shadows, and prophecies which testified of Him, any one of which He might have appropriated now? Yes, but no other passage so completely answered His design, no other was so clearly and fully declarative of His earthly mission. And so Jesus selected this picture of Isaiah, which was at once a prophecy and an epitome of His own Gospel, as His inaugural message, His manifesto.

The Mosaic Code, in its play upon the temporal octaves, had made provision, not only for a weekly Sabbath, and for a Sabbath year, but it completed its cycle of festivals by setting apart each fiftieth year as a year of special grace and gladness. It was the year of redemption and restoration, when all debts were remitted, when the family inheritance, which by the pressure of the times had been alienated, reverted to its original owner, and when those who had mortgaged their personal liberty regained their freedom. The "Jubilee" year, as they called it--putting into its name the play of the priestly trumpets which ushered it in--was thus the Divine safeguard against monopolies, a Divine provision for a periodic redistribution of the wealth and privileges of the theocracy; while at the same time it served to keep intact the separate threads of family life, running its lines of lineage down through the centuries, and across into the New Testament. Seizing upon this, the gladdest festival of Hebrew life, Jesus likens Himself to one of the priests, who with trumpet of silver proclaims "the acceptable year of the Lord." He finds in that Jubilee a type of His Messianic year, a year that shall bring, not to one chosen race alone, but to a world of debtors and captives, remissions and manumissions without number, ushering in an era of liberty and gladness. And so in these words, adapted and adopted from Isaiah, Jesus announces Himself as the world's Evangelist, and Healer, and Emancipator; or separating the general message into its prismatic colours, we have the three characteristics of Christ's Gospel--(1) as the Gospel of Love; (2) the Gospel of Light; and (3) the Gospel of Liberty.

1. The Gospel of Jesus was the Gospel of Love. "He anointed Me to preach good tidings to the poor." That there is a Gospel even in the Old Testament no one will attempt to deny, and able writers have delighted in tracing out the evangelism that, like hidden veins of gold, runs here and there, now embedded deep in historical strata, and now cropping out in the current of prophetical speech. Still, an ear but little trained to harmonies can detect a marvellous difference between the tone of the Old and the tone of the New Dispensation. "Evangelists" is scarcely the name we should give to the prophets and preachers of the Old Testament, if we except that prophet of the dawn, Isaiah. They came, not as the bearers of glad tidings, but with the pressure, the burden of a terrible "woe" upon them. With a voice of threat and doom they recall Israel back to the ways of fidelity and purity, and with the caustic of biting words they seek to burn out the cancer of national corruption. They were no doves, those old-time prophets, building their nests in the blossoming olives, in soft accents telling of a winter past and a summer near; they were storm-birds rather, beating with swift, sad wings on the crest of sullen waves, or whirling about among the torn shrouds. Even the eremite Baptist brought no evangel. He was a sad man, with a sad message, telling, not of the right which men should do, but of the wrong they should not do, his ministry, like that of the law, being a ministry of condemnation. Jesus, however, announces Himself as the world's Evangelist. He declares that He is anointed and commissioned to be the bearer of good, glad tidings to man. At once the Morning Star and Sun, He comes to herald a new day; nay, He comes to make that day. And so it was. We cannot listen to the words of Jesus without noticing the high and heavenly pitch to which their music is set. Beginning with the Beatitudes, they move on in the higher spaces, striking the notes of courage, hope, and faith, and at last, in the guest-chamber, dropping down to their key-note, as they close with an eirenicon and a benediction. How little Jesus played upon men's fears! how, instead, He sought to inspire them with new hopes, telling of the possibilities of goodness, the perfections which were within reach of even the human endeavour! How seldom you catch the tone of despondency in His words! As He summons men to a life of purity, unselfishness, and faith, His are not the voice and mien of one who commands to a forlorn hope. There is the ring of courage, conviction, certainty about His tone, a hopefulness that was itself half a victory. Jesus was no Pessimist, reading over the grave of departed glories His "ashes to ashes;" He who knew our human nature best had most hopes of it, for He saw the Deity that was around it and within it.

And just here we touch what we may call the fundamental chord in the Gospel of Jesus, the Fatherhood of God; for though we can detect other strains running through the music of the Gospel, such as the Love of God, the Grace of God, and the Kingdom of God, yet these are but the consonant notes completing the harmonic scale, or the variations that play about the Divine Fatherhood. To the Hebrew conception of God this was an element altogether new. To their mind Jehovah is the Lord of hosts, an invisible, absolute Power, inhabiting the thick darkness, and speaking in the fire. Sinai thus throws its shadow across the Old Testament Scriptures, and men inhale an atmosphere of law rather than of love.

But what a transformation was wrought in the world's thought and life as Jesus unfolded the Divine Fatherhood! It altered the whole aspect of man's relation to God, with a change as marked and glorious as when our earth turns its face more directly to the sun, to find its summer. The Great King, whose will commanded all forces, became the Great Father, in whose compassionate heart the toiling children of men might find refuge and rest. The "Everlasting Arms" were none the less strong and omnipotent; but as Jesus uncovered them they seemed less distant, less rigid; they became so near and so gentle, the weakest child of earth might not fear to lay its tired heart upon them. Law was none the less mighty, none the less majestic, but it was now a transfigured law, all lighted up and suffused with love. No longer was life one round of servile tasks, demanded by an inexorable, invisible Pharaoh; no longer was it a trampled playground, where all the flowers are crushed, as Fate and Chance take their alternate innings. No; life was ennobled, adorned with new and rare beauties; and when Jesus opened the gate of the Divine Fatherhood the light that was beyond, and that "never was on sea or land," shone through, putting a heavenliness upon the earthly, and a Divineness upon the human life. What better, gladder tidings could the poor (whether in spirit or in life) hear than this--that heaven was no longer a distant dream, but a present and most precious reality, touching at every point, and enfolding their little lives; that God was no longer hostile, or even indifferent to them, but that He cared for them with an infinite care, and loved them with an infinite love? Thus did Jesus proclaim the "good tidings;" for love, grace, redemption, and heaven itself are all found within the compass of the Fatherhood. And He who gave to His disciples, in the Paternoster, a golden key for heaven's audience-chamber, speaks that sacred name "Father" even amid the agonies of the cross, putting the silver trumpet to His parched and quivering lips, so that earth may hear once again the music of its new and more glorious Jubilee.

2. The Gospel of Jesus was a Gospel of Light. "And recovering of sight to the blind," which is the Septuagint rendering of the Hebrew passage in Isaiah, "the opening of the prison to them that are bound." At first sight this appears to be a break in the Jubilee idea; for physical cures, such as the healing of the blind, did not come within the scope of Jubilatic mercies. The original expression, however, contains a blending of figures, which together preserve the unity of the prophetic picture. Literally it reads, "The opening of the eyes to them that are bound;" the figure being that of a captive, whose long captivity in the darkness has filmed his vision, and who now passes through the opened door of his prison into the light of day.

In what way shall we interpret these words? Are they to be taken literally, or spiritually? or are both methods equally legitimate? Evidently they are both intended, for Jesus was the Light-bringer in more senses than one. That the Messiah should signalize His advent by performing wonders and signs, and by working physical cures, was certainly the teaching of prophecy, as it was a fixed and prominent hope in the expectation of the Jews. And so, when the despondent Baptist sent two of his disciples to ask "Art Thou He that should come?" Jesus gave no direct answer, but turning from His questioners to the multitude of sick who pressed around Him, He healed their sick, and gave sight to many that were blind. Then returning to the surprised strangers, He bids them carry back to their master these visible proofs of His Messiahship--how that "lepers are cleansed, and the blind receive their sight." Jesus Himself had a wonderful power of vision. His eyes were divinely bright, for they carried their own light. Not only had He the gift of prescience, the forward-looking eye; He had what for want of a word we may call the gift of perscience, the eye that looked within, that saw the heart and soul of things. What a strange fascination there was in His very look! how it flashed like a subtle lightning, striking and scathing with its holy indignation the half-veiled meanness and hypocrisy! and how again, like a beam of light, it fell upon Peter's soul, thawing the chilled heart, and opening the closed fountain of his tears, as an Alpine summer falls on the rigid glacier, and sends it rippling and singing through the lower vales. And had not Jesus an especial sympathy for cases of ophthalmic distress, paying to the blind a peculiar attention? How quickly He responded to Bartimæus--"What is it that I shall do for thee?"--as if Bartimæus were conferring the benefit by making his request. Where on the pages of the four Gospels do we find a picture more full of beauty and sublimity than when we read of Jesus taking the blind man by the hand, and leading him out of the town? What moral grandeur and what touching pathos are there! and how that stoop of gentleness makes Him great! No other case is there of such prolonged and tender sympathy, where He not only opens the gates of day for the benighted, but leads the benighted one up to the gates. And why does Jesus make this difference in His miracles, that while other cures are wrought instantly, even the raising of the dead, with nothing more than a look, a word, or a touch, in healing the blind He should work the cure, as it were, in parts, or by using such intermediaries as clay, saliva, or the water of Siloam's pool? Must it not have been intentional? It would seem so, though what the purpose might be we can only guess. Was it so gradual an inletting of the light, because a glare too bright and sudden would only confuse and blind? or did Jesus linger over the cure with the pleasure of one who loves to watch the dawn, as it paints the east with vermilion and gold? or did Jesus make use of the saliva and clay, that like crystal lenses, they might magnify His power, and show how His will was supreme, that He had a thousand ways of restoring sight, and that He had only to command even unlikely things, and light, or rather sight, should be? We do not know the purpose, but we do know that physical sight was somehow a favourite gift of the Lord Jesus, one that He handed to men carefully and tenderly. Nay, He Himself said that the man of Jerusalem had been born blind "that the works of God should be manifest in him;" that is, his firmament had been for forty years darkened that his age, and all coming ages, might see shining within it the constellations of Divine Pity and Divine Power.

But while Jesus knew well the anatomy of the natural eye, and could and did heal it of its disorders, putting within the sunken socket the rounded ball, or restoring to the optic nerve its lost powers, this was not the only sight He brought. To the companion clauses of this prophecy, where Jesus proclaims deliverance to the captives, and sets at liberty them that are bruised, we are

*The Expositor's Bible: The Gospel According to St. Luke*

compelled to give a spiritual interpretation; and so "the recovering of sight to the blind" demands a far wider horizon than the literalistic sense offers. It speaks of the true Light which lighteth every man, that spiritual photosphere that environs and enswathes the soul, and of the opening and adjusting of the spiritual sense; for as sight without light is darkness, so light without sight is darkness still. The two facts are thus related, each useless apart from the other, but together producing what we call vision. The recovering of sight to the blind is thus the universal miracle. It is the "Let light be" of the new Genesis, or, as we prefer to call it, the "regeneration." It is the dawn, which, breaking over the soul, broadens unto the perfect day, the heavenly, the eternal noon. Jesus Himself recognized this binoculism, this double vision. He says (John xvi. 16), "A little while, and ye behold Me no more; and again a little while, and ye shall see Me," using two altogether different words--the one speaking of the vision of the sense, the other of the deeper vision of the soul. And it was so. The disciples' vision of the Christ, at least so long as the bodily presence was with them, was the earthly, physical vision. The spiritual Christ was, in a sense, lost, masked in the corporeal. The veil of His flesh hung dense and heavy before their eyes, and not until it was uplifted on the cross, not until it was rent in twain, did they see the mysterious Holy Presence that dwelt within the veil. Nor was the clearer vision given them even now. The dust of the sepulchre was in their eyes, blurring, and for a time half-blinding them--the anointing with the clay. The emptied grave, the Resurrection, was their "pool of Siloam," washing away the blinding clay, the dust of their gross, materialistic thoughts. Henceforth they saw Christ, not, as before, ever coming and going, but as the ever-present, the abiding One. In the fuller light of the Pentecostal flames the unseen Christ became more near and more real than the seen Christ ever was. Seeing Him as visible, their minds were holden, somewhat perplexed; they could neither accomplish much nor endure much; but seeing Him who had become invisible, they were a company of invincibles. They could do and they could endure anything; for was not the I AM with them always?

Now, even in the physical vision there is a wonderful correspondence between the sight and the soul, the prospect and introspect. As men read the outward world they see pretty much the shadow of themselves, their thoughts, feelings, and ideas. In the German fable the travelled stork had nothing to say about the beauty of the fields and wonders of the cities over which it passed, but it could discourse at length about the delicious frogs it had found in a certain ditch. Exactly the same law rules up in the higher vision. Men see what they themselves love and are; the sight is but a sort of projection of the soul. As St. Paul says, "The natural man receiveth not the things of God;" the things which God hath prepared for them that love Him are "things which eye saw not, and ear heard not." And so Jesus gives sight by renewing the soul; He creates around us a new heaven and a new earth, by creating a new, a clean heart within us. Within every soul there are the possibilities of a Paradise, but these possibilities are dormant. The natural heart is a chaos of confusion and darkness, until it turns towards Jesus as its Saviour and its Sun, and henceforth revolves around Him in its ever-narrowing circles.

3. The Gospel of Jesus was a Gospel of Liberty. "He hath sent Me to proclaim release to the captives," "to set at liberty them that are bruised." The latter clause is not in the original prophecy, but is a rough adaptation of another passage in Isaiah (lviii. 6). Probably it was quoted by Jesus in His address, and so was inserted by the Evangelist with the passages read; for in the New Testament the quotations from the Old are grouped together by affinities of spirit, rather than by the law of textual continuity. The two passages are one in their proclamation and promise of liberty, but they by no means cover the same ground. The former speaks of the liberation of captives, those whom the exigencies of war or some change of fortune have thrown into prison; the latter speaks of deliverance to the oppressed, those whose personal liberties may not be impawned, but whose lives are made hard and bitter under severe exactions, and whose spirits are broken, crushed beneath a weight of accumulated ills. Speaking generally, we should call the one an amnesty, and the other an enfranchisement; for one is the offer of freedom to the captive, the other of freedom to the slave; while together they form an act of emancipation for humanity, enfranchising and ennobling each individual son of man, and giving to him, even the poorest, the freedom of God's world.

In what sense, then, is Jesus the great Emancipator? It would be easy to show that Jesus, personally, was a lover of freedom. He could not brook restraints. Antiquity, conventionalism, had no charms for Him. Keenly in touch with the present, He did not care to take the cold, clammy hand of a dead Past, or allow it to prescribe His actions. Between the right and the wrong, the good and the evil, He put a wall of adamant, God's eternal "No;" but within the sphere of the right, the good, He left room for largest liberties. He observed forms--occasionally, at least--but formalism He could not endure. And so Jesus was constantly coming into collision with the Pharisaic school of thought, the school of routinists, casuists, whose religion was a glossary of terms, a volume of formulas and negations. To the Pharisee religion was a cold, dead thing, a mummy, all enswathed in the cerecloths of tradition; to Jesus it was a living soul within a living form, an angel of grace and beauty, whose wings would bear her aloft to higher, heavenlier spheres, and whose feet and hands fitted her just as well for the common walks of life, in a beautiful, every-day ministry of blessing. And how Jesus loved to give personal liberty to man--to remove the restrictions disease had put around their activities, and to leave them physically, mentally free! And what were His miracles of healing but proclamations of liberty, in the lowest sense of that word? He found the human body enfeebled, enslaved; here it was an arm, there an eye, so held in the grip of disease that it was as if dead. But Jesus said to Disease, "Loose that half-strangled life and let it go," and in an instant it was free to act and feel, finding its lesser jubilee. Jesus saw the human mind led into captivity. Reason was dethroned and immured in the dungeon, while the feet of lawless passions were trampling overhead. But when Jesus healed the demoniac, the imbecile, the lunatic, what was it but a mental jubilee, as He gives peace to a distracted soul, and leads banished Reason back to her Jerusalem?

But these deliverances and liberties, glorious as they are, are but figures of the true, which is the enfranchisement of the soul. The disciples were perplexed and sorely disappointed that Jesus should die without having wrought any "redemption" for Israel. This was their one dream, that the Messiah should break in pieces the hated Roman yoke, and effect a political deliverance. But they see Him moving steadily to His goal, taking no note of their aspirations, or noticing them only to rebuke them, and scarce giving a passing glance to these Roman eagles, which darken the sky, and cast their ominous shadows over the homes and fields of Israel. But Jesus had not come into the world to effect any local, political redemption; another Moses could have done that. He had come to lead captive the captivity of Sin, as Zacharias had foretold, "that being delivered out of the hand of our (spiritual) enemies, we might serve Him without fear, in holiness and righteousness all the days of our life." The sphere of His mission was where His kingdom should be, in the great interior of the heart. A Prophet like unto Moses, but infinitely greater than he, He too leaves the palace, of the Eternal, laying aside, not the robes of a prospective royalty, but the glories He possessed with the Father; He too assumes the dress, the speech, nay, the very nature, of the race He has come to redeem. And when no other ransom was sufficient He "offered Himself without spot to God," "our Passover, sacrificed for us," so sprinkling the doorway of the new Exodus with His own blood. But here we stand on the threshold of a great mystery; for if angels bend over the mercyseat, desiring, but in vain, to read the secret of redemption, how can our finite minds grasp the great thought and purpose of God? We do know this, however, for it is the oft-repeated truth of Scripture, that the life, or, as St. Peter puts it, "the precious blood of Christ," was, in a certain sense, our ransom, the price of our redemption. We say "in a certain sense," for the figure breaks down if we press it unduly, as if Heaven had held a parley with the power that had enslaved man, and, at a stipulated price, had bought him off. That certainly was no part of the Divine purpose and fact of redemption. But an atonement was needed in order to make salvation possible; for how could God, infinitely holy and just, remit the penalty due to sin with no expression of His abhorrence of sin, without destroying the dignity of law, and reducing justice to a mere name? But the obedience and death of Christ were a satisfaction of infinite worth. They upheld the majesty of law, and at the same time made way for the interventions of Divine Love. The cross of Jesus was thus the place where Mercy and Truth met together, and Righteousness and Peace kissed each other. It was at once the visible expression of God's deep hatred of sin, and of His deep love to the sinner. And so, not virtually simply, in some far-off sense, but in truest reality, Jesus "died for our sins," Himself tasting death that we might have life, even the life "more abundant," the life everlasting; suffering Himself to be led captive by the powers of sin, bound to the cross and imprisoned in a grave, that men might be free in all the glorious liberty of the children of God.

But this deliverance from sin, the pardon for past offences, is but one part of the salvation Jesus provides and proclaims. Heaven's angel may light up the dungeon of the imprisoned soul; he may strike off its fetters, and lead it forth into light and liberty; but if Satan can reverse all this, and fling back the soul into captivity, what is that but a partial, intermittent salvation, so unlike Him whose name is Wonderful? The angel said, "He shall save His people," not from the effects of their sin, from its guilt and condemnation alone, but "from their sins." That is, He shall give to the pardoned soul power over sin; it shall no longer have dominion over him; captivity itself shall be led captive; for

> "His grace, His love, His care
> Are wider than our utmost need,
> And higher than our prayer."

Yes, verily; and the life that is hid with Christ in God, that, with no side-glances at self, is set apart utterly to do the Divine will, that abandons itself to the perfect keeping of the perfect Saviour, will find on earth the "acceptable year of the Lord," its years, henceforth, years of liberty and victory, a prolonged Jubilee.

# CHAPTER IX - A SABBATH IN GALILEE

We should naturally expect that our physician-Evangelist would have a peculiar interest in Christ's connection with human suffering and disease, and in this we are not mistaken.

It is almost a superfluous task to consider what our Gospels would have been had there been no miracles of healing to record; but we may safely say that such a blank would be inexplicable, if not impossible. Even had prophecy been utterly silent on the subject, should we not look for the Christ to signalize His advent and reign upon earth by manifestations of His Divine power? A Man amongst men, human yet superhuman, how can He manifest the Divinity that is within, except by the flashings forth of His supernatural power? Speech, however eloquent, however true, could not do this. There must be a background of deeds, visible credentials of authority and power, or else the words are weak and vain--but the play of a borealis in the sky, beautiful and bright indeed, but distant, inoperative, and cold. If the prophets of old, who were but acolytes swinging their lamps and singing their songs before the coming Christ, were allowed to attest their commission by occasional enduements of miraculous power, must not the Christ Himself prove His super-humanity by fuller measures and exhibitions of the same power? And where can He manifest this so well as in connection with the world's suffering, need, and pain? Here is a background prepared, and all dark enough in sooth; where can He write so well that men may read His messages of good-will, love, and peace? Where can He put His sign manual, His Divine autograph, better than on this firmament of human sorrow, disease, and woe? And so the miracles of healing fall naturally into the story; they are the natural and necessary accompaniments of the Divine life upon earth.

The first miracle that Jesus wrought was in the home at Cana; His first miracle of healing was in the synagogue. He thus placed Himself in the two pivotal centres of our earthly life; for that life, with its heavenward and earthward aspects, revolves about the synagogue and the home. He touches our human life alike on its temporal and its spiritual side. To a nature like that of Jesus, which had an intense love for what was real and true, and as intense a scorn for what was superficial and unreal, it would seem as if a Hebrew synagogue would offer but few attractions. True, it served as the visible symbol of religion; it was the shrine where the Law and the Prophets spoke; what spiritual life there was circled and eddied around its door; while its walls, pointing to Jerusalem, kept the scattered populations in touch with the Temple, that marbled dream of Hebraism; but in saying this we say nearly all. The tides of worldliness and formality, which, sweeping through the Temple gates, had left a scum of mire even upon the sacred courts, chilling devotion and almost extinguishing faith, had swept over the threshold of the synagogue. There the scribes had usurped Moses' seat, exalting Tradition as a sort of essence of Scripture, and deadening the majestic voices of the law in the jargon of their vain repetitions. But Jesus does not absent Himself from the service of the synagogue because the fires upon its altars are dulled and quenched by the down-draught of the times. To Him it is the house of God, and if others see it not, He sees a ladder of light, with ascending and descending angels. If others hear but the voices of man, all broken and confused, He hears the Diviner voice, still and small; He hears the music of the heavenly host, throwing down their Glorias upon earth. The pure in heart can find and see God anywhere. He who worships truly carries his Holy of holies within him. He who takes his own fire need never complain of the cold, and with wood and fire all prepared, he can find or he can build an altar upon any mount. Happy is the soul that has learned to lean upon God, who can say, amid all the distractions and interventions of man, "My soul, wait thou only upon God." To such a one, whose soul is athirst for God, the Valley of Baca becomes a well, while the hot rock pours out its streams of blessing. The art of worship avails nothing if the heart of worship is gone; but if that remain, subtle attractions will ever draw it to the place where "His name is recorded, and where His honour dwelleth."

In his earlier chapters St. Luke is careful to light his Sabbath lamp, telling that such and such miracles were wrought on that day, because the Sabbath question was one on which Jesus soon came into collision with the Pharisees. By their traditions, and the withs of dry and sharp legalities, they had strangled the Sabbath, until life was well-nigh extinct. They had made rigorous and exacting what God had made bright and restful, fencing it around with negations, and burdening it with penalties. Jesus broke the withs that bound her, let the freer air play upon her face, and then led her back to the sweet liberties of her earlier years. How He does it the sequel will show.

The Sabbath morning finds Jesus repairing to the synagogue at Capernaum, a sanctuary built by a Gentile centurion, and presided over by Jairus, both of whom are yet to be brought into close personal relationship with Christ. From the silence of the narrative we should infer that the courtesy offered at Nazareth was not repeated at Capernaum--that of being invited to read the lesson from the Book of the Prophets. But whether so or not, He was allowed to address the congregation, a privilege which was often accorded to any eminent stranger who might be present. Of the subject of the discourse we know nothing. Possibly it was suggested by some passing scene or incident, as the sculptured pot of manna, in this same synagogue, called forth the remarkable address about the earthly and the heavenly bread (John vi. 31). But if the substance of the discourse is lost to us, its effect is not. It awoke the same feeling of surprise at Capernaum as it had done before among the more rustic minds of Nazareth. There, however, it was the graciousness of His words, their mingled "sweetness and light," which so caused them to wonder; here at Capernaum it was the "authority" with which He spoke that so astonished them, so different from the speech of the scribes, which, for the most part, was but an iteration of quibbles and trivialities, with just as much of originality as the "old clo'" cries of our modern streets. The speech of Jesus came as a breath from the upper air; it was the intense language of One who possessed the truth, and who was Himself possessed by the truth. He dealt in principles, not platitudes; in eternal facts, and not in the fancies of gossamer that tradition so delighted to spin. Others might speak with the hesitancy of doubt; Jesus spoke in "verilys" and verities, the very essences of truth. And so His word fell upon the ears of men with the tones of an oracle; they felt themselves addressed by the unseen Deity who was behind; they had not learned, as we have, that the Deity of their oracle was within. No wonder that they are astonished at His authority--an authority so perfectly free from any assumptions; they will wonder still more when they find that demons, too, recognize this authority, and obey it.

While Jesus was still speaking--the tense of the verb implies an unfinished discourse-- suddenly He was interrupted by a loud, wild shout: "Ah, what have we to do with Thee, Thou Jesus of Nazareth? Art Thou come to destroy us? I know Thee, who Thou art, the Holy One of God." It was the cry of a man who, as our Evangelist expresses it, "had a spirit of an unclean devil." The phrase is a singular one, in fact unique, and savours a little of tautology; for St. Luke uses the words "spirit" and "devil" as synonyms (ix. 39). Later in his Gospel he would simply have said "he had an unclean devil;" why, then, does he here amplify the phrase, and say he had "a spirit of an unclean devil"? We can, of course, only conjecture, but might it not be because to the Gentile mind--to which he is writing--the powers of evil were represented as personifications, having a corporeal existence? And so in his first reference to demoniacal possession he pauses to explain that these demons are evil "spirits," with existences altogether separate from the diseased humanity which temporarily they were allowed to inhabit and to rule. Neither can we determine with certainty the meaning of the phrase "an unclean devil," though probably it was so called because it drove its victim to haunt unclean places, like the Gadarene, who had his dwelling among the tombs.

The whole subject of demonology has been called in question by certain modern critics. They aver that it is simply an after-growth of Paganism, the seeds of worn-out mythologies which had been blown over into the Christian mind; and eliminating from them all that is supernatural, they reduce the so-called "possessions" to the natural effects of purely natural causes, physical and mental. It is confessedly a subject difficult as it is mysterious; but we are not inclined, at the bidding of rationalistic clamour, so to strike out the supernatural. Indeed, we cannot, without impaling ourselves upon this dilemma, that Jesus, knowingly or unknowingly, taught as the truth what was not true. That Jesus lent the weight of His testimony to the popular belief is evident; never once, in all His allusions, does He call it in question, nor hint that He is speaking now only in an accommodated sense, borrowing the accents of current speech. To Him the existence and presence of evil spirits was just as patent and as solemn a fact as was the existence of the arch-spirit, even Satan himself. And granting the existence of evil spirits, who will show us the line of limitation, the "Hitherto, but no farther," where their influence is stayed? Have we not seen, in mesmerism, cases of real possession, where the weaker human will has been completely overpowered by the stronger will? when the subject was no longer himself, but his thoughts, words, and acts were those of another? And are there not, in the experiences of all medical men, and of ministers of religion, cases of depravity so utterly foul and loathsome that they cannot be explained except by the Jewish taunt, "He hath a devil"? According to the teaching of Scripture, the evil spirit possessed the man in the entirety of his being, commanding his own spirit, ruling both body and mind. Now it touched the tongue with a certain glibness of speech, becoming a "spirit of divination," and now it touched it with dumbness, putting upon the life the spell of an awful silence. Not that the obscurity of the eclipse was always the same. There were more lucid moments, the penumbras of brightness, when, for a brief interval, the consciousness seemed to awake, and the human will seemed struggling to assert itself; as is seen in the occasional dualism of its speech, when the "I" emerges from the "we," only, however, to be drawn back again, to have its identity swallowed up as before.

Such is the character who, leaving the graves of the dead for the abodes of the living, now breaks through the ceremonial ban, and enters the synagogue. Rushing wildly within--for we can scarcely suppose him to be a quiet worshipper; the rules of the synagogue would not have allowed that--and approaching Jesus, he abruptly breaks in upon the discourse of Jesus with his cry of mingled fear and passion. Of the cry itself we need not speak, except to notice its question and its confession. "Art Thou come to destroy us?" he asks, as if, somehow, the secret of the Redeemer's mission had been told to these powers of darkness. Did they know that He had come to "destroy" the works of the devil, and ultimately to destroy, with an everlasting destruction, him who had the power of death, that is, the devil? Possibly they did, for, citizens of two worlds, the visible and the invisible, should not their horizon be wider than our own? At any rate, their knowledge, in some points, was in advance of the nascent faith of the disciples. They knew and confessed the Divinity of Christ's mission, and the Divinity of His Person, crying, "I know Thee, who Thou art, the Holy One of God;" "Thou art the Son of God" (iv. 41), when as yet the faith of the disciples was only a nebula of mist, made up in part of unreal hopes and random guesses. Indeed, we seldom find the demons yielding to the power of Christ, or to the delegated power of His disciples, but they make their confession of superior knowledge as if they possessed a more intimate acquaintance with Christ. "Jesus I know, and Paul I know," said the demon, which the sons of Sceva could not exorcise (Acts xix. 15), while now the demon of Capernaum boasts, "I know Thee, who Thou art, the Holy One of God." Nor was it a vain boast either, for our Evangelist asserts that Jesus did not suffer the demons to speak, "because they knew that He was the Christ" (ver. 41). They knew Jesus, but they feared and hated Him. In a certain sense they believed, but their belief only caused them to tremble, while it left them demons still. Just so is it now:--

"There are, too, who believe in hell and lie;
There are who waste their souls in working out
Life's problem, on these sands betwixt two tides,
And end, 'Now give us the beasts' part, in death.'"

Saving faith is thus more than a bare assent of the mind, more than some cold belief, or vain repetition of a creed. A creed may be complete and beautiful, but it is not the Christ; it is only the vesture the Christ wears; and alas, there are many still who will chaffer about, and cast lots for, a creed, who will go directly and crucify the Christ Himself! The faith that saves, besides the assent of the mind, must have the consent of the will and the surrender of the life. It is "with the heart," and not only with the mind, man "believeth unto righteousness."

The interruption brought the discourse of Jesus to an abrupt end, but it served to point the discourse with further exclamations of surprise, while it offered space for a new manifestation of Divine authority and power. It did not in the least disconcert the Master, though it had doubtless sent a thrill of excitement through the whole congregation. He did not even rise from His seat (ver. 38), but retaining the teaching posture, and not deigning a reply to the questions of the demon, He rebuked the evil spirit, saying, "Hold thy peace, and come out of him," thus recognizing the dual will, and distinguishing between the possessor and the possessed. The command was obeyed instantly and utterly; though, as if to make one last supreme effort, he throws his victim down upon the floor of the synagogue, like Samson Agonistes, pulling to the ground the temple of his imprisonment. It was, however, a vain attempt, for he did him "no hurt." The roaring lion had indeed been "muzzled"--which is the primitive meaning of the verb rendered "Hold thy peace"--by the omnipotent word of Jesus.

They were "astonished at His teaching" before, but how much more so now! Then it was a convincing word; now it is a commanding word. They hear the voice of Jesus, sweeping like suppressed thunder over the boundaries of the invisible world, and commanding even devils, driving them forth, just with one rebuke, from the temple of the human soul, as afterwards He drove the traders from His Father's house with His whip of small cords. No wonder that "amazement came upon all," or that they asked, "What is this word? for with authority and power He commandeth the unclean spirits, and they come out."

And so Jesus began His miracles of healing at the outmost marge of human misery. With the finger of His love, with the touch of His omnipotence, He swept the uttermost circle of our human need, writing on that far and low horizon His wonderful name, "Mighty to save." And since none are outcasts from His mercy save those who outcast themselves, why should we limit "the Holy One of Israel"? why should we despair of any? Life and hope should be coeval.

Immediately on retiring from the synagogue, Jesus passes out of Capernaum, and along the shore to Bethsaida, and enters, together with James and John, the house of Peter and Andrew (John i. 44). It is a singular coincidence that the Apostle Peter, with whose name the Romish Church takes such liberties, and who is himself the "Rock" on which they rear their huge fabric of priestly assumptions, should be the only Apostle of whose married life we read; for though John afterwards possesses a "home," its only inmate besides, as far as the records show, is the new "mother" he leads away from the cross. It is true we have not the name of Peter's wife, but we find her shadow, as well as that of her husband, thrown across the pages of the New Testament; cleaving to her mother even while she follows another; ministering to Jesus, and for a time finding Him a home; while later we see her sharing the privations and the perils of her husband's wandering life (1 Cor. ix. 5). Verily, Rome has drifted far from the "Rock" of her anchorage, the example of her patron saint; and between the Vatican of the modern Pontiff and the sweet domesticities of Bethsaida is a gulf of divergence which only a powerful imagination can cross.

No sooner, however, has Jesus entered the house than He is told how Peter's mother-in-law has been suddenly stricken down by a violent fever, probably a local fever for which that lake-shore was notorious, and which was bred from the malaria of the marsh. Our physician-Evangelist does not stay to diagnose the malady, but he speaks of it as "a great fever," thus giving us an idea of its virulence and consequent danger. "And they besought Him for her;" not that He was at all reluctant to grant their request, for the tense of the verb implies that once asking was sufficient; but evidently there was the "beseeching" look and tone of a mingled love and fear. Jesus responds instantly; for can He come fresh from the healing of a stranger, to allow a dread shadow to darken the home and the hearts of His own? Seeking the sick chamber, He bends over the fever-stricken one, and taking her hand in His (Mark i. 31), He speaks some word of command, "rebuking the fever," as St. Luke expresses it. In a moment the fatal fire is quenched, the throbbing heart regains its normal beat, a delicious coolness takes the place of the burning heat, while the fever-flush steals away to make place for the bloom of health. The cure was perfect and instant. The lost strength returned, and "immediately she arose and ministered unto them," preparing, doubtless, the evening meal.

May we not throw the light of this narrative upon one of the questions of the day? Men speak of the reign of law, and the drift of modern scientific thought is against any interference--even Divine--with the ordinary operations of physical law. As the visible universe is opened up and explored the heavens are crowded back and back, until they seem nothing but a golden mist, some distant dream. Nature's laws are seen to be so uniform, so ruthlessly exact, that certain of those who should be teachers of a higher faith are suggesting the impossibility of any interference with their ordinary operations. "You do but waste your breath," they say, "in asking for any immunities from Nature's penalties, or for any deviation from her fixed rules. They are invariable, inviolate. Be content rather to be conformed, mentally and morally, to God's will." But is prayer to have so restricted an area? is the physical world to be buried so deep in "law" that it shall give no rest to prayer, not even for the sole of her foot? Entire conformity to God's will is, indeed, the highest aim and privilege of life, and he who prays the most seeks most for this; but has God no will in the world of physics, in the realm of matter? Shall we push Him back to the narrow ledge of a primal Genesis? or shall we leave Him chained to that frontier coast, another Prometheus bound? It is well to respect and to honour law, but Nature's laws are complex, manifold. They can form combinations numberless, working different or opposite results. He who searches for "the springs of life" will

"Reach the law within the law;"

and who can tell whether there is not a law of prayer and faith, thrown by the Unseen Hand across all the warp of created things, binding "the whole round earth" about "the feet of God"? Reason says, "It might be so," and Scripture says, "It is so." Was Jesus angry when they told Him of the fever-stricken, and they implored His intervention? Did He say, "You mistake My mission. I must not interfere with the course of the fever; it must have its range. If she lives, she lives; and if she dies, she dies; and whether the one or the other, you must be patient, you must be content"? But such were not the words of Jesus, with their latent fatalism. He heard the prayer, and at once granted it, not by annulling Nature's laws, nor even suspending them, but by introducing a higher law. Even though the fever was the result of natural causes, and though it probably might have been prevented, had they but drained the marsh or planted it with the eucalyptus, yet this does not shut out all interventions of Divine mercy. The Divine compassion makes some allowance for our human ignorance, when it is not wilful, and for our human impotence.

The fever "left her, and immediately she rose up and ministered unto them." Yes, and there are fevers of the spirit as well as of the flesh, when the heart is quick and flurried, the brain hot with anxious thought, when the fret and jar of life seem eating our strength away, and our disquiet spirit finds its rest broken by the pressure of some fearful nightmare. And how soon does this soul-fever strike us down! how it unfits us for our ministry of blessing, robbing us of the "heart at leisure from itself," and filling the soul with sad, distressing fears, until our life seems like the helpless, withered leaf, whirled and tossed hither and thither by the wind! For the fever of the body there may not always be relief, but for the fever of the spirit there is a possible and a perfect cure. It is the touch of Jesus. A close personal contact with the living and loving Christ will rebuke the fever of your heart; it will give to your soul a quietness and restfulness that are Divine; and with the touch of His omnipotence upon you, and with all the elation of conscious strength, you too will arise into a nobler life, a life which will find its supremest joy in ministering unto others, and so ministering unto Him.

Such was the Sabbath in Galilee in which Jesus began His miracles of healing. But if it saw the beginning of His miracles, it did not see their end; for soon as the sun had set, and the Sabbath restraint was over, "all that had any sick with divers diseases brought them unto Him, and He laid His hands on every one of them, and healed them." A marvellous ending of a marvellous day! Jesus throws out by handfuls His largesse of blessing, health, which is the highest wealth, showing that there is no end to His power, as there is no limit to His love; that His will is supreme over all forces and all laws; that He is, and ever will be, the perfect Saviour, binding up the broken in heart, assuaging all griefs, and healing all wounds!

Henry Burton

## CHAPTER X - THE CALLING OF THE FOUR

When Peter and his companions had the interview with Jesus by the Jordan, and were summoned to follow Him, it was the designation, rather than the appointment, to the Apostleship. They did accompany Him to Cana, and thence to Capernaum; but here their paths diverged for a time, Jesus passing on alone to Nazareth, while the novitiate disciples fall back again into the routine of secular life. Now, however, His mission is fairly inaugurated, and He must attach them permanently to His person. He must lay His hand, where His thoughts have long been, upon the future, making provision for the stability and permanence of His work, that so the kingdom may survive and flourish when the Ascension clouds have made the King Himself invisible.

St. Matthew and St. Mark insert their abridged narrative of the call before the healing of the demoniac and the cure of Peter's mother-in-law; and most expositors think that St. Luke's setting "in order," in this case at least, is wrong; that he has preferred to have a chronological inaccuracy, so that His miracles may be gathered into related groups. But that our Evangelist is in error is by no means certain; indeed, we are inclined to think that the balance of probability is on the side of his arrangement. How else shall we account for the crowds who now press upon Jesus so importunately and with such Galilean ardour? It was not the rumour of His Judæan miracles which had awoke this tempest of excitement, for the journey to Jerusalem was not yet taken. And what else could it be, if the miraculous draught of fishes was the first of the Capernaum miracles? But suppose that we retain the order of St. Luke, that the call followed closely upon that memorable Sabbath, then the crowds fall into the story naturally; it is the multitude which had gathered about the door when the Sabbath sun had set, putting an after-glow upon the hills, and on whose sick He wrought His miracles of healing. Nor does the fact that Jesus went to be a guest in Peter's house require us to invert the order of St. Luke; for the casual acquaintance by the Jordan had since ripened into intimacy, so that Peter would naturally offer hospitality to his Master on His coming to Capernaum. Again, too, going back to the Sabbath in the synagogue, we read how they were astonished at His doctrine; "for His word was with authority;" and when that astonishment was heightened into amazement, as they saw the demon cowed and silenced, this was their exclamation, "What a word is this!" And does not Peter refer to this, when the same voice that commanded the demon now commands them to "Let down the nets," and he answers, "At Thy word I will"? It certainly seems as if the "word" of the sea-shore were an echo from the synagogue, and so a "word" that justifies the order of our Evangelist.

It was probably still early in the morning--for the days of Jesus began back at the dawn, and very often before--when He sought the quiet of the sea-shore, possibly to find a still hour for devotion, or perhaps to see how His friends had fared with their all-night fishing. Little quiet, however, could He find, for from Capernaum and Bethsaida comes a hurrying and intrusive crowd, surging around Him with the swirl and roar of confused voices, and pressing inconveniently near. Not that the crowd was hostile; it was a friendly but inquisitive multitude, eager, not so much to see a repetition of His miracles, as to hear Him speak, in those rare, sweet accents, "the word of God." The expression characterizes the whole teaching of Jesus. Though His words were meant for earth, for human ears and for human hearts, there was no earthliness about them. On the topics in which man is most exercised and garrulous, such as local or national events, Jesus is strangely silent. He scarcely gives them a passing thought; for what were the events of the day to Him who was "before Abraham," and who saw the two eternities? what to Him was the gossip of the hour, how Rome's armies marched and fought, or how "the dogs of faction" bayed? To His mind these were but as dust caught in the eddies of the wind. The thoughts of Jesus were high. Like the figures of the prophet's vision, they had feet indeed, so that they could alight and rest awhile on earthly things-- though even here they only touched earth at points which were common to humanity, and they were winged, too, having the sweep of the lower spaces and of the highest heavens. And so there was a heavenliness upon the words of Jesus, and a sweetness, as if celestial harmonies were imprisoned within them. They set men looking upwards, and listening; for the heavens seemed nearer as He spoke, and they were no longer dumb. And not only did the words of Jesus bring to men a clearer revelation of God, correcting the hard views which man, in his fears and his sins, had formed of Him, but men felt the Divineness of His speech; that Jesus was the Bearer of a new evangel, God's latest message of hope and love. And He was the Bearer of such a message; He was Himself that

Evangel, the Word of God incarnate, that men might hear of heavenly things in the common accents of earthly speech.

Nor was Jesus loth to deliver His message; He needed no constraining to speak of the things pertaining to the kingdom of God. Only let Him see the listening heart, the void of a sincere longing, and His speech distilled as the dew. And so no time was to Him inopportune; the break of day, the noon, the night were all alike to Him. No place was out of harmony with His message--the Temple-court, the synagogue, the domestic hearth, the mountain, the lake-shore; He consecrated all alike with the music of His speech. Nay, even upon the cross, amid its agonies, He opens His lips once more, though parched with terrible thirst, to speak peace within a penitent soul, and to open for it the gate of Paradise.

Drawn up on the shore, close by the water's edge, are two boats, empty now, for Simon and his partners are busy washing their nets, after their night of fruitless toil. Seeking for freer space than the pushing crowd will allow Him, and also wanting a point of vantage, where His voice will command a wider range of listeners, Jesus gets into Simon's boat, and requests him to put out a little from the land. "And He sat down, and taught the multitudes out of the boat," assuming the posture of the teacher, even though the occasion partook so largely of the impromptu character. When He dispensed the material bread He made the multitudes "sit down;" but when He dispensed the living bread, the heavenly manna, He left the multitudes standing, while He Himself sat down, so claiming the authority of a Master, as His posture emphasized His words. It is somewhat singular that when our Evangelist has been so careful and minute in his description of the scene, giving us a sort of photograph of that lakeside group, with bits of artistic colouring thrown in, that then he should omit entirely the subject-matter of the discourse. But so he does, and we try in vain to fill up the blank. Did He, as at Nazareth, turn the lamps of prophecy full upon Himself, and tell them how the "great Light" had at last risen upon Galilee of the nations? or did He let His speech reflect the shimmer of the lake, as He told in parable how the kingdom of heaven was "like unto a net that was cast into the sea, and gathered of every kind"? Possibly He did, but His words, whatever they were, "like the pipes of Pan, died with the ears and hearts of those who heard them."

"When He had left speaking," having dismissed the multitude with His benediction, He turns to give to His future disciples, Peter and Andrew, a private lesson. "Put out into the deep," He said, including Andrew now in His plural imperative, "and let down your nets for a draught." It was a commanding voice, altogether different in its tone from the last words He addressed to Peter, when He "requested" him to put out a little from the land. Then He spoke as the Friend, possibly the Guest, with a certain amount of deference; now He steps up to a very throne of power, a throne which in Peter's life He never more abdicates. Simon recognizes the altered conditions, that a Higher Will is now in the boat, where hitherto his own will has been supreme; and saluting Him as "Master," he says, "We toiled all night, and took nothing; but at Thy word I will let down the nets." He does not demur; he does not hesitate one moment. Though himself weary with his night-long labours, and though the command of the Master went directly against his nautical experiences, he sinks his thoughts and his doubts in the word of his Lord. It is true he speaks of the failure of the night, how they have taken nothing; but instead of making that a plea for hesitancy and doubt, it is the foil to make his unquestioning faith stand out in bolder relief. Peter was the man of impulse, the man of action, with a swift-beating heart and an ever-ready hand. To his forward-stepping mind decision was easy and immediate; and so, almost before the command was completed, his swift lips had made answer, "I will let down the nets." It was the language of a prompt and full obedience. It showed that Simon's nature was responsive and genuine, that when a Christly word struck upon his soul it set his whole being vibrating, and drove out all meaner thoughts. He had learned to obey, which was the first lesson of discipleship; and having learned to obey, he was therefore fit to rule, qualified for leadership, and worthy of being entrusted with the keys of the kingdom.

And how much is missed in life through feebleness of resolve, a lack of decision! How many are the invertebrate souls, lacking in will and void of purpose, who, instead of piercing waves and conquering the flow of adverse tides, like the medusæ, can only drift, all limp and languid, in the current of circumstance! Such men do not make apostles; they are but ciphers of flesh and blood, of no value by themselves, and only of any worth as they are attached to the unit of some stronger will. A poor broken thing is a life spent in the subjunctive mood, among the "mights" and "shoulds," where the "I will" waits upon "I would". That is the truest, worthiest life that is divided between the indicative and the imperative. As in shaking pebbles the smaller ones drop down to the bottom, their place determined by their size, so in the shaking together of human lives, in the rub and jostle of the world, the strong wills invariably come to the top.

And how much do even Christians lose, through their partial or their slow obedience! How we hesitate and question, when our duty is simply to obey! How we cling to our own ways, modes, and wills, when the Christ is commanding us forward to some higher service! How strangely we forget that in the grammar of life the "Thou willest" should be the first person, and the "I will" a far-off second! When the soldier hears the word of command he becomes deaf to all other voices, even the voice of danger, or the voice of death itself; and when Christ speaks to us His word should completely fill the soul, leaving no room for hesitancy, no place for doubt. Said the mother to the servants of Cana, "Whatsoever He saith unto you, do it." That "whatsoever" is the line of duty, and the line of beauty too. He who makes Christ's will his will, who does implicitly "whatsoever He saith," will find a Cana anywhere, where life's water turns to wine, and where life's common things are exalted into sacraments. He who walks up to the light will surely walk in the light.

We can imagine with what alacrity Simon obeys the Master's word, and how the disappointment of the night and all sense of fatigue are lost in the exhilaration of the new hopes. Seconded by the more quiet Andrew, who catches the enthusiasm of his brother's faith, he pulls out into deep water, where they let down the nets. Immediately they enclosed "a great multitude" of fishes, a weight altogether beyond their power to lift; and as they saw the nets beginning to give way with the strain, Peter "beckoned" to his partners, James and John, whose boat, probably, was still drawn up on the shore. Coming to their assistance, together they secured the spoil, completely filling the two boats, until they were in danger of sinking with the over-weight.

Here, then, we find a miracle of a new order. Hitherto, in the narrative of our Evangelist, Jesus has shown His supernatural power only in connection with humanity, driving away the ills and diseases which preyed upon the human body and the human soul. And not even here did Jesus make use of that power randomly, making it common and cheap; it was called forth by the constraint of a great need and a great desire. Now, however, there is neither the desire nor the need. It was not the first time, nor was it to be the last, that Peter and Andrew had spent a night in fruitless toil. That was a lesson they had early to learn, and which they were never allowed long to forget. They had been quite content to leave their boat, as indeed they had intended, on the sands, until the evening should recall them to their task. But Jesus volunteers His help, and works a miracle--whether of omnipotence, or omniscience, or of both, it matters not, and not either to relieve some present distress, or to still some pain, but that He might fill the empty boats with fishes. We must not, however, assess the value of the miracle at the market-price of the take, for evidently Jesus had some ulterior motive and design. As the leaden types, lying detached and meaningless in the "case," can be arranged into words and be made to voice the very highest thought, so these boats and oars, nets and fish are but so many characters, the Divine "code" as we may call it, spelling out, first to these fishermen, and then to mankind in general, the deep thought and purpose of Christ. Can we discover that meaning? We think we may.

In the first place, the miracle shows us the supremacy of Christ. We may almost read the Divineness of Christ's mission in the manner of its manifestation. Had Jesus been man only, His thoughts running on human lines, and His plans built after human models, He would have arranged for another Epiphany at the beginning of His ministry, showing His credentials at the first, and announcing in full the purpose of His mission. That would have been the way of man, fond as he is of surprises and sudden transitions; but such is not the way of God. The forces of heaven do not move forward in leaps and somersaults; their advances are gradual and rhythmic. Evolution, and not revolution, is the Divine law, in the realm of matter and of mind alike. The dawn must precede the day. And just so the life of the Divine Son is manifested. He who is the "Light of the world" comes into that world softly as a sunrise, lighting up little by little the horizon of His disciples' thought, lest a revelation which was too full and too sudden should only dazzle and blind them. So far they have seen Him exercise His power over diseases and demons, or, as at Cana, over inorganic matter; now they see that power moving out in new directions. Jesus sets up His throne to face the sea, the sea with which they were so familiar, and over which they claimed some sort of lordship. But even here, upon their own element, Jesus is supreme. He sees what they do not; He knows these deeps, filling up with His omniscience the blanks they seek to fill with their random guesses. Here, hitherto, their wills have been all-powerful; they could take their boats and cast their nets just when and where they would; but now they feel the touch of a Higher Will, and Christ's word fills their hearts, impelling them onward, even as their boats were driven of the wind. Jesus now assumes the command. His Will, like a magnet, attracts to itself and controls their lesser wills; and as His word now launches out the boat and casts the nets, so shortly, at that same "word," will boats and nets, and the sea itself, be left behind.

And did not that Divine Will move beneath the water as well as above it, controlling the movements of the shoal of fishes, as on the surface it was controlling the thoughts and moving the hands of the fishermen? It is true that in Gennesaret, as in our modern seas, the fish sometimes moved in such dense shoals that an enormous "take" would be an event purely natural, a wonder indeed, but no miracle. Possibly it was so here, in which case the narrative would resolve itself into a miracle of omniscience, as Jesus saw, what even the trained eyes of the fishermen had not seen, the movements of the shoal, then regulating His commands, so making the oars above and the fins below strike the water in unison. But was this all? Evidently not, to Peter's mind, at any rate. Had it been all to him, a purely natural phenomenon, or had he seen in it only the prescience of Christ, a vision somewhat clearer and farther than his own, it would not have created such feelings of surprise and awe. He might still have wondered, but he scarcely would have worshipped. But Peter feels himself in the presence of a Power that knows no limit, One who has supreme authority over diseases and demons, and who now commands even the fishes of the sea. In this sudden wealth of spoil he reads the majesty and glory of the new-found Christ, whose word, spoken or unspoken, is omnipotent, alike in the heights above and in the depths beneath. And so the moment his thoughts are disengaged from the pressing task he prostrates himself at the feet of Jesus, crying with awe-stricken speech, "Depart from me; for I am a sinful man, O Lord!" We are not, perhaps, to interpret this literally, for Peter's lips were apt to become tremulous with the excitement of the moment, and to say words which in a cooler mood he would recall, or at least modify. So here, it surely was not his meaning that "the Lord," as he now calls Jesus, should leave him; for how indeed should He depart, now that they are afloat upon the deep, far from land? But such had been the revelation of the power and holiness of Jesus, borne in by the miracle upon Peter's soul, that he felt himself thrown back, morally and in every way, to an infinite distance from Christ. His boat was unworthy to carry, as the house of the centurion was unworthy to receive, such infinite perfections as now he saw in Jesus. It was an apocalypse indeed, revealing, together with the purity and power of Christ, the littleness, the nothingness of his sinful self; that, as Elijah covered his face when the Lord passed by, so Peter feels as if he ought to draw the veil of an infinite distance around himself--the distance which would ever be between him and the Lord, were not His mercy and His love just as infinite as His power.

    The fuller meaning of the miracle, however, becomes apparent when we interpret it in the light of the call which immediately followed. Reading the sudden fear which has come over Peter's soul, and which has thrown his speech somewhat into confusion, Jesus first stills the agitation of his heart by a word of assurance and of cheer. "Fear not," He says, for "from henceforth thou shalt catch men." It will be observed that St. Luke puts the commission of Christ in the singular number, as addressed to Peter alone, while St. Matthew and St. Mark put it in the plural, as including Andrew as well: "I will make you to become fishers of men." The difference, however, is but immaterial, and possibly the reason why St. Luke introduces the Apostle Peter with such a frequent nomination--for "Simon" is a familiar name in these early chapters--making his call so emphatic and prominent, was because in the partisan times which came but too early in the Church the Gentile Christians, for whom our Evangelist is writing, might think unworthily and speak disparagingly of him who was the Apostle of the Circumcision. Be this as it may, Simon and Andrew are now summoned to, and commissioned for, a higher service. That "henceforth" strikes across their life like a high watershed, severing the old from the new, their future from their past, and throwing all the currents of their thoughts and plans into different and opposite directions. They are to be "fishers of men," and Jesus, who so delights in giving object-lessons to His disciples, uses the miracle as a sort of background, on which He may write their commission in large and lasting characters; it is the Divine seal upon their credentials.

    Not that they understood the full purport of His words at once. The phrase "fishers of men" was one of those seed-thoughts which needed pondering in the heart; it would gradually unfold itself in the after-months of discipleship, ripening at last in the summer heat and summer light of the Pentecost. They were now to be fishers of the higher art, their quest the souls of men. This must now be the one object, the supreme aim of their life, a life now ennobled by a higher call. Plans, journeys, thoughts, and words, all must bear the stamp of their great commission, which is to "catch men," not unto death, however, as the fish expire when taken from their native element, but unto life--for such is the meaning of the word. And to "take them alive" is to save them; it is to take them out of an element which stifles and destroys, and to draw them, by the constraints of truth and love, within the kingdom of heaven, which kingdom is righteousness and life, even eternal life.

    But if the full meaning of the Master's words grows upon them--an aftermath to be harvested in later months--enough is understood to make the line of present duty plain. That "henceforth" is clear, sharp, and imperative. It leaves room neither for excuse nor postponement. And so immediately, "when they had brought their boats to land, they left all and followed Him," to learn by following how they too might be winners of souls, and in a lesser, lower sense, saviours of men.

    The story of St. Luke closes somewhat abruptly, with no further reference to Simon's partners; and having "beckoned" them into his central scene, and filled their boat, then, as in a dissolving-view, the pen of our Evangelist draws around them the haze of silence, and they disappear. The other Synoptists, however, fill up the blank, telling how Jesus came to them, probably later in the day, for they were mending the nets, which had been tangled and somewhat torn with the weight of spoil they had just taken. Speaking no word of explanation, and giving no word of promise, He simply says, with that commanding voice of His, "Follow Me," thus putting Himself above all associations and all relationships, as Leader and Lord. James and John recognize the call, for which doubtless they had been prepared, as being for themselves alone, and instantly leaving the father, the "hired servants," and the half-mended nets, and breaking utterly with their past, they follow Jesus, giving to Him, with the exception of one dark, hesitating hour, a life-long devotion. And forsaking all, the four disciples found all. They exchanged a dead self for a living Christ, earth for heaven. Following the Lord fully, with no side-glances at self or selfish gain--at any rate after the enduement and the enlightenment of Pentecost--they found in the presence and friendship of the Lord the "hundredfold" in the present life. Allying themselves with Christ, they too rose with the rising Sun. Obscure fishermen, they wrote their names among the immortals as the first Apostles of the new faith, bearers of the keys of the kingdom. Following Christ, they led the world; and as the Light that rose over Galilee of the nations becomes ever more intense and bright, so it makes ever more intense and vivid the shadows of these Galilean fishermen, as it throws them across all lands and times.

And such even now is the truest and noblest life. The life which is "hid with Christ" is the life that shines the farthest and that tells the most. Whether in the more quiet paths and scenes of discipleship or in the more responsible and public duties of the apostolate, Jesus demands of us a true, whole-souled, and life-long devotion. And, here indeed, the paradox is true, for by losing life we find it, even the life more abundant; for

> "Men may rise on stepping-stones
> Of their dead selves to higher things."

Nay, they may attain to the highest things, even to the highest heavens.

## CHAPTER XI – CONCERNING PRAYER

When the Greeks called man ho anthropos, or the "uplooking one," they did but crystallize in a word what is a universal fact, the religious instinct of humanity. Everywhere, and through all times, man has felt, as by a sort of intuition, that earth was no Ultima Thule, with nothing beyond but oceans of vacancy and silence, but that it lay in the over-shadow of other worlds, between which and their own were subtle modes of correspondence. They felt themselves to be in the presence of Powers other and higher than human, who somehow influenced their destiny, whose favour they must win, and whose displeasure they must avert. And so Paganism reared her altars, almost numberless, dedicating them even to the "Unknown God," lest some anonymous deity should be grieved at being omitted from the enumeration. The prevalence of false religions in the world, the garrulous babble of mythology, does but voice the religious instinct of man; it is but another Tower of Babel, by which men hope to find and to scale the heavens which must be somewhere overhead.

In the Old Testament, however, we find the clearer revelation. What to the unaided eye of reason and of nature seemed but a wave of golden mist athwart the sky--"a meeting of gentle lights without a name"--now becomes a wide-reaching and shining realm, peopled with intelligences of divers ranks and orders; while in the centre of all is the city and the throne of the Invisible King, Jehovah, Lord of Sabaoth. In the breath of the new morning the gossamer threads Polytheism had been spinning through the night were swept away, and on the pillars of the New Jerusalem, that celestial city of which their own Salem was a far-off and broken type, they read the inscription, "Hear, O Israel: the Lord our God is one Lord." But while the Old Testament revealed the unity of the Godhead, it emphasized especially His sovereignty, the glories of His holiness, and the thunders of His power. He is the great Creator, arranging His universe, commanding evolutions and revolutions, and giving to each molecule of matter its secret affinities and repulsions. And again He is the Lawgiver, the great Judge, speaking out of the cloudy pillar and the windy tempest, dividing the firmaments of Right and Wrong, whose holiness hates sin with an infinite hatred, and whose justice, with sword of flame, pursues the wrong-doer like an unforgetting Nemesis. It is only natural, therefore, that with such conceptions of God, the heavens should appear distant and somewhat cold. The quiet that was upon the world was the hush of awe, of fear, rather than of love; for while the goodness of God was a familiar and favourite theme, and while the mercy of God, which "endureth for ever," was the refrain, oft repeated, of their loftiest songs, the love of God was a height the Old Dispensation had not explored, and the Fatherhood of God, that new world of perpetual summer, lay all undiscovered, or but dimly apprehended through the mist. The Divine love and the Divine Fatherhood were truths which seemed to be held in reserve for the New Dispensation; and as the light needs the subtle and sympathetic ether before it can reach our outlying world, so the love and the Fatherhood of God are borne in upon us by Him who was Himself the Divine Son and the incarnation of the Divine love.

It is just here where the teaching of Jesus concerning prayer begins. He does not seek to explain its philosophy; He does not give hints as to any observance of time or place; but leaving these questions to adjust themselves, He seeks to bring heaven into closer touch with earth. And how can He do this so well as by revealing the Fatherhood of God? When the electric wire linked the New with the Old World the distances were annihilated, the thousand leagues of sea were as if they were not; and when Jesus threw across, between earth and heaven, that word "Father," the wide distances vanished, and even the silences became vocal. In the Psalms, those loftiest utterances of devotion, Religion only once ventured to call God "Father;" and then, as if frightened at her own temerity, she lapses into silence, and never speaks the familiar word again. But how different the language of the Gospels! It is a name that Jesus is never weary of repeating, striking its music upwards of seventy times, as if by the frequent iteration He would lodge the heavenly word deep within the world's heart. This is His first lesson in the science of prayer: He drills them on the Divine Fatherhood, setting them on that word, as it were, to practise the scales; for as he who has practised well the scales has acquired the key to all harmonies, so he who has learned well the "Father" has learned the secret of heaven, the sesame that opens all its doors and unlocks all its treasures.

"When ye pray," said Jesus, replying to a disciple who sought instruction in the heavenly language, "say, Father," thus giving us what was His own pass-word to the courts of heaven. It is as if He said, "If you would pray acceptably put yourself in the right position. Seek to realize, and then to claim, your true relationship. Do not look upon God as a distant and cold abstraction, or as some blind force; do not regard Him as being hostile to you or as careless about you. Else your prayer will be some wail of bitterness, a cry coming out of the dark, and losing itself in the dark again. But look upon God as your Father, your living, loving, heavenly Father; and then step up with a holy boldness into the child-place, and all heaven opens before you there."

And not only does Jesus thus "show us the Father," but He takes pains to show us that it is a real, and not some fictitious Fatherhood. He tells us that the word means far more in its heavenly than in its earthly use; that the earthly meaning, in fact, is but a shadow of the heavenly. For "if ye then," He says, "being evil, know how to give good gifts unto your children: how much more shall your heavenly Father give the Holy Spirit to them that ask Him?" He thus sets us a problem in Divine proportion. He gives us the human fatherhood, with all it implies, as our known quantities, and from these He leaves us to work out the unknown quantity, which is the Divine ability and willingness to give good gifts to men; for the Holy Spirit includes in Himself all spiritual gifts. It is a problem, however, which our earthly figures cannot solve. The nearest that we can approach to the answer is that the Divine Fatherhood is the human fatherhood multiplied by that "how much more"--a factor which gives us an infinite series.

Again, Jesus teaches that character is an important condition of prayer, and that in this realm heart is more than any art. Words alone do not constitute prayer, for they may be only like the bubbles of the children's play, iridescent but hollow, never climbing the sky, but returning to the earth whence they came. And so when the scribes and Pharisees make "long prayers," striking devotional attitudes, and putting on airs of sanctity, Jesus could not endure them. They were a weariness and abomination to Him; for He read their secret heart, and found it vain and proud. In His parable (xviii. 11) He puts the genuine and the counterfeit prayer side by side, drawing the sharp contrast between them. He gives us that of the Pharisee wordy, inflated, full of the self-eulogizing "I." It is the prayerless prayer, that had no need, and which was simply an incense burned before the clayey image of himself. Then He gives us the few brief words of the publican, the cry of a broken heart, "God be merciful to me, a sinner," a prayer which reached directly the highest heaven, and which came back freighted with the peace of God. "If I regard iniquity in my heart," the Psalmist said, "the Lord will not hear me." And it is true. If there be the least unforgiven sin within the soul we spread forth our hands, we make many prayers, in vain; we do but utter "wild, delirious cries" that Heaven will not hear, or at any rate regard. The first cry of true prayer is the cry for mercy, pardon; and until this is spoken, until we step up by faith into the child-position, we do but offer vain oblations. Nay, even in the regenerate heart, if there be a temporary lapse, and unholy tempers brood within, the lips of prayer become paralyzed at once, or they only stammer in incoherent speech. We may with filled hands compass the altar of God, but neither gifts nor prayers can be accepted if there be bitterness and jealousy within, or if our "brother has aught against" us. The wrong must be righted with our brother, or we cannot be right with God. How can we ask for forgiveness if we ourselves cannot forgive? How can we ask for mercy if we are hard and merciless, gripping the throat of each offender, as we demand the uttermost farthing? He who can pray for them who despitefully use him is in the way of the Divine commandment; he has climbed to the dome of the temple, where the whispers of prayer, and even its inarticulate aspirations, are heard in heaven. And so the connection is most close and constant between praying and living, and they pray most and best who at the same time "make their life a prayer."

Again, Jesus maps out for us the realm of prayer, showing the wide areas it should cover. St. Luke gives us an abbreviated form of the prayer recorded by St. Matthew, and which we call the "Lord's Prayer." It is a disputed point, though not a material one, whether the two prayers are but varied renderings of one and the same utterance, or whether Jesus gave, on a later occasion, an epitomized form of the prayer He had prescribed before, though from the circumstantial evidence of St. Luke we incline to the latter view. The two forms, however, are identical in substance. It is scarcely likely that Jesus intended it to be a rigid formula, to which we should be slavishly bound; for the varied renderings of the two Evangelists show plainly that Heaven does not lay stress upon the ipsissima verba. We must take it rather as a Divine model, laying down the lines on which our prayers should move. It is, in fact, a sort of prayer-microcosm, giving a miniature reflection of the whole world of prayer, as a drop of dew will give a reflection of the encircling sky. It gives us what we may call the species of prayer, whose genera branch off into infinite varieties; nor can we readily conceive of any petition, however particular or private, whose root-stem is not found in the few but comprehensive words of the Lord's Prayer. It covers every want of man, just as it befits every place and time.

Running through the prayer are two marked divisions, the one general, the other particular and personal; and in the Divine order, contrary to our human wont, the general stands first, and the personal second. Our prayers often move in narrow circles, like the homing birds coming back to this "centred self" of ours, and sometimes we forget to give them the wider sweeps over a redeemed humanity. But Jesus says, "When ye pray, say, Father, hallowed be Thy name. Thy kingdom come." It is a temporary erasure of self, as the soul of the worshipper is absorbed in God. In its nearness to the throne it forgets for awhile its own little needs; its low-flying thoughts are caught up into the higher currents of the Divine thought and purpose, moving outwards with them. And this is the first petition, that the name of God may be hallowed throughout the world; that is, that men's conceptions of the Deity may become just and holy, until earth gives back in echo the Trisagion of the seraphim. The second petition is a continuation of the first; for just in proportion as men's conceptions of God are corrected and hallowed will the kingdom of God be set up on earth. The first petition, like that of the Psalmist, is for the sending out of "Thy light and Thy truth;" the second is that humanity may be led to the "holy hill," praising God upon the harp, and finding in God their "exceeding joy." To find God as the Father-King is to step up within the kingdom.

The prayer now descends into the lower plane of personal wants, covering (1) our physical, and (2) our spiritual needs. The former are met with one petition, "Give us day by day our daily bread," a sentence confessedly obscure, and which has given rise to much dispute. Some interpret it in a spiritual sense alone, since, as they say, any other interpretation would break in upon the uniformity of the prayer, whose other terms are all spiritual. But if, as we have suggested, the whole prayer must be regarded as an epitome of prayer in general, then it must include somewhere our physical needs, or a large and important domain of our life is left uncovered. As to the meaning of the singular adjective epiousion we need not say much. That it can scarcely mean "to-morrow's" bread is evident from the warning Jesus gives against "taking thought" for the morrow, and we must not allow the prayer to traverse the command. The most natural and likely interpretation is that which the heart of mankind has always given it, as our "daily" bread, or bread sufficient for the day. Jesus thus selects, what is the most common of our physical wants, the bread which comes to us in such purely natural, matter-of-course ways, as the specimen need of our physical life. But when He thus lifts up this common, ever-recurring mercy into the region of prayer He puts a halo of Divineness about it, and by including this He teaches us that there is no want of even our physical life which is excluded from the realm of prayer. If we are invited to speak with God concerning our daily bread, then certainly we need not be silent as to aught else.

Our spiritual needs are included in the two petitions, "And forgive us our sins; for we ourselves also forgive everyone that is indebted to us. And bring us not into temptation." The parenthesis does not imply that all debts should be remitted, for payment of these is enjoined as one of the duties of life. The indebtedness spoken of is rather the New Testament indebtedness, the failure of duty or courtesy, the omission of some "ought" of life or some injury or offence. It is that human forgiveness, the opposite of resentment, which grows up under the shadow of the Divine forgiveness. The former of these petitions, then, is for the forgiveness of all past sin, while the latter is for deliverance from present sinning; for when we pray, "Bring us not into temptation," it is a prayer that we may not be tempted "above that we are able," which, amplified, means that in all our temptations we may be victorious, "kept by the power of God."

Such, then, is the wide realm of prayer, as indicated by Jesus. He assures us that there is no department of our being, no circumstance of our life, which does not lie within its range; that

*"The whole round world is every way*
*Bound with gold chains about the feet of God,"*

and that on these golden chains, as on a harp, the touch of prayer may wake sweet music, far-off or near alike. And how much we miss through restraining prayer, reserving it for special occasions, or for the greater crises of life! But if we would only loop up with heaven each successive hour, if we would only run the thread of prayer through the common events and the common tasks, we should find the whole day and the whole life swinging on a higher, calmer level. The common task would cease to be common, and the earthly would be less earthly, if we only threw a bit of heaven upon it, or we opened it out to heaven. If in everything we could but make our requests known unto God-- that is, if prayer became the habitual act of life--we should find that heaven was no longer the land "afar off," but that it was close upon us, with all its proffered ministries.

Again, Jesus teaches the importance of earnestness and importunity in prayer. He sketches the picture--for it is scarcely a parable--of the man whose hospitality is claimed, late at night, by a passing friend, but who has no provision made for the emergency. He goes over to another friend, and rousing him up at midnight, he asks for the loan of three loaves. And with what result? Does the man answer from within, "Trouble me not: the door is now shut, and my children are with me in bed; I cannot rise and give thee"? No, that would be an impossible answer; for "though he will not rise and give him because he is his friend, yet because of his importunity he will rise and give him as many as he needeth" (xi. 8). It is the unreasonableness, or at any rate the untimeliness of the request Jesus seems to emphasize. The man himself is thoughtless, improvident in his household management. He disturbs his neighbour, waking up his whole family at midnight for such a trivial matter as the loan of three loaves. But he gains his request, not, either, on the ground of friendship, but through sheer audacity, impudence; for such is the meaning of the word, rather than importunity. The lesson is easily learned, for the suppressed comparison would be, "If man, being evil, will put himself out of the way to serve a friend, even at this untimely hour, filling up by his thoughtfulness his friend's lack of thought, how much more will the heavenly Father give to His child such things as are needful?"

We have the same lesson taught in the parable of the Unjust Judge (xviii. 1), that "men ought always to pray, and not to faint." Here, however, the characters are reversed. The suppliant is a poor and a wronged widow, while the person addressed is a hard, selfish, godless man, who boasts of his atheism. She asks, not for a favour, but for her rights--that she may have due protection from some extortionate adversary, who somehow has got her in his power; for justice rather than vengeance is her demand. But "he would not for awhile," and all her cries for pity and for help beat upon that callous heart only as the surf upon a rocky shore, to be thrown back upon itself. But afterwards he said within himself, "Though I fear not God, nor regard man, yet because this widow troubleth me, I will avenge her, lest she wear me out by her continual coming." And so he is moved to take her part against her adversary, not for any motive of compassion or sense of justice, but through mere selfishness, that he may escape the annoyance of her frequent visits--lest her continual coming "worry" me, as the colloquial expression might be rendered. Here the comparison, or contrast rather, is expressed, at any rate in part. It is, "If an unjust and abandoned judge grants a just petition at last, out of base motives, when it is often urged, to a defenceless person for whom he cares nothing, how much more shall a just and merciful God hear the cry and avenge the cause of those whom He loves?"[1]

It is a resolute persistence in prayer the parable urges, the continued asking, and seeking, and knocking that Jesus both commended and commanded (xi. 9), and which has the promise of such certain answers, and not the tantalizing mockeries of stones for bread, or scorpions for fish. Some blessings lie near at hand; we have only to ask, and we receive--receive even while we ask. But other blessings lie farther off, and they can only be ours by a continuance in prayer, by a persistent importunity. Not that our heavenly Father needs any wearying into mercy; but the blessing may not be ripe, or we ourselves may not be fully prepared to receive it. A blessing for which we are unprepared would only be an untimely blessing, and like a December swallow, it would soon die, without nest or brood. And sometimes the long delay is but a test of faith, whetting and sharpening the desire, until our very life seems to depend upon the granting of our prayer. So long as our prayers are among the "may-be's" and "mights" there are fears and doubts alternating with our hope and faith. But when the desires are intensified, and our prayers rise into the "must-be's," then the answers are near at hand; for that "must be" is the soul's Mahanaim, where the angels meet us, and God Himself says "I will." Delays in our prayers are by no means denials; they are often but the lengthened summer for the ripening of our blessings, making them larger and more sweet.

And now we have only to consider, which we must do briefly, the practice of Jesus, the place of prayer in His own life; and we shall find that in every point it coincides exactly with His teaching. To us of the clouded vision heaven is sometimes a hope more than a reality. It is an unseen goal, luring us across the wilderness, and which one of these days we may possess; but it is not to us as the wide-reaching, encircling sky, throwing its sunshine into each day, and lighting up our nights with its thousand lamps. To Jesus, heaven was more and nearer than it is to us. He had left it behind; and yet He had not left it, for He speaks of Himself, the Son of man, as being now in heaven. And so He was. His feet were upon earth, at home amid its dust; but His heart, His truer life, were all above. And how constant His correspondence, or rather communion, with heaven! At first sight it appears strange to us that Jesus should need the sustenance of prayer, or that He could even adopt its language. But when He became the Son of man He voluntarily assumed the needs of humanity; He emptied Himself, as the Apostle expresses a great mystery, as if for the time divesting Himself of all Divine prerogatives, choosing to live as man amongst men. And so Jesus prayed. He was wont, even as we are, to refresh a wasted strength by draughts from the celestial springs; and as Antæus, in his wrestling, recovered himself as he touched the ground, so we find Jesus, in the great crises of His life, falling back upon Heaven.

St. Luke, in his narrative of the Baptism, inserts one fact the other Synoptists omit--that Jesus was in the act of prayer when the heavens were opened, and the Holy Ghost descended, in the semblance of a dove, upon Him. It is as if the opened heavens, the descending dove, and the audible voice were but the answer to His prayer. And why not? Standing on the threshold of His mission, would He not naturally ask that a double portion of the Spirit might be His--that Heaven might put its manifest seal upon that mission, if not for the confirmation of His own faith, yet for that of His forerunner? At any rate, the fact is plain that it was while He was in the act of prayer that He received that second and higher baptism, even the baptism of the Spirit.

A second epoch in that Divine life was when Jesus formally instituted the Apostleship, calling and initiating the Twelve into the closer brotherhood. It was, so to speak, the appointment of a regency, who should exercise authority and rule in the new kingdom, sitting, as Jesus figuratively expresses it (xxii. 30), "on thrones, judging the twelve tribes of Israel." It is easy to see what tremendous issues were involved in this appointment; for were these foundation-stones untrue, warped by jealousies and vain ambitions, the whole superstructure would have been weakened, thrown out of the square. And so before the selection is made, a selection demanding such insight and foresight, such a balancing of complementary gifts, Jesus devotes the whole night to prayer, seeking the solitude of the mountain-height, and in the early dawn coming down, with the dews of night upon His garment and with the dews of heaven upon His soul, which, like crystals or lenses of light, made the invisible visible and the distant near.

A third crisis in that Divine life was at the Transfiguration, when the summit was reached, the borderline between earth and heaven, where, amid celestial greetings and overshadowing clouds of glory, that sinless life would have had its natural transition into heaven. And here again we find the same coincidence of prayer. Both St. Mark and St. Luke state that the "high mountain" was climbed for the express purpose of communion with Heaven; they "went up into the mountain to pray." It is only St. Luke, however, who states that it was "as He was praying" the fashion of His countenance was altered, thus making the vision an answer, or at least a corollary, to the prayer. He is at a point where two ways meet: the one passes into heaven at once, from that high level to which by a sinless life He has attained; the other path sweeps suddenly downward to a valley of agony, a cross of shame, a tomb of death; and after this wide détour the heavenly heights are reached again. Which path will He choose? If He takes the one He passes solitary into heaven; if He takes the other He brings with Him a redeemed humanity. And does not this give us, in a sort of echo, the burden of His prayer? He finds the shadow of the cross thrown over this heaven-lighted summit—for when Moses and Elias appear they would not introduce a subject altogether new; they would in their conversation strike in with the theme with which His mind is already preoccupied, that is the decease He should accomplish at Jerusalem—and as the chill of that shadow settles upon Him, causing the flesh to shrink and quiver for a while, would He not seek for the strength He needs? Would He not ask, as later, in the garden, that the cup might pass from Him; or if that should not be possible, that His will might not conflict with the Father's will, even for a passing moment? At any rate we may suppose that the vision was, in some way, Heaven's answer to His prayer, giving Him the solace and strengthening that He sought, as the Father's voice attested His Sonship, and celestials came forth to salute the Well-beloved, and to hearten Him on towards His dark goal.

Just so was it when Jesus kept His fourth watch in Gethsemane. What Gethsemane was, and what its fearful agony meant, we shall consider in a later chapter. It is enough for our present purpose to see how Jesus consecrated that deep valley, as before He had consecrated the Transfiguration height, to prayer. Leaving the three outside the veil of the darkness, He passes into Gethsemane, as into another Holy of holies, there to offer up for His own and for Himself the sacrifice of prayer; while as our High Priest He sprinkles with His own blood, that blood of the everlasting covenant, the sacred ground. And what prayer was that! how intensely fervent! That if it were possible the dread cup might pass from Him, but that either way the Father's will might be done! And that prayer was the prelude to victory; for as the first Adam fell by the assertion of self, the clashing of his will with God's, the second Adam conquers by the total surrender of His will to the will of the Father. The agony was lost in the acquiescence.

But it was not alone in the great crises of His life that Jesus fell back upon Heaven. Prayer with Him was habitual, the fragrant atmosphere in which He lived, and moved, and spoke. His words glide as by a natural transition into its language, as a bird whose feet have lightly touched the ground suddenly takes to its wings; and again and again we find Him pausing in the weaving of His speech, to throw across the earthward warp the heavenward woof of prayer. It was a necessity of His life; and if the intrusive crowds allowed Him no time for its exercise, He was wont to elude them, to find upon the mountain or in the desert His prayer-chamber beneath the stars. And how frequently we read of His "looking up to heaven" amid the pauses of His daily task! stopping before He breaks the bread, and on the mirror of His upturned glance leading the thoughts and thanks of the multitude to the All-Father, who giveth to all His creatures their meat in due season; or pausing as He works some impromptu miracle, before speaking the omnipotent "Ephphatha," that on His upward look He may signal to the skies! And what a light is turned upon His life and His relation to His disciples by a simple incident that occurs on the night of the betrayal! Reading the sign of the times, in His forecast of the dark to-morrow, He sees the terrible strain that will be put upon Peter's faith, and which He likens to a Satanic sifting. With prescient eye He sees the temporary collapse; how, in the fierce heat of the trial, the "rock" will be thrown into a state of flux; so weak and pliant, it will be all rippled by agitation and unrest, or driven back at the mere breath of a servant-girl. He says mournfully, "Simon, Simon, behold. Satan asked to have you, that he might sift you as wheat: but I made supplication for thee, that thy faith fail not" (xxii. 31). So completely does Jesus identify Himself with His own, making their separate needs His care (for this doubtless was no solitary case); but just as the High Priest carried on his breastplate the twelve tribal names, thus bringing all Israel within the light of Urim and Thummim, so Jesus carries within His heart both the name and the need of each separate disciple, asking for them in prayer what, perhaps, they have failed to ask for themselves. Nor are the prayers of Jesus limited by any such narrow circle; they compassed the world, lighting up all horizons; and even upon the cross, amid the jeers and laughter of the crowd, He forgets His own agonies, as with parched lips He prays for His murderers, "Father, forgive them; for they know not what they do."

Thus, more than any son of man, did Jesus "pray without ceasing," "in everything by prayer and supplication with thanksgiving" making request unto God. Shall we not copy His bright example? shall we not, too, live, labour, and endure, as "seeing Him who is invisible"? He who lives a life of prayer will never question its reality. He who sees God in everything, and everything in God, will turn his life into a south land, with upper and nether springs of blessing in ceaseless flow; for the life that lies full heavenward lies in perpetual summer, in the eternal noon.

## Footnotes:
1. Farrar

## CHAPTER XII – THE FAITH OF THE CENTURION

*Luke vii. 1-10.*

Our Evangelist prefaces the narrative of the healing of the centurion's servant with one of his characteristic time-marks, the shadow upon his dial-plate being the shadow of the new mount of God: "After He had ended all His sayings in the ears of the people, He entered into Capernaum." The language is unusually weighty, almost solemn, as if the Sermon on the Mount were not so much a sermon as a manifesto, the formal proclamation of the kingdom of heaven. Our word "ended," too, is scarcely an equivalent of the original word, whose underlying idea is that of fullness, completion. It is more than a full-stop to point a sentence; it is a word that characterizes the sentence itself, suggesting, if not implying, that these "sayings" of His formed a complete and rounded whole, a body of moral and ethical truth which was perfect in itself. The Mount of Beatitudes thus stands before us as the Sinai of the New Testament, giving its laws to all peoples and to all times. But how different the aspect of the two mounts! Then the people dare not touch the mountain; now they press close up to the "Prophet like unto Moses" to hear the word of God. Then the Law came in a cluster of restrictions and negations; it now speaks in commands most positive, in principles permanent as time itself; while from this new Sinai the clouds have disappeared, the thunders ceased, leaving a sky serene and bright, and a heaven which is strangely near.

Returning to Capernaum--which city, after the ejection from Nazareth, became the home of Jesus, and the centre of His Galilean ministry--He was met by a deputation of Jewish elders, who came to intercede with Him on behalf of a centurion whose servant was lying dangerously ill and apparently at the point of death. The narrative thus gives us, as its dramatis personæ, the Sufferer, the Intercessor, and the Healer.

As we read the story our thought is arrested, and naturally so, by the central figure. The imposing shadow of the centurion so completely fills our range of vision that it throws into the background the nameless one who in his secret chamber is struggling vainly in the tightening grip of death. But who is he who can command such a service? around whose couch is such a multitude of ministering feet? who is he whose panting breath can throw over the heart of his master, and over his face, the ripple-marks of a great sorrow, which sends hither and thither, as the wind tosses the dry leaves, soldiers of the army, elders of the Jews, friends of the master, and which makes even the feet of the Lord hasten with His succour?

"And a certain centurion's servant, who was dear unto him, was sick and at the point of death." Such is the brief sentence which describes a character, and sums up the whole of an obscure life. We are not able to define precisely his position, for the word leaves us in doubt whether he were a slave or a servant of the centurion. Probably--if we may throw the light of the whole narrative upon the word--he was a confidential servant, living in the house of his master, on terms of more than usual intimacy. What those terms were we may easily discover by opening out the word "dear," reading its depths as well as its surface-meaning. In its lower sense it means "valuable," "worth-y" (putting its ancient accent upon the modern word). It sets the man, not over against the tables of the Law, but against the law of the tables, weighing him in the balances of trade, and estimating him by the scale of commercial values. But in this meaner, worldly mode of reckoning he is not found wanting. He is a servant proved and approved. Like Eliezer of old, he has identified himself with his master's interests, listening for his voice, and learning to read even the wishes which were unexpressed in words. Adjusting his will to the higher will, like a vane answering the currents of the wind, his hands, his feet, and his whole self have swung round to fall into the unit of his master's purpose. Faithful in his service, whether that service were under the master's eye or not, and faithful alike in the great and the little things, he has entered into his master's confidence, and so into his joy. Losing his own personality, he is content to be something between a cipher and a unit, only a "hand." But he is the master's right hand, strong and ever ready, so useful as to be almost an integral part of the master's self, without which the master's life would be incomplete and strangely bereaved. All this we may learn from the lower meaning of the phrase "was dear unto him."

But the word has a higher meaning, one that is properly rendered by our "dear." It implies esteem, affection, transferring our thought from the subject to the object, from the character of the servant to the influence it has exerted upon the master, The word is thus an index, a barometrical reading, measuring for us the pressure of that influence, and recording for us the high sentiments of regard and affection it has evoked. As the trees around the pond lean towards the water which laves their roots, so the strong soul of the centurion, drawn by the attractions of a lowly but a noble life, leans toward, until it leans upon, his servant, giving him its confidence, its esteem and love, that golden fruitage of the heart. That such was the mutual relation of the master and the servant is evident, for Jesus, who read motives and heard thoughts, would not so freely and promptly have placed His miraculous power at the disposal of the centurion had his sorrow been only the selfish sorrow of losing what was commercially valuable. To an appeal of selfishness, though thrown forward and magnified by the sounding-boards of all the synagogues, the ears of Jesus would have been perfectly deaf; but when it was the cry of a genuine sorrow, the moan of a vicarious pain, an unselfish, disinterested grief, then the ears of Jesus were quick to hear, and His feet swift to respond.

It is impossible for us to define exactly what the sickness was, though the statement of St. Matthew that it was "palsy," and that he was "grievously tormented," would suggest that it might be an acute case of inflammatory rheumatism. But whatever it might be, it was a most painful, and as every one thought a mortal sickness, one that left no room for hope, save this last hope in the Divine mercy. But what a lesson is here for our times, as indeed for all times, the lesson of humanity! How little does Heaven make of rank and station! Jesus does not even see them; He ignores them utterly. To His mind Humanity is one, and the broad lines of distinction, the impassable barriers Society is fond of drawing or setting up, to Him are but imaginary meridians of the sea, a name, but nothing more. It is but a nameless servant of a nameless master, one, too, of many, for a hundred others are ready, with military precision, to do that same master's will; but Jesus does not hesitate. He who voluntarily took upon Himself the form of a servant, as He came into the world "not to be ministered unto, but to minister," now becomes the Servant of a servant, saying to him who knew only how to obey, how to serve, "Here am I; command Me; use Me as thou wilt." All service is honourable, if we serve not ourselves, but our fellows, and it is doubly so if, serving man, we serve God too. As the sunshine looks down into, and strews with flowers, the lowest vales, so the Divine compassion falls on the lowliest lives, and the Divine grace makes them sweet and beautiful. Christianity is the great leveller, but it levels upwards, and if we possess the mind of Christ, His Spirit dwelling and ruling within, we too, like the great Apostle, shall know no man after the flesh; the accidents of birth, and rank, and fortune will sink back into the trifles that they are; for however these may vary, it is an eternal truth, though spoken by a son of the soil and the heather--

"A man's a man for a' that."

It is not easy to tell how the seed-thought is borne into a heart, there to germinate and ripen; for influences are subtle, invisible things. Like the pollen of a flower, which may be carried on the antennæ of some unconscious insect, or borne into the future by the passing breeze, so influences which will yet ripen into character and make destinies are thrown off unconsciously from our common deeds, or they are borne on the wings of the chance, casual word. The case of the centurion is no exception. By what steps he has been brought into the clearer light we cannot tell, but evidently this Pagan officer is now a proselyte to the Hebrew faith and worship, the window of his soul open towards Jerusalem, while his professional life still looks towards Rome, as he renders to Cæsar the allegiance and service which are Cæsar's due. And what a testimony it is to the vitality and reproductive power of the Hebrew faith, that it should boast of at least three centurions, in the imperial ranks, of whom Scripture makes honourable mention--one at Capernaum; another, Cornelius, at Cæsarea, whose prayers and alms were had in remembrance of Heaven; and the third in Jerusalem, witnessing a good confession upon Calvary, and proclaiming within the shadow of the cross the Divinity of the Crucified. It shows how the Paganism of Rome failed to satisfy the aspirations of the soul, and how Mars, red and lurid through the night, paled and disappeared at the rising of the Sun.

Although identifying himself with the religious life of the city, the centurion had not yet had any personal interview with Jesus. Possibly his military duties prevented his attendance at the synagogue, so that he had not seen the cures Jesus there wrought upon the demoniac and the man with the withered hand. The report of them, however, must soon have reached him, intimate as he was with the officials of the synagogue; while the nobleman, the cure of whose sick son is narrated by St. John (iv. 46), would probably be amongst his personal friends, an acquaintance at any rate. The centurion "heard" of Jesus, but he could not have heard had not some one spoken of Him. The

Christ was borne into his mind and heart on the breath of common speech; that is, the little human word grew into the Divine Word. It was the verbal testimony as to what Jesus had done that now led to the still greater things He was prepared to do. And such is the place and power of testimony to-day. It is the most persuasive, the most effective form of speech. Testimony will often win where argument has failed, and gold itself is all-powerless to extend the frontiers of the heavenly kingdom until it is melted down and exchanged for the higher currency of speech. It is first the human voice crying in the wilderness, and then the incarnate Word, whose coming makes the wilderness to be glad, and the desert places of life to sing. And so, while a sword of flame guards the Paradise Lost, it is a "tongue" of flame, that symbol of a perpetual Pentecost, which calls man back, redeemed now, to the Paradise Restored. If Christians would only speak more for Christ; if, shaking off that foolish reserve, they would in simple language testify to what they themselves have seen, and known, and experienced, how rapidly would the kingdom come, the kingdom for which we pray, indeed, but for which, alas, we are afraid to speak! Nations then would be born in a day, and the millennium, instead of being the distant or the forlorn hope it is, would be a speedy realization. We should be in the fringe of it directly. It is said that on one of the Alpine glaciers the guides forbid travellers to speak, lest the mere tremor of the human voice should loosen and bring down the deadly avalanche. Whether this be so or not, it was some unnamed voice that now sent the centurion to Christ, and brought the Christ to him.

It was probably a sudden relapse, with increased paroxysms of pain, on the part of the sufferer, which now decided the centurion to make his appeal to Jesus, sending a deputation of Jewish elders, as the day was on the wane, to the house to which Jesus had now returned. They make their request that "He would come and save the servant of the centurion, who was now lying at the point of death." True advocates, and skilful, were these elders. They made the centurion's cause their own, as if their hearts had caught the rhythmic beat of his great sorrow, and when Jesus held back a little--as He often did, to test the intensity of the desire and the sincerity of the suppliant--"they besought Him earnestly," or "kept on beseeching," as the tense of the verb would imply, crowning their entreaty with the plea, "He is worthy that Thou shouldest do this, for he loveth our nation, and himself built us our synagogue." Possibly they feared--putting a Hebrew construction upon His sympathies--that Jesus would demur, and perhaps refuse, because their client was a foreigner. They did not know, what we know so well, that the mercy of Jesus was as broad as it was deep, knowing no bounds where its waves of blessing are stayed. But how forceful and prevalent was their plea! Though they knew it not, these elders do but ask Jesus to illustrate the words He has just spoken, "Give, and it shall be given unto you." And had not Jesus laid this down as one of the laws of mercy, that action and reaction are equal? Had He not been describing the orbit in which blessings travel, showing that though its orbit be apparently eccentric at times, like the boomerang, that wheels round and comes back to the hand that threw it forward, the mercy shown will eventually come back to him who showed it, with a wealth of heavenly usury? And so their plea was the one of all others to be availing. It was the precept of the mount evolved into practice. It was, "Bless him, for he has richly blessed us. He has opened his hand, showering his favours upon us; do Thou open Thine hand now, and show him that the God of the Hebrews is a God who hears, and heeds, and helps."

It has been thought, from the language of the elders, that the synagogue built by the centurion was the only one that Capernaum possessed; for they speak of it as "the" synagogue. But this does not follow, and indeed it is most improbable. They might still call it "the" synagogue, not because it was the only one, but because it was the one foremost and uppermost in their thought, the one in which they were particularly interested. The definite article no more proves this to be the only synagogue in Capernaum than the phrase "the house" (ver. 10) proves the house of the centurion to be the only house of the city. The fact is that in the Gospel age Capernaum was a busy and important place, as shown by its possessing a garrison of soldiers, and by its being the place of custom, situated as it was on the great highway of trade. And if Jerusalem could boast of four hundred synagogues, and Tiberias--a city not even named by the Synoptists--fourteen, Capernaum certainly would possess more than one. Indeed, had Capernaum been the insignificant village that one synagogue would imply, then, instead of deserving the bitter woes Jesus pronounced upon it, it would have deserved the highest commendation, as the most fruitful field in all His ministry, giving Him, besides other disciples, a ruler of the Jews and the commandant of the garrison. That it deserved such bitter "woes" proves that Capernaum had a population both dense and, in the general, hostile to Jesus, compared with which His friends and adherents were a feeble few.

In spite of the negative manner Jesus purposely showed at the first, He fully intended to grant all the elders had asked, and allowing them now to guide Him, He "went with them." When, however, they were come near the house, the centurion sent other "friends" to intercept Jesus, and to urge Him not to take any further trouble. The message, which they deliver in the exact form in which it was given to them, is so characteristic and exquisitely beautiful that it is best to give it entire: "Lord, trouble not Thyself: for I am not worthy that Thou shouldest come under my roof: wherefore neither thought I myself worthy to come unto Thee: but say the word, and my servant shall be healed. For I also am a man set under authority, having under myself soldiers: and I say to this one, Go, and he goeth; and to another, Come, and he cometh; and to my servant, Do this, and he doeth it."

The narrative of St. Matthew differs slightly from that of St. Luke, in that he omits all reference to the two deputations, speaking of the interview as being personal with the centurion. But St. Matthew's is evidently an abbreviated narrative, and he passes over the intermediaries, in accordance with the maxim that he who acts through another does it per se. But both agree as to the terms of the message, a message which is at once a marvel and a rebuke to us, and one which was indeed deserving of being twice recorded and eulogized in the pages of the Gospels.

And how the message reveals the man, disclosing as in a transparency the character of this nameless foreigner! We have already seen how broad were his sympathies, and how generous his deeds, as he makes room in his large heart for a conquered and despised people, at his own cost building a temple for the exercises of their faith. We have seen, too, what a wealth of tenderness and benevolence was hiding beneath a somewhat stern exterior, in his affection for a servant, and his anxious solicitude for that servant's health. But now we see in the centurion other graces of character, that set him high amongst those "outside saints" who worshipped in the outer courts, until such time as the veil of the Temple was rent in twain, and the way into the Holiest was opened for all. And what a beautiful humility is here! what an absence of assumption or of pride! Occupying an honoured position, representing in his own person an empire which was world-wide, surrounded by troops of friends, and by all the comforts wealth could buy, accustomed to speak in imperative, if not in imperious ways, yet as he turns towards Jesus it is with a respectful, yea, a reverential demeanour. He feels himself in the presence of some Higher Being, an unseen but august Cæsar. Nay, not in His presence either, for into that audience-chamber he feels that he has neither the fitness nor the right to intrude. All that he can do is to send forward his petition by the hands of worthier advocates, who have access to Him, while he himself keeps back out of sight, with bared feet standing by the outer gate. Others can speak well and highly of him, recounting his noble deeds, but of himself he has nothing good to say; he can only speak of self in terms of disparagement, as he emphasizes his littleness, his unworthiness. Nor was it with him the conventional hyperbole of Eastern manners; it was the language of deepest, sincerest truth, when he said that he was not worthy even to speak with Christ, or to receive such a Guest beneath his roof. Between himself and the One he reverently addressed as "Lord" there was an infinite distance; for one was human, while the Other was Divine.

And what a rare and remarkable faith! In his thought Jesus is an Imperator, commanding all forces, as He rules the invisible realms. His will is supreme over all substances, across all distances. "Thou hast no need, Lord, to take any trouble about my poor request. There is no necessity that Thou shouldest take one step, or even lift up a finger; Thou hast only to speak the word, and it is done;" and then he gives that wonderfully graphic illustration borrowed from his own military life.

The passage "For I also am a man set under authority" is generally rendered as referring to his own subordinate position under the Chiliarch. But such a rendering, as it seems to us, breaks the continuity of thought, and grammatically is scarcely accurate. The whole passage is an amplification and description of the "word" of ver. 7, and the "also" introduces something the centurion and Jesus possess in common, i.e., the power to command; for the "I also" certainly corresponds with the "Thou" which is implied, but not expressed. But the centurion did not mean to imply that Jesus possessed only limited, delegated powers; this was farthest from his thought, and formed no part of the comparison. But let the clause "I also am a man set under authority" be rendered, not as referring to the authority which is above him, but to that which is upon him--"I also am vested with authority," or "Authority is put upon me"--and the meaning becomes clear. The "also" is no longer warped into an ungrammatical meaning, introducing a contrast rather than a likeness; while the clause which follows, "having under myself soldiers," takes its proper place as an enlargement and explanation of the "authority" with which the centurion is invested.

The centurion speaks in a soldierly way. There is a crispness and sharpness about his tones-- that shibboleth of militaryism. He says, "My word is all-powerful in the ranks which I command. I have but to say 'Come,' or 'Go,' and my word is instantly obeyed. The soldier upon whose ear it falls dare not hesitate, any more than he dare refuse. He 'goes' at my word, anywhither, on some forlorn hope it may be, or to his grave." And such is the obedience, instant and absolute, that military service demands. The soldier must not question, he must obey; he must not reason, he must act; for when the word of command--that leaded word of authority--falls upon his ear, it completely fills his soul, and makes him deaf to all other, meaner voices.

Such was the thought in the centurion's mind, and from the "go" and "come" of military authority to the higher "word" of Jesus the transition is easy. But how strong the faith that could give to Jesus such an enthronement, that could clothe His word with such superhuman power! Yonder, in his secluded chamber, lies the sufferer, his nerves quivering in their pain, while the mortal sickness physicians and remedies have all failed to touch, much less to remove, has dragged him close up to the gate of death. But this "word" of Jesus shall be all-sufficient. Spoken here and now, it shall pass over the intervening streets and through the interposing walls and doors; it shall say to these demons of evil, "Loose him, and let him go," and in a moment the torturing pain shall cease, the fluttering heart shall resume its healthy, steady beat, the rigid muscles shall become pliant as before, while through arteries and veins the life-blood--its poison all extracted now--shall regain its healthful, quiet flow. The centurion believed all this of the "word" of Jesus, and even more. In his heart it was a word all-potent, if not omnipotent, like to the word of Him who "spake, and it was done," who "commanded, and it stood fast." And if the word of Jesus in these realms of life and death was so imperative and all-commanding, could the Christ Himself be less than Divine?

To find such confidence reposed in Himself was to Jesus something new; and to find this rarest plant of faith growing up on Gentile soil was a still greater marvel and turning to the multitude which clustered thick and eager around, He said to them, "I have not found so great faith, no, not in Israel." And commending the centurion's faith, He honours it too, doing all he requested, and even more, though without the "word." Jesus does not even say "I will," or "Be it so," but He works the instant and perfect cure by a mere volition. He wills it, and it is done, so that when the friends returned to the house they found the servant "whole."

Of the sequel we know nothing. We do not even read that Jesus saw the man at whose faith He had so marvelled. But doubtless He did, for His heart was drawn strangely to him, and doubtless He gave to him many of those "words" for which his soul had longed and listened, words in which were held, as in solution, all authority and all truth. And doubtless, too, in the after-years, Jesus crowned that life of faithful but unnoted service with the higher "word," the heavenly "Well done."

Henry Burton

# CHAPTER XIII - THE ANOINTING OF THE FEET

*Luke vii. 36-50.*

Whether the narrative of the Anointing is inserted in its chronological order we cannot say, for the Evangelist gives us no word by which we may recognize either its time or its place-relation; but we can easily see that it falls into the story artistically, with a singular fitness. Going back to the context, we find Jesus pronouncing a high eulogium upon John the Baptist. Hereupon the Evangelist adds a statement of his own, calling attention to the fact that even John's ministry failed to reach and influence the Pharisees and lawyers, who rejected the counsel of God, and declined the baptism of His messenger. Then Jesus, in one of His brief but exquisite parables, sketches the character of the Pharisees. Recalling a scene of the market-place, where the children were accustomed to play at "weddings" and "funerals"--which, by the way, are the only games at which the children of the land play to-day--and where sometimes the play was spoiled and stopped by some of the children getting into a pet, and lapsing into a sullen silence, Jesus says that is just a picture of the childish perversity of the Pharisees. They respond neither to the mourning of the one nor to the music of the other, but because John came neither eating bread nor drinking wine, they can him a maniac, and say, "He hath a devil;" while of Jesus, who has no ascetic ways, but mingles in the gatherings of social life, a Man amongst men, they say, "Behold a gluttonous man and a wine-bibber, a friend of publicans and sinners." And having recorded this, our Evangelist inserts, as an appropriate sequel, the account of the supper in the Pharisee's house, with its idyllic interlude, played by a woman's hand, a narrative which shows how Wisdom is justified of all her children, and how these condescensions of Jesus, His intercourse with even those who were ceremonially or morally unclean, were both proper and beautiful.

It was in one of the Galilean towns, perhaps at Nain, where Jesus was surprised at receiving an invitation to the house of a Pharisee. Such courtesies on the part of a class who prided themselves on their exclusiveness, and who were bitterly intolerant of all who were outside their narrow circle, were exceptional and rare. Besides, the teaching of Jesus was diametrically opposed to the leaven of the Pharisees. Between the caste of the one and the Catholicism of the other was a wide gulf of divergence. To Jesus the heart was everything, and the outflowing issues were coloured by its hues; to the Pharisees the hand, the outward touch, was more than heart, and contact more than conduct. Jesus laid a Divine emphasis upon character; the cleanness He demanded was moral cleanness, purity of heart; that of the Pharisees was a ceremonial cleanness, the avoidance of things which were under a ceremonial ban. And so they magnified the jots and tittles, scrupulously tithing their mint and anise, while they overlooked completely the moralities of the heart, and reduced to a mere nothing those grander virtues of mercy and of justice. Between the Separatists and Jesus there was therefore constant friction, which afterwards developed into open hostility; and while they ever sought to damage Him with opprobrious epithets, and to bring His teaching into disrepute, He did not fail to expose their hollowness and insincerity, tearing off the veneer with which they sought to hide the brood of viperous things their creed had gendered, and to hurl against their whited sepulchres His indignant "woes."

It would almost seem as if Jesus hesitated in accepting the invitation, for the tense of the verb "desired" implies that the request was repeated. Possibly other arrangements had been made, or perhaps Jesus sought to draw out and test the sincerity of the Pharisee, who in kind and courteous words offered his hospitality. The hesitation would certainly not arise from any reluctance on His part, for Jesus refused no open door; he welcomed any opportunity of influencing a soul. As the shepherd of His own parable went over the mountainous paths in quest of his lone, lost sheep, so Jesus was glad to risk unkind aspersions, and to bear the "fierce light" of hostile, questioning eyes, if He might but rescue a soul, and win some erring one back to virtue and to truth.

The character of the host we cannot exactly determine. The narrative lights up his features but indistinctly, for the nameless "sinner" is the central object of the picture, while Simon stands in the background, out of focus, and so somewhat veiled in obscurity. To many he appears as the cold and heartless censor, distant and haughty, seeking by the guile of hospitality to entrap Jesus, hiding behind the mask of friendship some dark and sinister motive. But such deep shadows are cast by our own thoughts rather than by the narrative; they are the random "guesses after truth," instead of the truth itself. It will be noticed that Jesus does not impugn in the least his motive in proffering his hospitality; and this, though but a negative evidence, is not without its weight, when on a similar occasion the evil motive was brought to light. The only charge laid against him--if charge it be-- was the omission of certain points of etiquette that Eastern hospitality was accustomed to observe, and even here there is nothing to show that Jesus was treated differently from the other invited guests. The omission, while it failed to single out Jesus for special honour, might still mean no disrespect; and at the most it was a breach of manners, deportment, rather than of morals, just one of those lapses Jesus was most ready to overlook and forgive. We shall form a juster estimate of the man's character if we regard him as a seeker after truth. Evidently he has felt a drawing towards Jesus; indeed, ver. 47 would almost imply that he had received some personal benefit at His hands. Be this as it may, he is desirous of a closer and a freer intercourse. His mind is perplexed, the balances of his judgment swinging in alternate and opposite ways. A new problem has presented itself to him, and in that problem is one factor he cannot yet value. It is the unknown quantity, Jesus of Nazareth. Who is He? what is He? A prophet--the Prophet--the Christ? Such are the questions running through his mind--questions which must be answered soon, as his thoughts and opinions have ripened into convictions. And so he invites Jesus to his house and board, that in the nearer vision and the unfettered freedom of social intercourse he may solve the great enigma. Nay, he invites Jesus with a degree of earnestness, putting upon Him the constraint of a great desire; and leaving his heart open to conviction, ready to embrace the truth as soon as he recognizes it to be truth, he flings open the door of his hospitalities, though in so doing he shakes the whole fabric of Pharisaic exclusiveness and sanctity. Seeking after truth, the truth finds him.

There was a simplicity and freeness in the social life of the East which our Western civilization can scarcely understand. The door of the guest-chamber was left open, and the uninvited, even comparative strangers, were allowed to pass in and out during the entertainment; or they might take their seats by the wall, as spectators and listeners. It was so here. No sooner have the guests taken their places, reclining around the table, their bared feet projecting behind them, than the usual drift of the uninvited set in, amongst whom, almost unnoticed in the excitements of the hour, was "a woman of the city." Simon in his soliloquy speaks of her as "a sinner;" but had we his testimony only, we should hesitate in giving to the word its usually received meaning; for "sinner" was a pet term of the Pharisees, applied to all who were outside their circle, and even to Jesus Himself. But when our Evangelist, in describing her character, makes use of the same word, we can only interpret the "sinner" in one way, in its sensual, depraved meaning. And with this agrees the phrase "a woman which was in the city," which seems to indicate the loose relations of her too-public life.

Bearing in her hand "an alabaster cruse of ointment," for a purpose which soon became apparent, she passed over to the place where Jesus sat, and stood directly behind Him. Accustomed as she had been to hide her deeds in the veil of darkness, nothing but the current of a deep emotion could have carried her thus through the door of the guest-chamber, setting her, alone of her sex, full in the glare of the lamps and the light of scornful eyes; and no sooner has she reached her goal than the storm of the heart breaks in a rain of tears, which fall hot and fast upon the feet of the Master. This, however, is no part of her plan; they were impromptu tears she could not restrain; and instantly she stoops down, and with the loosened tresses of her hair she wipes His feet, kissing them passionately as she did so. There is a delicate meaning in the construction of the Greek verb, "she began to wet His feet with her tears;" it implies that the action was not continued, as when afterwards she "anointed" His feet. It was momentary, instantaneous, checked soon as it was discovered. Then pouring from her flask the fragrant nard, she proceeded with loving, leisurely haste to anoint His feet, until the whole chamber was redolent of the sweet perfume.

But what is the meaning of this strange episode, this "song without words," struck by the woman's hands as from a lyre of alabaster? It was evidently something determined, prearranged. The phrase "when she knew that He was sitting at meat" means something more than she "heard." Her knowledge as to where Jesus was had not come to her in a casual way, in the vagrant gossip of the town; it had come by search and inquiry on her part, as if the plan were already determined, and she were eager to carry it out. The cruse of ointment that she brings also reveals the settled resolve that she came on purpose, and she came only, to anoint the feet of Jesus. The word, too, rendered "she brought" has a deeper meaning than our translation conveys. It is a word that is used in ten other passages of the New Testament, where it is invariably rendered "receive," or "received," referring to something received as a wage, or as a gift, or as a prize. Used here in the narrative, it implies that the cruse of ointment had not been bought; it was something she had received as a gift, or possibly as the wages of her sin. And not only was it prearranged, part of a deliberate intention, but evidently it was not displeasing to Jesus. He did not resent it. He gives Himself up passively to the woman's will. He allows her to touch, and even to kiss His feet, though He knows that to society she is a moral leper, and that her fragrant ointment is possibly the reward of her shame. We must, then, look behind the deed to the motive. To Jesus the ointment and the tears were full of meaning, eloquent beyond any power of words. Can we discover that meaning, and read why they were so welcome? We think we may.

And here let us say that Simon's thoughts were perfectly natural and correct, with no word or tone that we can censure. Canon Farrar, it is true, detects in the "This man" with which he speaks of Jesus a "supercilious scorn;" but we fail to see the least scorn, or even disrespect, for the pronoun Simon uses is the identical word used by St. Matthew (Matt. iii. 3), of John the Baptist, when he says, "This is he that was spoken of by the prophet Esaias," and the word of the "voice from heaven" which said, "This is My beloved Son" (Matt. iii. 17). That the woman was a sinner Simon knew well; and would not Jesus know it too, if He were a prophet? Doubtless He would; but as Simon marks no sign of disapproval upon the face of Jesus, the enigmatical "if" grows larger in his mind, and he begins to think that Jesus has scarcely the keen insight--the power of seeing through things--that a true prophet would have. Simon's reasoning was right, but his facts were wrong. He imagined that Jesus did not know "who and what manner of woman" this was; whereas Jesus knew more than he, for He knew not only the past of shame, but a present of forgiveness and hope.

And what did the tears and the ointment mean, that Jesus should receive them so readily, and that He should speak of them so approvingly? The parable Jesus spoke to Simon will explain it. "Simon, I have somewhat to say unto thee," said Jesus, answering his thoughts--for He had heard them--by words. And falling naturally into the parabolic form of speech--as He did when He wanted to make His meaning more startling and impressive--He said, "A certain money-lender had two debtors: the one owed five hundred pence, and the other fifty. When they had not wherewith to pay, he forgave them both. Which of them therefore will love him most?" A question to which Simon could promptly answer, "He, I suppose, to whom he forgave the most." It is clear, then, whatever others might see in the woman's deed, that Jesus read in it the expression of her love, and that He accepted it as such; the tears and outpoured ointment were the broken utterances of an affection which was too deep for words. But if her offering--as it certainly was--was the gift of love, how shall we explain her tears? for love, in the presence of the beloved, does not weep so passionately, indeed does not weep at all, except, it may be, tears of joy, or tears of a mutual sorrow. In this way: As the wind blows landward from the sea, the mountain ranges cool the clouds, and cause them to unlock their treasures, in the fertile and refreshing rains; so in the heart of this "sinner" a cloud of recollections is blown up suddenly from her dark past; the memories of her shame--even though that shame be now forgiven--sweep across her soul with resistless force, for penitence does not end when forgiveness is assured; and as she finds herself in the presence of Infinite Purity, what wonder that the heart's great deeps are broken up, and that the wild storm of conflicting emotions within should find relief in a rain of tears? Tears of penitence they doubtless were, bitter with the sorrow and the shame of years of guilt; but they were tears of gratitude and holy love as well, all suffused and brightened by the touch of mercy and the light of hope. And so the passionate weeping was no acted grief, no hysterical tempest; it was the perfectly natural accompaniment of profound emotion, that storm of mingled but diverse elements which now swept through her soul. Her tears, like the dew-drops that hang upon leaf and flower, were wrought in the darkness, fashioned by the Night, and at the same time they were the jewels that graced the robe of a new dawn, the dawn of a better, a purer life.

But how came this new affection within her heart, an affection so deep that it must have tears and anointings for its expression--this new affection, which has become a pure and holy passion, and which breaks through conventional bonds, as it has broken through the old habits, the ill usages of a life? Jesus Himself traces for us this affection to its source. He tells us--for the parable is all meaningless unless we recognize in the five-hundred-pence debtor the sinning woman--that her great love grows out of her great forgiveness, a past forgiveness too, for Jesus speaks of the change as already accomplished: "Her sins, which were many, are (have been) forgiven." And here we touch an unwritten chapter of the Divine life; for as the woman's love flows up around Jesus, casting its treasures at His feet, so the forgiveness must first have come from Jesus. His voice it must have been which said, "Let there be light," and which turned the chaos of her dark soul into another Paradise. At any rate, she thinks she owes to Him her all. Her new creation, with its deliverance from the tyrannous past; her new joys and hopes, the spring-blossom of a new and heavenly existence; the conscious purity which has now taken the place of lust--she owes all to the word and power of Jesus. But when this change took place, or when, in the great transit, this Venus of the moral firmament passed across the disc of the Sun, we do not know. St. John inserts in his story one little incident, which is like a piece of mosaic dropped out from the Gospels of the Synoptists, of a woman who was taken in her sin and brought to Jesus. And when the hands of her accusers were not clean enough to cast the first stone, but they shrank one by one out of sight, self-condemned, Jesus bade the penitent one to "go in peace, and sin no more."[2] Are the two characters identical? and does the forgiven one, dismissed into peace, now return to bring to her Saviour her offering of gratitude and love? We can only say that such an identification is at least possible, and more so far than the improbable identification of tradition, which confounds this nameless "sinner" with Mary Magdalene, which is an assumption perfectly baseless and most unlikely.

And so in this erring one, who now puts her crown of fragrance upon the feet of Jesus, since she is unworthy to put it upon His head, we see a penitent and forgiven soul. Somewhere Jesus found her, out on the forbidden paths, the paths of sin, which, steep and slippery, lead down to death; His look arrested her, for it cast within her heart the light of a new hope; His presence, which was the embodiment of a purity infinite and absolute, shot through her soul the deep consciousness and conviction of her guilt; and doubtless upon her ears had fallen the words of the great absolution and the Divine benediction, "Thy sins are all forgiven; go in peace," words which to her made all things new--a new heart within, and a new earth around. And now, regenerate and restored, the sad past forgiven, all the currents of her thought and life reversed, the love of sin turned into a perfect loathing, her language, spoken in tears, kisses, and fragrant nard, is the language of the Psalmist, "O Lord, I will praise Thee; for though Thou wast angry with me, Thine anger is turned away, and Thou comfortedst me." It was the Magnificat of a forgiven and a loving soul.

Simon had watched the woman's actions in silence, though in evident displeasure. He would have resented her touch, and have forbade even her presence; but found under his roof, she became in a certain sense a guest, shielded by the hospitable courtesies of Eastern life. But if he said nothing, he thought much, and his thoughts were hard and bitter. He looked upon the woman as a moral leper, an outcast. There was defilement in her touch, and he would have shaken it off from him as if it were a viper, fit only to be cast into the fire of a burning indignation. Now Jesus must teach him a lesson, and throw his thoughts back upon himself. And first He teaches him that there is forgiveness for sin, even the sin of uncleanness; and in this we see the bringing in of a better hope. The Law said, "The soul that sinneth, it shall surely die;" it shall be cut off from the people of Israel. The Law had but one voice for the adulterer and adulteress, the voice which was the knell of a sharp and fearful doom, without reprieve or mercy of any kind. It cast upon them the deadly rain of stones, as if it would hurl a whole Sinai upon them. But Jesus comes to man with a message of mercy and of hope. He proclaims a deliverance from the sin, and a pardon for the sinner; nay, He offers Himself, as at once the Forgiver of sin and the Saviour from sin. Let Him but see it repented of; let Him but see the tears of penitence, or hear the sighs of a broken and contrite heart, and He steps forward at once to deliver and to save. The valley of Achor, where the Law sets up its memorial of shame, Jesus turns into a door of hope. He speaks life where the Law spoke death; He offers hope where the Law gave but despair; and where exacting Law gave pains and fearful punishment only, the Mediator of the New Covenant, to the penitent though erring ones, spoke pardon and peace, even the perfect peace, the eternal peace.

And Jesus teaches Simon another lesson. He teaches him to judge himself, and not either by his own fictitious standard, by the Pharisaic table of excellence, but by the Divine standard. Holding up as a mirror the example of the woman, Jesus gives to Simon a portrait of his own self, as seen in the heavenly light, all shrunken and dwarfed, the large "I" of Pharisaic complacency becoming, in comparison, small indeed. Turning to the woman, He said unto Simon, "Seest thou this woman?" (And Simon had not seen her; he had only seen her shadow, the shadow of her sinful past). "I entered into thine house; thou gavest Me no water for My feet: but she hath wetted My feet with her tears, and wiped them with her hair. Thou gavest Me no kiss: but she, since the time I came in, hath not ceased to kiss My feet. My head with oil thou didst not anoint: but she hath anointed My feet with ointment." It is a problem of the pronouns, in which the "I" being given, it is desired to find the relative values of "thou" and "she." And how beautifully does Jesus work it out, according to the rules of Divine proportions! With what antithetical skill does He make His comparison, or rather His contrast! "Thou gavest me no water for My feet; she hath wetted My feet with her tears, and wiped them with her hair. Thou gavest me no kiss: she hath not ceased to kiss my feet. My head with oil thou didst not anoint: she hath anointed My feet with ointment."

And so Jesus sets over against the omissions of Simon the loving and lavish attentions of the woman; and while reproving him, not for a lack of civility, but for a want of heartiness in his reception of Himself, He shows how deep and full run the currents of her affection, breaking through the banks and bounds of conventionality in their sweet overflow, while as yet the currents of his love were intermittent, shallow, and somewhat cold. He does not denounce this Simon as having no part or lot in this matter. No; He even credits him with a little love, as He speaks of him as a pardoned, justified soul. And it was true. The heart of Simon had been drawn toward Jesus, and in the urgent invitation and these proffered hospitalities we can discern a nascent affection. His love is yet but in the bud. It is there, a thing of life; but it is confined, constrained, and lacking the sweetness of the ripened and opened flower. Jesus does not cut off the budding affection, and cast it out amongst the withered and dead things, but sprinkling it with the dew of His speech, and throwing upon it the sunshine of His approving look, He leaves it to develop, ripening into an after-harvest of fragrance and of beauty. And why was Simon's love more feeble and immature than that of the woman? First, because he did not see so much in Jesus as she did. He was yet stumbling over the "if," with some lingering doubts as to whether He were "the prophet;" to her He is more than a "prophet," even her Lord and her Saviour, covering her past with a mantle of mercy, and opening within her heart a heaven. Then, too, Simon's forgiveness was not so great as hers. Not that any forgiveness can be less than entire; for when Heaven saves it is not a salvation by instalments--certain sins remitted, while others are held back uncancelled. But Simon's views of sin were not so sharp and vivid as were those of the woman. The atmosphere of Phariseeism in its moral aspects was hazy; it magnified human virtues, and created all sorts of illusive mirages of self-righteousness and reputed holiness, and doubtless Simon's vision had been impaired by the refracting atmosphere of his creed. The greatness of our salvation is ever measured by the greatness of our danger and our guilt. The heavier the burden and weight of condemnation, the deeper is the peace and the higher are the ecstasies of joy when that condemnation is removed. Shall we say, then, "We must sin more, that love may more abound"? Nay, we need not, we must not; for as Godet says, "What is wanting to the best of us, in order to love much, is not sin, but the knowledge of it." And this deeper knowledge of sin, the more vivid realization of its guilt, its virulence, its all-pervasiveness, comes just in proportion as we approach Christ. Standing close up to the cross, feeling the mortal agonies of Him whose death was necessary as sin's atonement, in that vivid light of redeeming love even the strict moralist, the Pharisee of the Pharisees, could speak of himself as the "chief" of sinners.

The lesson was over, and Jesus dismissed the woman--who, with her empty alabaster flask, had lingered at the feast, and who had heard all the conversation--with the double assurance of pardon: "Thy sins are forgiven; thy faith hath saved thee; go in peace." And such is the Divine order everywhere and always--Faith, Love, Peace. Faith is the procuring cause, or the condition of salvation; love and peace are its after-fruits; for without faith, love would be only fear, and peace itself would be unrest.

She went in peace, "the peace of God, which passeth all understanding;" but she left behind her the music of her tears and the sweet fragrance of her deed, a fragrance and a music which have filled the whole world, and which, floating across the valley of death, will pass up into heaven itself!

There was still one little whisper of murmuring, or questioning rather; for the guests were startled by the boldness of His words, and asked among themselves, "Who is this that even forgiveth sins?" But it will be noticed that Simon himself is no longer among the questioners, the doubters. Jesus is to him "the Prophet," and more than a prophet, for who can forgive sins but God alone? And though we hear no more of him or of his deeds, we may rest assured that his conquered heart was given without reserve to Jesus, and that he too learned to love with a true affection, even with the "perfect love," which "casteth out fear."

## *Footnotes:*

2. The narrative is of doubtful authenticity; but even should it be proved to be a postscript by some later scribe, it would still point to a tradition, which, as Stier says, was "well founded and genuine."

# CHAPTER XIV - THE PARABLE OF THE SOWER

Luke viii. 1-18.

In a single parenthetical sentence our Evangelist indicates a marked change in the mode of the Divine ministry. Hitherto "His own city," Capernaum, has been a sort of centre, from which the lines of light and blessing have radiated. Now, however, He leaves Capernaum, and makes a circuit through the province of Galilee, going through its cities and villages in a systematic, and as the verb would imply, a leisurely way, preaching the "good tidings of the kingdom of God." Though no mention is made of them, we are not to suppose that miracles were suspended; but evidently they were set in the background, as secondary things, the by-plays or "asides" of the Divine Teacher, who now is intent upon delivering His message, the last message, too, that they would hear from Him. Accompanying Him, and forming an imposing demonstration, were His twelve disciples, together with "many" women, who ministered unto them of their substance, among whom were three prominent ones, probably persons of position and influence--Mary of Magdala, Joanna, wife of Chuza, Herod's steward, and Susanna, who had been healed by Jesus of "evil spirits and infirmities"--which last word, in New Testament language, is a synonym for physical weakness and disorder. Of the particulars and results of this mission we know nothing, unless we may see, in the "great multitude" which followed and thronged Jesus on His return, the harvest reaped from the Galilean hills. Our Evangelist, at any rate, links them together, as if the "great multitude" which now lines the shore was, in part at least, the cloud of eager souls which had been caught up and borne along on His fervid speech, as the echoes of the kingdom went resounding among the hills and vales of Galilee.

Returning to Capernaum, whither the crowds follow Him, every city sending its contingent of curious or conquered souls, Jesus, as St. Matthew and St. Mark inform us, leaves the house, and seeks the open stretch of shore, where from a boat--probably the familiar boat of Simon--He addresses the multitudes, adopting now, as His favourite mode of speech, the amplified parable. It is probable that He had observed on the part of His disciples an undue elation of spirit. Reading the crowds numerically, and not discerning the different motives which had brought them together, their eyes deceived them. They imagined that these eager multitudes were but a wave-sheaf of the harvest already ripe, which only waited their gathering-in. But it is not so; and Jesus sifts and winnows His audience, to show His disciples that the apparent is not always the real, and that between the hearers of the word and the doers there will ever be a wide margin of disappointment and comparative failure. The harvest, in God's husbandry, as in man's, does not depend altogether upon the quality of the seed or the faithfulness of the sower, but upon the nature of the soil on which it falls.

As the sower went forth to sow his seed, "some fell by the way-side, and it was trodden under-foot, and the birds of the heaven devoured it." In his carefulness to cover all his ground, the sower had gone close up to the boundary, and some of the seed had fallen on the edge of the bare and trampled path, where it lay homeless and exposed. It was in contact with the earth, but it was a mechanical, and not a vital touch. There was no correspondence, no communion between them. Instead of welcoming and nourishing the seed, it held it aloof, in a cold, repelling way. Had the soil been sympathetic and receptive, it held within itself all the elements of growth. Touched by the subtle life that was hidden within the seed, the dead earth itself had lived, growing up into blades of promise, and from the full ear throwing itself forward into the future years. But the earth was hard and unreceptive; its possibilities of blessing were locked up and buried beneath a crust of trampled soil that was callous and unresponsive as the rock itself. And so the seed lay unwelcomed and alone, and the life which the warm touch of earth would have loosened and set free remained within its husk as a dead thing, without voice or hearing. There was nothing else for it but to be ground into dust by the passing foot or to be picked up by the foraging birds.

The parable was at once a prophecy and an experience. Forming a part of the crowd which surrounded Jesus was an outer ring of hearers who came but to criticize and to cavil. They had no desire to be taught--at any rate by such a teacher. They were themselves the "knowing ones," the learned, and they looked with suspicion and ill-concealed scorn upon the youthful Nazarene. Turning upon the Speaker a cold, questioning glance, or exchanging signals with one another, they were evidently hostile to Jesus, listening, it is true, but with a feline alertness, hoping to entrap the sweet Singer in His speech. Upon these, and such as these, the word of God, even when spoken by the Divine Son, made no impression. It was a speaking to the rocks, with no other result than the awaking of a few echoes of mockery and banter.

The experience is still true. Among those who frequent the house of God are many whose worship is a cold, conventional thing. Drawn thither by custom, by the social instinct, or by the love of change, they pass within the gates of the Lord's house, ostensibly to worship. But they are insincere, indifferent; they bring their body, and deposit it in the accustomed pew, but they might as well have put there a bag of ashes or an automaton of brass. Their mind is not here, and the cold, stolid features, unlighted by any passing gleam, tell too surely of a vacancy or vagrancy of thought. And even while the lips are throwing off mechanically Jubilates and Te Deums their heart is "far from Me," chasing some phantom "will o' the wisp," or dreaming their dreams of pleasure, gain, and ease. The worship of God they themselves would call it, but God does not recognize it. He calls their prayers a weariness, their incense an abomination. Theirs is but a worship of Self, as, setting up their image of clay, they summon earth's musicians to play their sweet airs about it. God, with them, is set back, ignored, proscribed. The personal "I" is writ so large, and is so all-pervasive, that there is no room for the I AM. Living for earth, all the fibres of their being growing downwards towards it, heaven is not even a cloud drifting across their distant vision; it is an empty space, a vacancy. To the voices of earth their ears are keenly sensitive; its very whispers thrill them with new excitements; but to the voices of Heaven they are deaf; the still, small voice is all unheard, and even the thunders of God are so muffled as to be unrecognized and scarcely audible. And so the word of God falls upon their ears in vain. It drops upon a soil that is impervious and antipathetic, a heart which knows no penitence, and a life whose fancied goodness has no room for mercy, or which finds such complete satisfaction in the gains of unrighteousness or the pleasures of sin that it is purposely and persistently deaf to all higher, holier voices. Ulysses filled his ears with wax, lest he should yield himself up to the enchantments of the sirens. The fable is true, even when read in reversed lines; for when Virtue, Purity, and Faith invite men to their resting-place, calling them to the Islands of the Blessed, and to the Paradise of God, they charm in vain. Deafening their ears, and not deigning to give a passing thought to the higher call, men drift past the heaven which might have been theirs, until these holier voices are silenced by the awful distance.

That the word of God is inoperative here is through no fault, either of the seed or of the sower. That word is still "quick and powerful," but it is sterile, because it finds nothing on which it may grow. It is not "understood," as Jesus Himself explains. It falls upon the outward ear alone, and there only as unmeaning sound, like the accents of some unknown tongue. And so the wicked one easily takes away the word from their heart; for, as the preposition itself implies, that word had not fallen into the heart; it was lying on it in a superficial way, like the seed cast upon the trampled path.

Is there, then, no hope for these way-side hearers? and sparing our strength and toil, shall we leave them for soils more promising? By no means. The fallow ground may be broken up; the ploughshare can loosen the hardened, unproductive earth. Pulverized by the teeth of the harrow or the teeth of the frost, the barren track itself disappears; it passes up into the advanced classes, giving back the seed with which it is now entrusted, with a thirty, sixty, or a hundredfold increase. And this is true in the higher husbandry, in which we are permitted to be "God's fellow-workers." The heart which to-day is indifferent or repellent, to-morrow, chastened by sickness or torn by the ploughshare of some keen grief, may hail with eagerness the message it rejected and even scorned before. Amid the penury and shame of the far country, the father's house, from which he had wantonly turned, now comes to the prodigal like a sweet dream, and even its bread has all the aroma and sweetness of ambrosial food. No matter how disappointing the soil, we are to do our duty, which is to "sow beside all waters;" nor should any calculations of imaginary productiveness make us slack our hand or cast away our hope. When the Spirit is poured out from on high, even "the wilderness becomes as a fruitful field," and death itself becomes instinct with life.

"And other fell on the rock; and as soon as it grew it withered away, because it had no moisture." Here is a second quality of soil. It is not, however, a soil that is weakened by an intermixture of gravel or of stones, but rather a soil that is thinly spread upon the rock. It is good soil as far as it goes, but it is shallow. It receives the seed gladly, as if that were its one mission, as indeed it is; it gives the seed a hiding-place, throwing over it a mantle of earth, so that the birds shall not devour it. It lays its warm touch upon the enveloping husk, as the Master once laid His finger upon the bier, and to the imprisoned life which was within it said, "Arise and multiply. Pass up into the sunlight, and give God's children bread." And the seed responds, obeys. The emerging life throws out its two wings--one downwards, as its roots clasp the soil; one upwards, as the blade, pushing the clods aside, makes for the light and the heavens that are above it. "Surely," we should say, if we read the future from the present merely, "the hundredfold is here. Pull down your barns and build greater, for never was seed received more kindly, never were the beginnings of life more auspicious, and never was promise so great." Ah that the promise should so soon be a disappointment, and the forecast be so soon belied! The soil has no depth. It is simply a thin covering spread over the rock. It offers no room for growth. The life it nourishes can be nothing more than an ephemeral life, which owns but a to-day, whose "to-morrow" will be in the oven of a burning heat. The growth is entirely superficial, for its roots come directly to the hard, impenetrable rock, which, yielding no support, but cutting off all supplies from the unseen reservoirs beneath, turns back the incipient life all starved and shrunken. The result is a sudden withering and decay. A foundling, left, not by some iron gate which the touch of mercy might open, but by a dead wall of cold, unresponsive stone, the plant throws up its arms into the air, in its vain struggle for life, and then wilts and droops, lying at last, a dead and shrivelled thing, on the dry bosom of the earth which had given it its untimely birth.

    Such, says Jesus, are many who hear the word. Unlike those by the way-side, these do not reject it. They listen, bending toward that word with attentive ears and eager hearts. Nay, they receive it with joy; it strikes upon their soul with the music of a new evangel. But the work is not thorough; it is superficial, external. They "have no root" in a deep and settled conviction, only a green blade of profession and of mock promise, and when the testing-time comes, as it comes to all, "the time of temptation," they fall away, or they "stand off," as the verb might be literally rendered.

    In this second class we must place a large proportion of those who heard and who followed Jesus. There was something attractive about His manner and about His message. Again and again we read how they "pressed upon Him" to hear His words, the multitude hanging on His lips as the bees will cluster upon a honeyed leaf. Thousands upon thousands thus came within the spell of His voice, now wondering at His gracious words, and now stunned with astonishment, as they marked the authority with which He spoke, the compressed thunder that was in His tones. But in how many cases are we forced to admit the interest to be but momentary! It was with many--shall we say with most?--merely a passing excitement, the effervescence of personal contact. The words of Jesus came "as a very lovely song of one that hath a pleasant voice," and for the moment the hearts of the multitudes were set vibrating in responsive harmonies. But the music ceased when the Singer was absent. The impressions were not permanent, and even the emotions had soon passed away, almost from memory. St. John speaks of one sifting in Galilee when "many of His disciples went back, and walked no more with Him" (vi. 66), showing that with them at least it was an attachment rather than an attachment that bound them to Himself. The bond of union was the hope of some personal gain, rather than the bond of a pure and deep affection. And so directly He speaks of His approaching death, of His "flesh and blood" which He shall give them to eat and to drink, like an icy breath from the north, those words chill their devotion, turning their zeal and ardour into a cold indifference, if not into an open hostility. And this same winnowing of Galilee is repeated in Judæa. We read of multitudes who escorted Jesus down the Mount of Olives, strewing His path with garments, giving Him a royal welcome to the "city of the Great King." But how soon a change "came o'er the spirit of their dream"! how soon the hosannahs died away! As a hawk in the sky will still in a moment the warbling of the birds, so the uplifted cross threw its cold shadow upon their hearts, drowning the brief hosannahs in a strange silence. The cross was the fan in the Masters hand, with which He "throughly purged His floor," separating the true from the false. It blew away into the deep valley of Oblivion the chaff, the dead superficialities, the barren yawns, leaving as the residuum of the sifted multitudes a mere handful of a hundred and twenty names.

    These pro tem. believers are indigenous to every soil. There never is a great movement afloat--philanthropic, political or spiritual--but numberless smaller craft are lifted up on its swell. For a moment they seem instinct with life, but having no propelling power in themselves, they drop behind, soon to be embedded in the mire. And especially is this true in the region of spiritual dynamics. In all so-called "revivals" of religion, when the Church rejoices in a deepened and quickened life, when a cooling zeal has been rewarmed at the heavenly fires, and converts are multiplied, in the accessions which follow almost invariably will be found a proportion of what we may call "casuals." We cannot say they are counterfeits, for the work, as far as it goes, seems real, and the change, both in their thought and life, is clearly marked. But they are unstable souls, prone to drifting, their direction given in the main by the set of the current in which they happen to be. And so when they reach the point--which all must reach sooner or later--where two seas meet, the cross current of enticement and temptation bears hard upon them, and they make shipwreck of faith. Others, again, are led by impulse. Religion with them is mainly a matter of feeling. Overlooking the fact that the emotions are easily stirred, that they respond to the passing breath just as the sea ripples to the breeze, they substitute emotion for conviction, feeling for faith. But these have no foundation, no root, no independent life, and when the excitements on which they feed are withdrawn, when the emotion subsides, the high tide of fervour falling back to its mean sea-level, they lose heart and hope. They are even ready to pity themselves as the objects of an illusion. But the illusion was one of their own making. They set the pleasant before the right, delight before duty, comfort before Christ, and instead of finding their heaven in doing the will of God, no matter what the emotions, they sought their heaven in their own personal happiness, and so they missed both.

"They endure for a while." And of how many are these words true! Verily we must not count our fruits from the blossoms of spring, nor must we reckon our harvest in that easy, hopeful way of multiplying each seed, or even each blade, by the hundredfold, for the blade may be only a short-lived blade and nothing more.

"And other fell amidst the thorns; and the thorns grew with it, and choked it." Here is a third quality of soil in the ascending series. In the first, the trampled path, life was not possible; the seed could find not the least response. In the second there was life. The thinly sprinkled soil gave the seed a home, a rooting; but lacking depth of earth and the necessary moisture, the life was precarious, ephemeral. It died away in the blade, and never reached its fruitage. Now, however, we have a deeper, richer soil, with an abundance of vitality, one capable of sustaining an exuberant life. But it is not clean; it is already thickly sown with thorns, and the two growths running up side by side, the hardier gets the mastery. And though the corn-life struggles up into the ear, bearing a sort of fruit, it is a grain that is dwarfed and shrivelled, a mere husk and shell, which no leaven can transmute into bread. It brings forth fruit, as the exposition of the parable indicates, but it has not strength to complete its task; it does not ripen it, bringing the fruit "to perfection."

Such, says Jesus, is another and a large class of hearers. They are naturally capable of doing great things. Possessing strong wills, and a large amount of energy, they are just the lives to be fruitful, impressing themselves upon others, and so throwing their manifold influence down into the future. But they do not, and for the simple reason that they do not give to the word a whole heart. Their attentions and energies are divided. Instead of seeking "first the kingdom of God," making that the supreme quest of life, it is with them but one of many things to be desired and sought. Chief among the hindrances to a perfected growth and fruitfulness, Jesus mentions three; namely, cares, riches, and pleasures. By the "cares of life" we must understand--interpreting the word by its related word in Matthew vi. 34--the anxieties of life. It is the anxious thought, mainly about the "to-morrow," which presses upon the heart as a sore and constant burden. It is the fearfulness and unrest of soul which gloom the spirit and shroud the life, making the Divine peace itself a fret and worry. And how many Christians find this to be the normal experience! They love God, they seek to serve Him; but they are weighted and weary. Instead of having the hopeful, buoyant spirit which rises to the crest of passing waves, it is a heart depressed and sad, living in the deeps. And so the brightness of their life is dimmed; they walk not "in the light, as He is in the light," but beneath a sky frequently overcast, their days bringing only "a little glooming light, much like a shade." And so their spiritual life is stunted, their usefulness impaired. Instead of having a heart "at leisure from itself," they are engrossed with their own unsatisfactory experiences. Instead of looking upwards to the heavens which are their own, or outwards upon the crying needs of earth, they look inward with frequent and morbid introspection; and instead of lending a hand to the fallen, that a brotherly touch might help them to rise, their hands find full employment in steadying the world, or worlds, of care which, Atlas-like, they are doomed to carry. Self-doomed, we should have said; for the Divine Voice invites us to cast "all our anxiety upon Him," assuring us that He careth for us, an assurance and an invitation which make our anxieties, the fret and fever of life, altogether superfluous.

Exactly the same effect of making the spiritual life incomplete, and so unproductive, is caused by riches and pleasures, or, as we might render the expression, by the pursuit after riches or after pleasure. Not that the Scriptures condemn wealth in itself. It is, per se, of a neutral character, whether a blessing or a bane depends on how it is earned and how it is held. Nor do the Scriptures condemn legitimate modes and measures of business; they condemn waste and indolence, but they commend industry, diligence, thrift. But the evil is in making wealth the chief aim of life. It is deceptive, promising satisfaction which it never gives, creating a thirst which it is powerless to slake, until the desire, ever more greedy and clamorous, grows into a "love of money," a pure worship of Mammon. Religion and business may well go together, for God has joined them in one. Each keeping its proper place, religion first and most, and business a far-off second, together they are the centrifugal and centripetal forces that keep the life revolving steadily around its Divine centre. But let the positions be reversed; let business be the first, chief thought, let religion sink down to some second or third place, and the life swings farther and farther from its pivotal centre, into wildernesses of dearth and cold. To give due thought to earthly things is right; nay, we may give all diligence to make our earthly, as well as our heavenly calling sure; but when business gets imperious in its demands, swallowing up all our thought and energy, leaving no time for spiritual exercises or for personal service for Christ, then the religious life declines. Crowded back into the chance corners, with nothing left it but the brief interstices of a busy life, religion can do little more than maintain a profession; its helpfulness is, in the main, remitted to the past, and its fruitfulness is postponed to that uncertain nowhere of the Greek calends.

The same is true with regard to the pleasures of life. The word "pleasure" is a somewhat infrequent word in the New Testament, and generally it is used of the lower, sensual pleasures. We are not obliged, however, to give the word its lowest meaning; indeed, the analogy of the parable would scarcely allow such an interpretation. Sinful pleasure would not check growth; it would simply prevent it, making a spiritual life impossible. We must therefore interpret the "pleasures" which retard the upward growth, and render it infertile, as the lawful pleasures of life, such as the delights of the eye and ear, the gratification of the tastes, the enjoyments of domestic or social life. Perfectly innocent and pure in themselves, purposely designed for our enjoyment, as St. Paul plainly intimates (1 Tim. vi. 17), they are pleasures which we have no right to treat with the stoic's disdain, nor with the ascetic's aversion. But the snare is in permitting these desires to step out of their proper place, in allowing them to have a controlling influence. As servants their ministry is helpful and benign; but if we make them "lords," then, like "the ill uses of a life," we find it difficult to put them down; they rather put us down, making us their thrall. To please God should be the one absorbing pursuit and passion of life, and wholly bent on this, if other pure enjoyments come in our way we may receive them thankfully. But if we make our personal gratification the aim, if our thoughts and plans are set on this rather than upon the pleasing of God, then our spiritual life is enfeebled and stifled, and the fruit we should bear shrivels up into chaff. Then we become selfish and self-willed, and the pure pleasures of life, which like Vestal Virgins minister within the temple of God, leading us ever to Him, turn round to burn perpetual incense before our enlarged and exalted Self. He who stops to confer with flesh and blood, who is ever consulting his own likes and leanings, can never be an apostle to others.

"And other fell into the good ground, and grew, and brought forth fruit a hundredfold." Here is the highest quality of soil. Not hard, like the trampled path, nor shallow, like the covering of the rock, not preoccupied with the roots of other growths, this is mellow, deep, clean, and rich. The seed falls, not "by," or "in," or "among," but "into" it, while seed and soil together grow up in an affluence of life, and passing through the blade-age and the earing, it ripens into a harvest of a hundredfold. Such, says Jesus, are they who, in an honest and good heart, having heard the word, hold it fast, and bring forth fruit with patience. Here, then, we reach the germ of the parable, the secret of fruitfulness. The one difference between the saint and the sinner, between the hundredfold hearer and him whose life is spent in throwing out promises of a harvest which never ripens, is their different attitude towards the word of God. In the one case that word is rejected altogether, or it is a concept of the mind alone, an aurora of the Arctic night, distant and cold, which some mistake for the dawn of a new day. In the other the word passes through the mind into the deepest heart; it conquers and rules the whole being; it becomes a part of one's very self, the soul of the soul. "Thy word have I hid in my heart," said the Psalmist, and he who puts the Divine word there, before all earthly and selfish voices, letting that Divine Voice fill up that most sacred temple of the heart, will make his outer life both beautiful and fruitful. He will walk the earth as one of God's seers, ever beholding Him who is invisible, speaking by life or lips in heavenly tones, and by his own steadfast, upward gaze lifting the hearts and thoughts of men "above the world's uncertain haze." Such is the Divine law of life; the measure of our faith is the measure of our fruitfulness. If we but half believe in the promises of God or in the eternal realities, then the sinews of our soul are houghed, and there comes over us the sad paralysis of doubt. How can we bring forth fruit except we abide in Him? and how can we abide in Him but by letting His words abide in us? But having His words abiding in us, then His peace, His joy, His life are ours, and we, who without Him are poor, dead things, now become strong in His infinite strength, and fruitful with a Divine fruitfulness; and to our lives, which were all barren and dead, will men come for the words that "help and heal," while the Master Himself gathers from them His thirty, sixty, or hundredfold, the fruitage of a whole-hearted, patient faith.

Let us take heed, therefore, how we hear, for on the character of the hearing depends the character of the life. Nor is the truth given us for ourselves alone; it is given that it may become incarnate in us, so that others may see and feel the truth that is in us, even as men cannot help seeing the light which is manifest.

And so the parable closes with the account of the visit of His mother and brethren, who came, as St. Matthew informs us, "to take Him home;" and when the message was passed on to Him that His mother and His brethren wished to see Him, this was His remarkable answer, claiming relationship with all whose hearts vibrate to the same "word:" "My mother and My brethren are those which hear the word of God, and DO IT." It is the secret of the Divine life on earth; they hear, and they do.

*Henry Burton*

## CHAPTER XV – THE KINGDOM OF GOD

In considering the words of Jesus, if we may not be able to measure their depth or to scale their height, we can with absolute certainty discover their drift, and see in what direction they move, and we shall find that their orbit is an ellipse. Moving around the two centres, sin and salvation, they describe what is not a geometric figure, but a glorious reality, "the kingdom of God." It is not unlikely that the expression was one of the current phrases of the times, a golden casket, holding within it the dream of a restored Hebraism; for we find, without any collusion or rehearsal of parts, the Baptist making use of the identical words in his inaugural address, while it is certain the disciples themselves so misunderstood the thought of their Master as to refer His "kingdom" to that narrow realm of Hebrew sympathies and hopes. Nor did they see their error until, in the light of Pentecostal flames, their own dream disappeared, and the new kingdom, opening out like a receding sky, embraced a world within its folds. That Jesus adopted the phrase, liable to misconstruction as it was, and that He used it so repeatedly, making it the centre of so many parables and discourses, shows how completely the kingdom of God possessed both His mind and heart. Indeed, so accustomed were His thoughts and words to flow in this direction that even the valley of Death, "lying darkly between" His two lives, could not alter their course, or turn His thoughts out of their familiar channel; and as we find the Christ beyond the cross and tomb, amid the resurrection glories, we hear Him speaking still of "the things pertaining to the kingdom of God."

It will be observed that Jesus uses the two expressions "the kingdom of God" and "the kingdom of heaven" interchangeably. But in what sense is it the "kingdom of heaven"? Does it mean that the celestial realm will so far extend its bounds as to embrace our outlying and low-lying world? Not exactly, for the conditions of the two realms are so diverse. The one is the perfected, the visible kingdom, where the throne is set, and the King Himself is manifest, its citizens, angels, heavenly intelligences, and saints now freed from the cumbering clay of mortality, and for ever safe from the solicitations of evil. This New Jerusalem does not come down to earth, except in the vision of the seer, as it were in a shadow. And yet the two kingdoms are in close correspondence, after all; for what is the kingdom of God in heaven but His eternal rule over the spirits of the redeemed and of the unredeemed? what are the harmonies of heaven but the harmonies of surrendered wills, as, without any hesitation or discord, they strike in with the Divine Will in absolute precision? To this extent, then, at least, heaven may project itself upon earth; the spirits of men not yet made perfect may be in subjection to the Supreme Spirit; the separate wills of a redeemed humanity, striking in with the Divine Will, may swell the heavenly harmonies with their earthly music.

And so Jesus speaks of this kingdom as being "within you." As if He said, "You are looking in the wrong direction. You expect the kingdom of God to be set up around you, with its visible symbols of flags and coins, on which is the image of some new Cæsar. You are mistaken. The kingdom, like its King, is unseen; it seeks, not countries, but consciences; its realm is in the heart, in the great interior of the soul." And is not this the reason why it is called, with such emphatic repetition, "the kingdom," as if it were, if not the only, at any rate the highest kingdom of God on earth? We speak of a kingdom of Nature, and who will know its secrets as He who was both Nature's child and Nature's Lord? And how far-reaching a realm is that! from the motes that swim in the air to the most distant stars, which themselves are but the gateway to the unseen Beyond! What forces are here, forces of chemical affinities and repulsions, of gravitation and of life! What successions and transformations can Nature show! what infinite varieties of substance, form, and colour! what a realm of harmony and peace, with no irruptions of discordant elements! Surely one would think, if God has a kingdom upon earth, this kingdom of Nature is it. But no; Jesus does not often refer to that, except as He makes Nature speak in His parables, or as He uses the sparrows, the grass, and the lilies as so many lenses through which our weak human vision may see God. The kingdom of God on earth is as much higher than the kingdom of Nature as spirit is above matter, as love is more and greater than power.

We said just now how completely the thought of "the kingdom" possessed the mind and heart of Jesus. We might go one step farther, and say how completely Jesus identified Himself with that kingdom. He puts. Himself in its pivotal centre, with all possible naturalness, and with an ease that assumption cannot feign. He gathers up its royalties and draws them around His own Person. He speaks of it as "My kingdom;" and this, not alone in familiar discourse with His disciples, but when face to face with the representative of earth's greatest power. Nor is the personal pronoun some chance word, used in a far-off, accommodated sense; it is the crucial word of the sentence, underscored and emphasized by a threefold repetition; it is the word He will not strike out, nor recall, even to save Himself from the cross. He never speaks of the kingdom but even His enemies acknowledge the "authority" that rings in His tones, the authority of conscious power, as well as of perfect knowledge. When His ministry is drawing to a close He says to Peter, "I will give unto thee the keys of the kingdom of heaven;" which language may be understood as the official designation of the Apostle Peter to a position of pre-eminence in the Church, as its first leader. But whatever it may mean, it shows that the keys of the kingdom are His; He can bestow them on whom He will. The kingdom of heaven is not a realm in which authority and honours move upwards from below, the blossoming of "the people's will;" it is an absolute monarchy, an autocracy, and Jesus Himself is here King supreme, His will swaying the lesser wills of men, and rearranging their positions, as the angel had foretold: "He shall reign over the house of David for ever, and of His kingdom there shall be no end." Given Him of the Father it is (xxii. 29; i. 32), but the kingdom is His, not either as a metaphor, but really, absolutely, inalienably; nor is there admittance within that kingdom but by Him who is the Way, as He is the Life. We enter into the kingdom, or the kingdom enters into us, as we find, and then crown the King, as we sanctify in our hearts "Christ as Lord" (1 Pet. iii. 15).

This brings us to the question of citizenship, the conditions and demands of the kingdom; and here we see how far this new dynasty is removed from the kingdoms of this world. They deal with mankind in groups; they look at birth, not character; and their bounds are well defined by rivers, mountains, seas, or by accurately surveyed lines. The kingdom of heaven, on the other hand, dispenses with all space-limits, all physical configurations, and regards mankind as one group, a unity, a lapsed but a redeemed world. But while opening its gates and offering its privileges to all alike, irrespective of class or circumstance, it is most eclectic in its requirements, and most rigid in the application of its test, its one test of character. Indeed, the laws of the heavenly kingdom are a complete reversal of the lines of worldly policy. Take, for instance, the two estimates of wealth, and see how different the position it occupies in the two societies. The world makes wealth its summum bonum; or if not exactly in itself the highest good, in commercial values it is equivalent to the highest good, which is position. Gold is all-powerful, the goal of man's vain ambitions, the panacea of earthly ill. Men chase it in hot, feverish haste, trampling upon each other in the mad scramble, and worshipping it in a blind idolatry. But where is wealth in the new kingdom? The worlds first becomes the last. It has no purchasing-power here; its golden key cannot open the least of these heavenly gates. Jesus sets it back, far back, in His estimate of the good. He speaks of it as if it were an encumbrance, a dead weight, that must be lifted, and that handicaps the heavenly athlete. "How hardly," said Jesus, when the rich ruler turned away "very sorrowful," "shall they that have riches enter into the kingdom of God!" (xviii. 24); and then, by way of illustration, He shows us the picture of the camel passing through the so-called "needle's eye" of an Eastern door. He does not say that such a thing is impossible, for the camel could pass through the "needle's eye," but it must first kneel down and be stripped of all its baggage, before it can pass the narrow door, within the larger, but now closed gate. Wealth may have its uses, and noble uses too, within the kingdom--for it is somewhat remarkable how the faith of the two rich disciples shone out the brightest, when the faith of the rest suffered a temporary eclipse from the passing cross--but he who possesses it must be as if he possessed it not. He must not regard it as his own, but as talents given him in trust by his Lord, their image and superscription being that of the Invisible King.

Again, Jesus sets down vacillation, hesitancy, as a disqualification for citizenship in His kingdom. At the close of His Galilean ministry our Evangelist introduces us to a group of embryo disciples. The first of the three says, "Lord, I will follow Thee whithersoever Thou goest" (ix. 57). Bold words they were, and doubtless well meant, but it was the language of a passing impulse, rather than of a settled conviction; it was the coruscation of a glowing, ardent temperament. He had not counted the cost. The large word "whithersoever" might, indeed, easily be spoken, but it held within it a Gethsemane and a Calvary, paths of sorrow, shame, and death he was not prepared to face. And so Jesus neither welcomed nor dismissed him, but opening out one part of his "whithersoever," He gave it back to him in the words, "The foxes have holes, and the birds of the heaven have nests; but the Son of man hath not where to lay His head." The second responds to the "Follow Me" of Christ with the request that he might be allowed first to go and bury his father. It was a most natural request, but participation in these funeral rites would entail a ceremonial uncleanness of seven days, by which time Jesus would be far away. Besides, Jesus must teach him, and the ages after him, that His claims were paramount; that when He commands obedience must be instant and absolute, with no interventions, no postponement. Jesus replies to him in that enigmatical way of His, "Leave the dead to bury their own dead: but go thou and publish abroad the kingdom of God;" indicating that this supreme crisis of his life is virtually a passing from death to life, a "resurrection from earth to things above." The last in this group of three volunteers his pledge, "I will follow Thee, Lord; but first suffer me to bid farewell to them that are at my house" (ix. 61); but to him Jesus replies, mournfully and sorrowfully, "No man, having put his hand to the plough, and looking back, is fit for the kingdom of God" (ix. 62). Why does Jesus treat these two candidates so differently? They both say, "I will follow Thee," the one in word, the other by implication; they both request a little time for what they regard a filial duty; why, then, be treated so differently, the one thrust forward to a still higher service, commissioned to preach the kingdom, and afterwards, if we may accept the tradition that he was Philip the Evangelist, passing up into the diaconate; the other, unwelcomed and uncommissioned, but disapproved as "not fit for the kingdom"? Why there should be this wide divergence between the two lives we cannot see, either from their manner or their words. It must have been a difference in the moral attitude of the two men, and which He who heard thoughts and read motives detected at once. In the case of the former there was the fixed, determined resolve, which the bier of a dead father might hold back a little, but which it could not break or bend. But Jesus saw in the other a double-minded soul, whose feet and heart moved in diverse, opposite ways, who gave, not his whole, but a very partial, self to his work; and this halting, wavering one He dismissed with the words of forecasted doom, "Not fit for the kingdom of God."

It is a hard saying, with a seeming severity about it; but is it not a truth universal and eternal? Are any kingdoms, either of knowledge or power, won and held by the irresolute and wavering? Like the stricken men of Sodom, they weary themselves to find the door of the kingdom; or if they do see the Beautiful Gates of a better life, they sit with the lame man, outside, or they linger on the steps, hearing the music indeed, but hearing it from afar. It is a truth of both dispensations, written in all the books; the Reubens who are "unstable as water" can never excel; the elder born, in the accident of years, they may be, but the birthright passes by them, to be inherited and enjoyed by others.

But if the gates of the kingdom are irrevocably closed against the half-hearted, the self-indulgent, and the proud, there is a sesame to which they open gladly. "Blessed are ye poor," so reads the first and great Beatitude: "for yours is the kingdom of God" (vi. 20); and beginning with this present realization, Jesus goes on to speak of the strange contrasts and inversions the perfected kingdom will show, when the weepers will laugh, the hungry be full, and those who are despised and persecuted will rejoice in their exceeding great reward. But who are the "poor" to whom the gates of the kingdom are open so soon and so wide? At first sight it would appear as if we must give a literal interpretation to the word, reading it in a worldly, temporal sense; but this is not necessary. Jesus was now directly addressing His disciples (vi. 20), though, doubtless, His words were intended to pass beyond them, to those ever-enlarging circles of humanity who in the after-years should press forward to hear Him. But evidently the disciples were in no weeping mood to-day; they would be elated and joyful over the recent miracles. Neither should we call them "poor," in the worldly sense of that word, for most of them had been called from honourable positions in society, while some had even "hired servants" to wait upon and assist them. Indeed, it was not the wont of Jesus to recognize the class distinctions Society was so fond of drawing and defining. He appraised men, not by their means, but by the manhood which was in them; and when He found a nobility of soul--whether in the higher or the lower walks of life it made no difference--He stepped forward to recognize and to salute it. We must therefore give to these words of Jesus, as to so many others, the deeper meaning, making the "blessed" of this Beatitude, who are now welcomed to the opened gate of the kingdom, the "poor in spirit," as, indeed, St. Matthew writes it.

What this spirit-poverty is, Jesus Himself explains, in a brief but wonderfully realistic parable. He draws for us the picture of two men at their Temple devotions. The one, a Pharisee, stands erect, with head uplifted, as if it were quite on a level with the heaven he was addressing, and with supercilious pride he counts his beads of rounded egotisms. He calls it a worship of God, when it is but a worship of self. He inflates the great "I," and then plays upon it, making it strike sharp and loud, like the tom-tom of a heathen fetish. Such is the man who fancies that he is rich toward God, that he has need of nothing, not even of mercy, when all the time he is utterly blind and miserably poor. The other is a publican, and so presumably rich. But how different his posture! With heart broken and contrite, self with him is a nothing, a zero; nay, in his lowly estimate it had become a minus quantity, less than nothing, deserving only rebuke and chastisement. Disclaiming any good, either inherent or acquired, he puts the deep need and hunger of his soul into one broken cry, "God be merciful to me a sinner (xviii. 13). Such are the two characters Jesus portrays as standing by the gate of the kingdom, the one proud in spirit, the other "poor in spirit;" the one throwing upon the heavens the shadow of his magnified self, the other shrinking up into the pauper, the nothing that he was. But Jesus tells us that he was "justified," accepted, rather than the other. With nought he could call his own, save his deep need and his great sin, he finds an opened gate and a welcome within the kingdom; while the proud in spirit is sent empty away, or carrying back only the tithed mint and anise, and all the vain oblations Heaven could not accept.

"Blessed" indeed are such "poor;" for He giveth grace unto the lowly, while the proud He knoweth afar off. The humble, the meek, these shall inherit the earth, ay, and the heavens too, and they shall know how true is the paradox, having nothing, yet possessing all things. The fruit of the tree of life hangs low, and he must stoop who would gather it. He who would enter God's kingdom must first become "as a little child," knowing nothing as yet, but longing to know even the mysteries of the kingdom, and having nothing but the plea of a great mercy and a great need. And are they not "blessed" who are citizens of the kingdom--with righteousness, peace, and joy all their own, a peace which is perfect and Divine, and a joy which no man taketh from them? Are they not blessed, thrice blessed, when the bright shadow of the Throne covers all their earthly life, making its dark places light, and weaving rainbows out of their very tears? He who through the strait gate of repentance passes within the kingdom finds it "the kingdom of heaven" indeed, his earthly years the beginnings of the heavenly life.

And now we touch a point Jesus ever loved to illustrate and emphasize, the manner of the kingdom's growth, as with ever-widening frontiers it sweeps outward in its conquest of a world. It was a beautiful dream of Hebrew prophecy that in the latter days the kingdom of God, or the kingdom of the Messiah, should overlap the bounds of human empires, and ultimately cover the whole earth. Looking through her kaleidoscope of ever-shifting but harmonious figures, Prophecy was never weary of telling of the Golden Age she saw in the far future, when the shadows would lift, and a new Dawn, breaking out of Jerusalem, would steal over the world. Even the Gentiles should be drawn to its light, and kings to the brightness of its rising; the seas should offer their abundance as a willing tribute, and the isles should wait for and welcome its laws. Taking up into itself the petty strifes and jealousies of men, the discords of earth should cease; humanity should again become a unit, restored and regenerate fellow-citizens of the new kingdom, the kingdom which should have no end, no boundaries either of space or time.

Such was the dream of Prophecy, the kingdom Jesus sets Himself to found and realize upon earth. But how? Disclaiming any rivalry with Pilate, or with his imperial master, Jesus said, "My kingdom is not of this world," so lifting it altogether out of the mould in which earthly dynasties are cast. "This world" uses force; its kingdoms are won and held by metallic processes, tinctures of iron and steel. In the kingdom of God carnal weapons are out of place; its only forces are truth and love, and he who takes the sword to advance this cause wounds but himself, after the vain manner of Baal's priests. "This world" counts heads or hands; the kingdom of God numbers its citizens by hearts alone. "This world" believes in pomp and show, in outward visibilities and symbols; the kingdom of God cometh not "with observation;" its voices are gentle as a zephyr, its footsteps noiseless as the coming of spring. If man had had the ordering of the kingdom he would have summoned to his aid all kinds of portents and surprises; he would have arranged processions of imposing events; but Jesus likens the coming of the kingdom to a grain of mustard-seed cast into a garden, or to a handful of leaven hid in three sata of meal. The two parables, with minor distinctions, are one in their import, the leading thought common to both being the contrast between its ultimate growth and the smallness and obscurity of its beginnings. In both the recreative force is a hidden force, buried out of sight, in the soil or in the meal. In both the force works outward from its centre, the invisible becoming visible, the inner life assuming an outer, external form. In both we see the touch of life upon death; for left to itself, the soil never would be anything more than dead earth, as the meal would be nothing more than dust, the broken ashes of a life that was departed. In both there is extension by assimilation, the leaven throwing itself out among the particles of kindred meal, while the tree attracts to itself the kindred elements of the soil. In both there is the mediation of the human hand; but as if to show that the kingdom offers equal privilege to male and female, with like possibilities of service, the one parable shows us the hand of a man, the other the hand of a woman. In both there is a perfect work, a consummation, the one parable showing us the whole mass leavened, the other showing us the wide-spreading tree, with the birds nesting in its branches.

Such, in outline, is the rise and progress of the kingdom of God in the heart of the individual man, and in the world; for the human soul is the protoplasm, the germ-cell, out of which this world-wide kingdom is evolved. The mass is leavened only by the leavening of the separate units. And how comes the kingdom of God within the soul and life of man? Not with observation or supernatural portents, but silently as the flashing forth of light. Thought, desire, purpose, prayer--these are the wheels of the chariot in which the Lord comes to His temple, the King into His kingdom. And when the kingdom of God is set up "within you" the outer life shapes itself to the new purpose and aim, the writ and will of the King running unhindered through every department, even to its outmost frontier, while thoughts, feelings, desires, and all the golden coinage of the heart bear, not, as before, the image of Self, but the image and superscription of the Invisible King--the "Not I, but Christ."

*Henry Burton*

And so the honour of the kingdom is in our keeping, as the growths of the kingdom are in our hands. The Divine Cloud adjusts its pace to our human steps, alas, often far too slow! Shall the leaven stop with us, as we make religion a kind of sanctified selfishness, doing nothing but gauging the emotions and singing its little doxologies? Do we forget that the weak human hand carries the Ark of God, and pushes forward the boundaries of the kingdom? Do we forget that hearts are only won by hearts? The kingdom of God on earth is the kingdom of surrendered wills and of consecrated lives. Shall we not, then, pray, "Thy kingdom come," and living "more nearly as we pray," seek a redeemed humanity as subjects of our King? So will the Divine purpose become a realization, and the "morning" which now is always "somewhere in the world" will be everywhere, the promise and the dawn of a heavenly day, the eternal Sabbath!

# CHAPTER XVI - THE MIRACLES OF HEALING

It is only natural that our Evangelist should linger with a professional as well as a personal interest over Christ's connection with human suffering and disease, and that in recounting the miracles of healing he should be peculiarly at home; the theme would be in such thorough accord with his studies and tastes. It is true he does not refer to these miracles as being a fulfilment of prophecy; it is left for St. Matthew, who weaves his Gospel on the unfinished warp of the Old Testament, to recall the words of Isaiah, how "Himself took our infirmities and bare our diseases;" yet our physician-Evangelist evidently lingers over the pathological side of his Gospel with an intense interest. St. John passes by the miracles of healing in comparative silence, though he stays to give us two cases which are omitted by the Synoptists--that of the nobleman's son at Capernaum, and that of the impotent man at Bethesda. But St. John's Gospel moves in more etherial spheres, and the touches he chronicles are rather the touches of mind with mind, spirit with spirit, than the physical touches through the coarser medium of the flesh. The Synoptists, however, especially their earlier chapters, bring the works of Christ into prominence, travelling too very much over the same ground, though each introduces some special facts omitted by the rest, while in their record of the same fact each Evangelist throws some additional colouring.

Grouping together the miracles of healing--for our space will not allow a separate treatment of each--our thought is first arrested by the variety of forms in which suffering and disease presented themselves to Jesus, the wideness of the ground, physical and psychical, the miracles of healing cover. Our Evangelist mentions fourteen different cases, not, however, as including the whole, or even the greater part, but rather as being typical, representative cases. They are, as it were, the nearer constellations, localized and named; but again and again in his narrative we find whole groups and clusters lying farther back, making a sort of Milky Way of light, whose thickly clustered worlds baffle all our attempts at enumeration. Such are the "women" of chap. viii. ver. 2, who had been healed of their infirmities, but whose record is omitted in the Gospel story; and such, too, are those groups of cures mentioned in chapters iv. 40, v. 15, vi. 19, and vii. 21, when the Divine power seemed to culminate, throwing itself out in a largesse of blessing, fairly raining down its bright gifts of healing like meteoric showers.

Turning now to the typical cases mentioned by St. Luke, they are as follows: the man possessed of an unclean demon; Peter's wife's mother, who was sick of a fever; a leper, a paralytic, the man with the withered hand, the servant of the centurion, the demoniac, the woman with an issue, the boy possessed with a demon, the man with a dumb demon, the woman with an infirmity, the man with the dropsy, the ten lepers, and blind Bartimæus. The list, like so many lines of dark meridians, measures off the entire circumference of the world of suffering, beginning with the withered hand, and going on and down to that "sacrament of death," leprosy, and to that yet further deep, demoniacal possession. Some diseases were of more recent origin, as the case of fever; others were chronic, of twelve or eighteen years' standing, or lifelong, as in the case of the possessed boy. In some a solitary organ was affected, as when the hand had withered, or the tongue was tied by some power of evil, or the eyes had lost their gift of vision. In others the whole person was diseased, as when the fires of the fever shot through the heated veins, or the leprosy was covering the flesh with the white scales of death. But whatever its nature or its stage, the disease was acute, as far as human probabilities went, past all hope of healing. It was no slight attack, but a "great fever" which had stricken down the mother-in-law of Peter, the intensive adjective showing that it had reached its danger-point. And where among human means was there hope for a restored vision, when for years the last glimmer of light had faded away, when even the optic nerve was atrophied by the long disuse? and where, among the limited pharmacopoeias of ancient or even among the vastly extended lists of modern times, was there a cure for the leper, who carried, burned into his very flesh, his sentence of death? No, it was not the trivial, temporary cases of sickness Jesus took in hand; but He passed into that innermost shrine of the temple of suffering, the shrine that lay in perpetual night, and over whose doorway was the inscription of Dante's "Inferno," "All hope abandon, ye who enter here!" But when Jesus entered this grim abode He turned its darkness to light, its sighs to songs, bringing hope to despairing ones, and leading back into the light of day these captives of Death, as Orpheus is fabled to have brought back to earth the lost Eurydice.

And not only are the cases so varied in their character, and humanly speaking, hopeless in their nature, but they were presented to Jesus in such a diversity of ways. They are none of them arranged for, studied. They could not have formed any plan or routine of mercy, nor were they timed for the purpose of producing spectacular effects. They were nearly all of them impromptu, extemporary events, coming without His seeking, and coming often as interruptions to His own plans. Now it is in the synagogue, in the pauses of public worship, that Jesus rebukes an unclean devil, or He bids the cripple stretch out his withered hand. Now it is in the city, amid the crowd, or out upon the plain; now it is within the house of a chief Pharisee, in the very midst of an entertainment; while at other times He is walking on the road, when, without even stopping in His journey, He wills the leper clean, or He throws the gift of life and health forward to the centurion's servant, whom He has not seen. No times were inopportune to Him, and no places were foreign to the Son of man, where men suffered and pain abode. Jesus refused no request on the ground that the time was not well chosen, and though He did again and again refuse the request of selfish interest or vain ambition, He never once turned a deaf ear to the cry of sorrow or of pain, no matter when or whence it came.

And if we consider His methods of healing we find the same diversity. Perhaps we ought not to use that word, for there was a singular absence of method. There was nothing set, artificial in His way, but an easy freedom, a beautiful naturalness. In one respect, and perhaps in one only, are all similar, and that is in the absence of intermediaries. There was no use of means, no prescription of remedies; for in the seeming exception, the clay with which He anointed the eyes of the blind, and the waters of Siloam which He prescribed, were not remedial in themselves; the washing was rather the test of the man's faith, while the anointing was a sort of "aside," spoken, not to the man himself, but to the group of onlookers, preparing them for the fresh manifestation of His power. Generally a word was enough, though we read of His healing "touch," and twice of the symbolic laying on of hands. And by-the-way, it is somewhat singular that Jesus made use of the touch at the healing of the leper, when the touch meant ceremonial uncleanness. Why does He not speak the word only, as He did afterwards at the healing of the "ten"? And why does He, as it were, go out of His way to put Himself in personal contact with a leper, who was under a ceremonial ban? Was it not to show that a new era had dawned, an era in which uncleanness should be that of the heart, the life, and no longer the outward uncleanness, which any accident of contact might induce? Did not the touching of the leper mean the abrogation of the multiplied bans of the Old Dispensation, just as afterwards a heavenly vision coming to Peter wiped out the dividing-line between clean and unclean meats? And why did not the touch of the leper make Jesus ceremonially unclean? for we do not read that it did, or that He altered His plans one whit because of it. Perhaps we find our answer in the Levitical regulations respecting the leprosy. We read (Lev. xiv. 28) that at the cleansing of the leper the priest was to dip his right finger in the blood and in the oil, and put it on the ear, and hand, and foot of the person cleansed. The finger of the priest was thus the index or sign of purity, the lifting up of the ban which his leprosy had put around and over him. And when Jesus touched the leper it was the priestly touch; it carried its own cleansing with it, imparting power and purity, instead of contracting the defilement of another.

But if Jesus touched the leper, and permitted the woman of Capernaum to touch Him, or at any rate His garment, He studiously avoided any personal contact with those possessed of devils. He recognized here the presence of evil spirits, the powers of darkness, which have enthralled the weaker human spirit, and for these a word is enough. But how different a word to His other words of healing, when He said to the leper, "I will; be thou clean," and to Bartimæus, "Receive thy sight"! Now it is a word sharp, imperative, not spoken to the poor helpless victim, but thrown over and beyond him, to the dark personality, which held a human soul in a vile, degrading bondage. And so while the possessed boy lay writhing and foaming on the ground, Jesus laid no hand upon him; it was not till after He had spoken the mighty word, and the demon had departed from him, that Jesus took him by the hand and lifted him up.

But whether by word or by touch, the miracles were wrought with consummate ease; there were none of those artistic flourishes which mere performers use as a blind to cover their sleight of hand. There was no straining for effect, no apparent effort. Jesus Himself seemed perfectly unconscious that He was doing anything marvellous or even unusual. The words of power fell naturally from His lips, like the falling of leaves from the tree of life, carrying, wheresoever they might go, healing for the nations.

But if the method of the cures is wonderful, the unstudied ease and simple naturalness of the Healer, the completeness of the cures is even more so. In all the multitudes of cases there was no failure. We find the disciples baffled and chagrined, attempting what they cannot perform, as with the possessed boy; but with Jesus failure was an impossible word. Nor did Jesus simply make them better, bringing them into a state of convalescence, and so putting them in the way of getting well. The cure was instant and complete; "immediately" is St. Luke's frequent and favourite word; so much so that she who half an hour ago was stricken down with malignant fever, and apparently at the point of death, now is going about her ordinary duties as if nothing had happened, "ministering" to Peter's many guests. Though Nature possesses a great deal of resilient force, her periods of convalescence, when the disease itself is checked, are more or less prolonged, and weeks, or sometimes months, must elapse before the spring-tides of health return, bringing with them a sweet overflow, an exuberance of life. Not so, however, when Jesus was the Healer. At His word, or at the mere beckoning of His finger, the tides of health, which had gone far out in the ebb, suddenly returned in all their spring fulness, lifting high on their wave the bark which through hopeless years had been settling down into its miry grave. Eighteen years of disease had made the woman quite deformed; the contracting muscles had bent the form God made to stand erect, so that she could "in no wise lift herself up;" but when Jesus said, "Woman, thou art loosed from thine infirmity," and laid His hands upon her, in an instant the tightened muscles relaxed, the bent form regained its earlier grace, for "she was made straight, and glorified God." One moment, with the Christ in it, was more than eighteen years of disease, and with the most perfect ease it could undo all the eighteen years had done. And this is but a specimen case, for the same completeness characterizes all the cures that Jesus wrought. "They were made whole," as it reads, no matter what the malady might be; and though disease had loosened all the thousand strings, so that the wonderful harp was reduced to silence, or at best could but strike discordant notes, the hand of Jesus has but to touch it, and in an instant each string recovers its pristine tone, the jarring sounds vanish, and body, "mind, and soul according well, awake sweet music as before."

But though Jesus wrought these many and complete cures, making the healing of the sick a sort of pastime, the interludes in that Divine "Messiah," still He did not work these miracles indiscriminately, without method or conditions. He freely placed His service at the disposal of others, giving Himself up to one tireless round of mercy; but it is evident there was some selection for these gifts of healing. The healing power was not thrown out randomly, falling on any one it might chance to strike; it flowed out in certain directions only, in ordered channels; it followed certain lines and laws. For instance, these circles of healing were geographically narrow. They followed the personal presence of Jesus, and with one or two exceptions, were never found apart from that presence; so that, many as they were, they would form but a small part of suffering humanity. And even within these circles of His visible presence we are not to suppose that all were healed. Some were taken, and others were left, to a suffering from which only death would release them. Can we discover the law of this election of mercy? We think we may.

(1) In the first place, there must be the need for the Divine intervention. This perhaps goes without saying, and does not seem to mean much, since among those who were left unhealed there were needs just as great as those of the more favoured ones. But while the "need" in some cases was not enough to secure the Divine mercy, in other cases it was all that was asked. If the disease was mental or psychical, with reason all bewildered, and the firmaments of Right and Wrong mixed confusedly together, making a chaos of the soul, that was all Jesus required. At other times He waited for the desire to be evoked and the request to be made; but for these cases of lunacy, epilepsy, and demoniacal possession He waived the other conditions, and without waiting for the request, as in the synagogue (iv. 34) or on the Gadarene coast, He spoke the word, which brought order to a distracted soul, and which led Reason back to her Jerusalem, to the long-vacant throne.

For others the need itself was not sufficient; there must be the request. Our desire for any blessing is our appraisement of its value, and Jesus dispensed His gifts of healing on the Divine conditions, "Ask, and ye shall receive; seek, and ye shall find." How the request came, whether from the sufferer himself or through some intercessor, it did not matter; for no request for healing came to Jesus to be disregarded or denied. Nor was it always needful to put the request into words. Prayer is too grand and great a thing for the lips to have a monopoly of it, and the deepest prayers may be put into acts as well as into words, as they are sometimes uttered in inarticulate sighs, and in groans which are too deep for words. And was it not truest prayer, as the multitudes carried their sick and laid them down at the feet of Jesus, even had their voice spoken no solitary word? and was it not truest prayer, as they put themselves, with their bent forms and withered hands right in His way, not able to speak one single word, but throwing across to Him the piteous but hopeful look? The request was thus the expression of their desire, and at the same time the expression of their faith, telling of the trust they reposed in His pity and His power, a trust He was always delighted to see, and to which He always responded, as He Himself said again and again, "Thy faith hath saved thee." Faith then, as now, was the sesame to which all Heaven's gates fly open; and as in the case of the paralytic who was borne of four, and let down through the roof, even a vicarious faith prevails with Jesus, as it brings to their friend a double and complete salvation. And so they who sought Jesus as their Healer found Him, and they who believed entered into His rest, this lower rest of a perfect health and perfect life; while they who were indifferent and they who doubted were left behind, crushed by the sorrow that He would have removed, and tortured by pains that His touch would have completely stilled.

*Henry Burton*

And now it remains for us to gather up the light of these miracles, and to focus it on Him who was the central Figure, Jesus, the Divine Healer. And (1) the miracles of healing speak of the knowledge of Jesus. The question, "What is man?" has been the standing question of the ages, but it is still unanswered, or answered but in part. His complex nature is still a mystery, the eternal riddle of the Sphinx, and OEdipus comes not. Physiology can number and name the bones and muscles, can tell the forms and functions of the different organs; chemistry can resolve the body into its constituent elements, and weigh out their exact proportions; philosophy can map out the departments of the mind; but man remains the great enigma. Biology carries her silken clue right up to the primordial cell; but here she finds a Gordian knot, which her keenest instruments cannot cut, or her keenest wit unravel. Within that complex nature of ours are oceans of mystery which Thought may indeed explore, but which she cannot fathom, paths which the vulture eye of Reason hath not seen, whose voices are the voices of unknown tongues, answering each other through the mist. But how familiar did Jesus seem with all these life-secrets! how intimate with all the life-forces! How versed He was in etiology, knowing without possibility of mistake whence diseases came, and just where they looked! It was no mystery to Him how the hand had shrunk, shrivelling into a mass of bones, with no skill in its fingers, and no life in its cloyed-up veins, or how the eyes had lost their power of vision. His knowledge of the human frame was an exact and perfect knowledge, reading its innermost secrets, as in a transparency, knowing to a certainty what links had dropped out of the subtle mechanism, and what had been warped out of place, and knowing well just at what point and to what an extent to apply the healing remedy, which was His own volition. All earth and all heaven were without a covering to His gaze; and what was this but Omniscience?

(2) Again, the miracles of healing speak of the compassion of Jesus. It was with no reluctance that He wrought these works of mercy; it was His delight. His heart was drawn towards suffering and pain by the magnetism of a Divine sympathy, or rather, we ought to say, towards the sufferers themselves; for suffering and pain, like sin and woe, were exotics in His Father's garden, the deadly nightshade an enemy had sown. And so we mark a great tenderness in all His dealings with the afflicted. He does not apply the caustic of bitter and biting words. Even when, as we may suppose, the suffering is the harvest of earlier sin, as in the case of the paralytic, Jesus speaks no harsh reproaches; He says simply and kindly, "Go in peace, and sin no more." And do we not find here a reason why these miracles of healing were so frequent in His ministry? Was it not because in His mind sickness was somehow related to sin? If miracles were needed to attest the Divineness of His mission, there was no need of the constant succession of them, no need, that they should form a part, and a large part, of the daily task. Sickness is, so to speak, something unnaturally natural. It results from the transgression of some physical law, as sin is the transgression of some moral law; and He who is man's Saviour brings a complete salvation, a redemption for the body as well as a redemption for the soul. Indeed, the diseases of the body are but the shadows, seen and felt, of the deeper diseases of the soul, and with Jesus the physical healing was but a step to the higher truth and higher experience, that spiritual cleansing, that inner creation of a right spirit, a perfect heart. And so Jesus carried on the two works side by side; they were the two parts of His one and great salvation; and as He loved and pitied the sinner, so He pitied and loved the sufferer; His sympathies all went out to meet him, preparing the way for His healing virtues to follow.

(3) Again, the miracles of healing speak of the power of Jesus. This was seen indirectly when we considered the completeness of the cures, and the wide field they covered, and we need not enlarge upon it now. But what a consciousness of might there was in Jesus! Others, prophets and apostles, have healed the sick, but their power was delegated. It came as in waves of Divine impulse, intermittent and temporary. The power that Jesus wielded was inherent and absolute, deeps which knew neither cessation nor diminution. His will was supreme over all forces. Nature's potencies are diffused and isolated, slumbering in herb or metal, flower or leaf, in mountain or sea. But all are inert and useless until man distils them with his subtle alchemies, and then applies them by his slow processes, dissolving the tinctures in the blood, sending on its warm currents the healing virtue, if haply it may reach its goal and accomplish its mission. But all these potencies lay in the hand or in the will of Christ. The forces of life all were marshalled under His bidding. He had but to say to one "Go," and it went, here or there, or anywhither; nor does it go for nought; it accomplishes its high behest, the great Master's will. Nay, the power of Jesus is supreme even in that outlying and dark world of evil spirits. The demons fly at His rebuke; and let Him throw but one healing word across the dark, chaotic soul of one possessed, and in an instant Reason dawns; bright thoughts play on the horizon; the firmaments of Right and Wrong separate to infinite distances; and out of the darkness a Paradise emerges, of beauty and light, where the new son of God resides, and God Himself comes down in the cool and the heat of the days alike. What power is this? Is it not the power of God? is it not Omnipotence?

# CHAPTER XVII - THE MIRACLE OF THE LOAVES

Luke ix. 1-17.

The Galilean ministry was drawing to a close, for the "great Light" which had risen over the northern province must now move southward, to set behind a cross and a grave. Jesus, however, is reluctant to leave these borders, amid whose hills the greater part of His life has been spent, and among whose composite population His greatest successes have been won, without one last effort. Calling together the Twelve, who hitherto have been Apostles in promise and in name rather than in fact, He lays His plans before them. Dividing the district into sections, so as to equalize their labours and prevent any overlapping, He sends them out in pairs; for in the Divine arithmetic two are more than twice one, more than the sum of the separate units by all the added force and strength of fellowship. They are to be the heralds of the new kingdom, to "preach the kingdom of God," their insignia no outward, visible badge, but the investiture of authority over all demons, and power over all diseases. Apostles of the Unseen, servants of the Invisible King, they must dismiss all worldly cares; they must not even make provision for their journey, weighting themselves with such impedimenta as wallets stored with bread or changes of raiment. They must go forth in an absolute trust in God, thus proving themselves citizens of the heavenly kingdom, whose gates they open to all who will repent and step up into them. They may take a staff, for that will help rather than hinder on the steep mountain paths; but since the King's business requireth haste, they must not spend their time in the interminable salutations of the age, nor in going about from house to house; such changes would only distract, diverting to themselves the thought which should be centred upon their mission. Should any city not receive them, they must retire at once, shaking off, as they depart, the very dust from their feet, as a testimony against them.

Such were the directions, as Jesus dismissed the Twelve, sending them to reap the Galilean harvest, and at the same time to prepare them for the wider fields which after the Pentecost would open to them on every side. It is only by incidental allusions that we learn anything as to the success of the mission, but when our Evangelist says "they went throughout the villages, preaching the Gospel and healing everywhere," these frequent miracles of healing would imply that they found a sympathetic and receptive people. Nor were the impulses of the new movement confined to the lower reaches of society; for even the palace felt its vibrations, and St. Luke, who seems to have had private means of information within the Court, possibly through Chuza and Manaen, pauses to give us a kind of silhouette of the Tetrarch. Herod himself is perplexed. Like a vane, "that fox" swings round to the varying gusts of public opinion that come eddying within the palace from the excited world outside; and as some say that Jesus is Elias, and others "one of the old prophets," while others aver that He is John himself, risen from the dead, this last rumour falls upon the ears of Herod like alarming thunders, making him quiver like an aspen. "And he sought to see Jesus." The "conscience that makes cowards of us all" had unnerved him, and he longed by a personal acquaintance with Jesus to waive back out of his sight the apparition of the murdered prophet. Who Jesus might be did not much concern Herod. He might be Elias, or one of the old prophets, anything but John; and so when Herod did see Jesus afterwards, and saw that He was not the risen Baptist, but the Man of Galilee, his courage revived, and he gave Jesus into the hands of his cohorts, that they might mock Him with the faded purple.

What steps Herod took to secure an interview we do not know; but the verb indicates more than a wish on his part; it implies some plan or attempt to gratify the wish; and probably it was these advances of Herod, together with the Apostles' need of rest after the strain and excitements of their mission, which prompted Jesus to seek a place of retirement outside the bounds of Antipas. On the northern shore of the Sea of Galilee, and on the eastern bank of the Jordan, was a second Bethsaida, or "House of Fish" as the name means, built by Philip, and to which, in honour of Cæsar's daughter, he gave the surname of "Julias." The city itself stood on the hills, some three or four miles back from the shore; while between the city and the lake swept a wide and silent plain, all untilled, as the New Testament "desert" means, but rich in pasturage, as the "much grass" of John vi. 10 would show. This still shore offered, as it seemed, a safe refuge from the exacting and intrusive crowds of Capernaum, whose constant coming and going left them no leisure so much as to eat; and bidding them launch the familiar boat, Jesus and the twelve sail away to the other side. The excited crowds, however, which followed them to the water's edge, are not so easily to be shaken off; but guessing the direction of the boat, they seek to head her off by a quick detour round the shore. And some of them do; for when the boat grates on the northern shingle some of the swift-footed ones are already there; while stretching back for miles is a stream of humanity, of both sexes and of all ages, but all fired with one purpose. The desert has suddenly grown populous.

And how does Jesus bear this interruption to His plans? Does He chafe at this intrusion of the people upon His quiet hours? Does He resent their importunity, calling it impertinence, then driving them from Him with a whip of sharp words? Not so. Jesus was accustomed to interruptions; they formed almost the staple of His life. Nor did He repulse one solitary soul which sought sincerely His mercy, no matter how unseasonable the hour, as men would read the hours. So now Jesus "received" them, or "welcomed" them, as it is in the R.V. It is a favourite word with St. Luke, found in his Gospel more frequently than in the other three Gospels together. Applied to persons, it means nearly always to receive as guests, to welcome to hospitality and home. And such is its meaning here. Jesus takes the place of the host. True, it is a desert place, but it is a part of the All-Father's world, a room of the Father's house, carpeted with grass and ablaze with flowers; and Jesus, by His welcome, transforms the desert into a guest-chamber, where in a new way He keeps the Passover with His disciples, at the same time entertaining His thousands of self-bidden guests, giving to them truth, speaking of the kingdom of God, and giving health, healing "those that had need of healing."

It was toward evening, "when the day began to wear away," that Jesus gave to a bright and busy day its crowning benediction. The thought had already ripened into purpose, in His mind, to spread a table for them in the wilderness; for how could He, the compassionate One, send them to their homes famishing and faint? These poor, shepherdless sheep have put themselves into His care. Their simple, unproviding confidence has made Him in a sense responsible, and can He disappoint that confidence? It is true they have been thoughtless and improvident. They have let the enthusiasm of the hour carry them away, without making any provision of the necessary food; but even this does not check the flow of the Divine compassion, for Jesus proceeds to fill up their lack of thought by His Divine thoughtfulness, and their scarcity with His Divine affluence.

According to St. John, it was Jesus who took the initiative, as He put the test-question to Philip, "Whence shall we buy bread, that these may eat?" Philip does not reply to the "whence;" that may stand aside awhile, as in mathematical language he speaks to the previous question, which is their ability to buy. "Two hundred pennyworth of bread," he said, "is not sufficient for them, that every one may take a little." He does not say how much would be required to satisfy the hunger of the multitude; his reckoning is not for a feast, but for a taste, to every one "a little." Nor does he calculate the full cost of even this, but says simply, "Two hundred pennyworth would not be sufficient." Evidently, in Philip's mind the two hundred, pence is the known quantity of the equation, and he works out his calculation from that, as he proves the impossibility of buying bread for this vast company anywhere. We may therefore conclude that the two hundred pence represented the value of the common purse, the purchasing power of the Apostolic community; and this was a sum altogether inadequate to meet the cost of providing bread for the multitude. The only alternative, as far as the disciples see, is to dismiss them, and let them requisition for themselves; and in a peremptory manner they ask Jesus to "send the multitude away," reminding Him of what certainly they had no need to remind Him, that they were here "in a desert place."

The disciples had spoken in their subjunctive, non possumus, way; it is now time for Jesus to speak, which He does, not in interrogatives longer, but in His imperative, commanding tone: "Give ye them to eat," a word which throws the disciples back upon themselves in astonishment and utter helplessness. What can they do? The whole available supply, as Andrew reports it, is but five barley loaves and two small fishes, which a lad has brought, possibly for their own refreshment. Five flat loaves of barley, which was the food of the poorest of the poor, and "two small fishes," as St. John calls them, throwing a bit of local colouring into the narrative by his diminutive word-- these are the foundation repast, which Jesus asks to be brought to Himself, that from Himself it may go, broken and enlarged, to the multitude of guests. Meantime the crowd is just as large, and perhaps more excited and impatient than before; for they would not understand these "asides" between the disciples and the Master, nor could they read as yet His compassionate and benevolent thought. It would be a pushing, jostling crowd, as these thousands were massed on the hill-side. Some are gathered in little groups, discussing the Messiahship; others are clustered round some relative or friend, who to-day has been wonderfully healed; while others, of the forward sort, are selfishly elbowing their way to the front. The whole scene is a kaleidoscope of changing form and colour, a perfect chaos of confusion. But Jesus speaks again: "Make them sit down in companies;" and those words, thrown across the seething mass, reduce it to order, crystallizing it, as it were, into measured and numbered lines. St. Mark, half-playfully, likens it to a garden, with its parterres of flowers; and such indeed it was, but it was a garden of the higher cult, with its variegated beds of humanity, a hundred men broad, and fifty deep.

When order was secured, and all were in their places, Jesus takes His place as the host at the head of the extemporized table, and though it is most frugal fare, He holds the barley loaves heavenward, and lifting up His eyes, He blesses God, probably in the words of the usual formula, "Blessed art Thou, Jehovah our God, King of the world, Who causeth to come forth bread from the earth." Then breaking the bread, He distributes it among the disciples, bidding them bear it to the people. It is not a matter of moment as to the exact point where the supernatural came in, whether it was in the breaking or the distributing. Somewhere a power which must have been Divine touched the bread, for the broken pieces strangely grew, enlarging rapidly as they were diminished. It is just possible that we have a clue to the mystery in the tense of the verb, for the imperfect, which denotes continued action, would read, "He brake," or "He kept on breaking," from which we might almost infer that the miracle was coincident with the touch. But whether so or not, the power was equal to the occasion, and the supply over and above the largest need, completely satisfying the hunger of the five thousand men, besides the off-group of women and children, who, though left out of the enumeration, were within the circle of the miracle, the remembered and satisfied guests of the Master.

It now remains for us to gather up the meaning and the practical lessons of the miracle. And first, it reveals to us the Divine pity. When Jesus called Himself the Son of man it was a title full of deep meaning, and most appropriate. He was the true, the ideal Humanity, humanity as it would have been without the warps and discolourations that sin has made, and within His heart were untold depths of sympathy, the "fellow-feeling that makes man wondrous kind." To the haughty and the proud He was stern, lowering upon them with a withering scorn; to the unreal, the false, the unclean He was severity itself, with lightnings in His looks and terrible thunders in His "woes;" but for troubled and tired souls He had nothing but tenderness and gentleness, and a compassion that was infinite. Even had He not called the weary and heavy-laden to Himself, they would have sought Him; they would have read the "Come" in the sunlight of His face. Jesus felt for others a vicarious pain, a vicarious sorrow, His heart responding to it at once, as the delicately poised needle responds to the subtle sparks that flash in upon it from without. So here; He receives the multitude kindly, even though they are strangers, and though they have thwarted His purpose and broken in upon His rest, and as this stream of human life flows out to Him His compassion flows out to them. He commiserates their forlorn condition, wandering like straying sheep upon the mountains; He gives Himself up to them, healing all that were sick, assuaging the pain or restoring the lost sense; while at the same time He ministers to a higher nature, telling them of the kingdom of God, which had come nigh to them, and which was theirs if they would surrender themselves to it and obey. Nor was even this enough to satisfy the promptings of His deep pity, but all-forgetful of His own weariness, He lengthens out this day of mercy, staying to minister to their lower, physical wants, as He spreads for them a table in the wilderness. Verily He was, incarnate, as He is in His glory, "touched with the feelings of our infirmities."

Again, we see the Divine love of order and arrangement. Nothing was done until the crowding and confusion had ceased, and even the Divine beneficence waits until the turbulent mass has become quiet, settled down into serried lines, the five thousand making two perfect squares. "Order," it is said, "is Heaven's first law;" but whether the first or the second, certain it is that Heaven gives us the perfection of order. It is only in the lawless wills of man that "time is broke, and no proportion kept." In the heavenly state nothing is out of place or out of time. All wills there play into each other with such absolute precision that life itself is a song, a Gloria in Excelsis. And how this is seen in all the works of God! What rhythmic motions are in the marches of the stars and the processions of the seasons! To everything a place, to everything a time; such is the unwritten law of the realm of physics, where Law is supreme, and anarchy is unknown. So in our earthly lives, on their secular and on their spiritual side alike, order is time, order is strength, and he who is deficient in this grace should practise on it the more. Avoid slovenliness; it is a distant relation of sin itself. Arrange your duties, and do not let them crowd one upon the other. Set the greater duties, not abreast, but one behind the other, filling up the spaces with the smaller ones. Do not let things drift, or your life, built for carrying precious argosies, and accomplishing something, will break up into pieces, the flotsam and jetsam of a barren shore. In prayer be orderly. Arrange your desires. Let some come first, while others stand back in the second or the third row, waiting their turn. If your relations with your fellows have got a little disarranged, atwist, seek to readjust the disturbed relation. Oppose what is evil and mean with all your might; but if no principle is involved, even at the cost of a little feeling, seek to have things put square. To get things into a tangle requires no great skill; but he who would be a true artist, keeping the Divine pattern before him, and ever working towards it, if not up to it, may reduce the tangled skein to harmony, and like the Gobelin tapestry-makers, weave a life that is noble and beautiful, a life on which men will love to gaze.

Again, we see the Divine concern for little things. Abundance always tempts to extravagance and waste. And so here; the broken remnants of the repast might have been thrown away as of no account; but Jesus bade them, "Gather up the fragments, that nothing be lost;" and we read they filled with the broken bread, which remained over and above to them that had eaten, twelve baskets full--and, by the way, the word rendered "basket" here corresponds with the frugal fare, for, made of willow or of wicker, it was of the coarsest kind, used only by the poor. What became of the fragments, which outweighed the original supply, we do not read; but though they were only the crumbs of the Divine bounty, and though there was no present use for them, Jesus would not allow them to be wasted.

But the true meaning of the narrative lies deeper than this. It is a miracle of a new order, this multiplying of the loaves. In His other miracles Jesus has wrought on the line of Nature, accelerating her slower processes, and accomplishing in an instant, by His mere volition, what by natural causes must have been the work of time, but which in the specific cases would have been purely impossible, owing to the enfeeblement of nature by disease. Sight, hearing, even life itself, come to man through channels purely natural; but Nature never yet has made bread. She grows the corn, but there her part ends, while Science must do the rest, first reducing the corn to flour, then kneading it into dough, and by the burning fires of the oven transmuting the dough to bread. Why does Jesus here depart from His usual order, creating what neither nature nor science can produce alone, but which requires their concurrent forces? Let us see. To Jesus these visible, tangible things were but the dead keys His hand touched, as He called forth some deeper, farther-off music, some spiritual truth that by any other method men would be slow to learn. Of what, then, is this bread of the desert the emblem? St. John tells us that when the miracle occurred "the Passover was nigh at hand," and this time-mark helps to explain the overcrowding into the desert, for probably many of the five thousand were men who were now on their way to Jerusalem, and who had stayed at Capernaum and the neighbouring cities for the night. This supposition, too, is considerably strengthened by the words of the disciples, as they suggest that they should go and "lodge" in the neighbouring cities and villages, which word implies that they were not residents of that locality, but passing strangers. And as Jesus cannot now go up to Jerusalem to the feast, He gathers the shepherdless thousands about Him, and keeps a sort of Passover in the open guest-chamber of the mountainside. That such was the thought of the Master, making it an anterior sacrament, is evident from the address Jesus gave the following day at Capernaum, in which He passes, by a natural transition, from the broken bread with which He satisfied their physical hunger to Himself as the Bread come down from heaven, the "living Bread" as He called it, which was His flesh. There is thus a Eucharistic meaning in the miracle of the loaves, and this northern hill signals in its subtle correspondences on to Jerusalem, to another hill, where His body was bruised and broken "for our iniquities," and His blood was poured out, a precious oblation for sin. And as that Blood was typified by the wine of the first miracle at Cana, so now Jesus completes the prophetic sacrament by the miraculous creation of bread from the five seminal loaves, bread which He Himself has consecrated to the holier use, as the visible emblem of that Body which was given for us, men, women, and children alike, even for a redeemed humanity. Cana and the desert-place thus draw near together, while both look across to Calvary; and as the Church keeps now her Eucharistic feast, taking from the one the consecrated bread, and from the other the consecrated wine, she shows forth the Lord's death "till He come."

## CHAPTER XVIII - THE TRANSFIGURATION

The Transfiguration of Christ marks the culminating point in the Divine life; the few remaining months are a rapid descent into the valley of Sacrifice and Death. The story is told by each of the three Synoptists, with an almost equal amount of detail, and all agree as to the time when it occurred; for though St. Matthew and St. Mark make the interval six days, while St. Luke speaks of it as "about eight," there is no real disagreement; St. Luke's reckoning is inclusive. As to the locality, too, they all agree, though in a certain indefinite way. St. Matthew and St. Mark leave it indeterminate, simply saying that it was "a high mountain," while St. Luke calls it "the mountain." Tradition has long localised the scene upon Mount Tabor, but evidently she has read off her bearings from her own fancies, rather than from the facts of the narrative. To say nothing of the distance of Mount Tabor from Cæsarea Philippi--which, though a difficulty, is not an insuperable one, since it might easily be covered in less than the six intervening days--Tabor is but one of the group of heights which fringe the Plain of Esdraelon, and so one to which the definite article would not, and could not, be applied. Besides, Tabor now was crowned by a Roman fortress, and so could scarcely be said to be "apart" from the strifes and ways of men, while it stood within the borders of Galilee, whereas St. Mark, by implication, sets his "high mountain" outside the Galilean bounds (ix. 30). But if Tabor fails to meet the requirements of the narrative, Mount Hermon answers them exactly, throwing its spurs close up to Cæsarea Philippi, while its snow-crowned peak shone out pure and white above the lesser heights of Galilee.

It is not an unmeaning coincidence that each of the Evangelists should introduce his narrative with the same temporal word, "after." That word is something more than a connecting link, a bridge thrown over a blank space of days; it is rather, when taken in connection with the preceding narrative, the key which unlocks the whole meaning and mystery of the Transfiguration. "After these sayings," writes St. Luke. What sayings? Let us go back a little, and see. Jesus had asked His disciples as to the drift of popular opinion about Himself, and had drawn from Peter the memorable confession--that first Apostle's Creed--"Thou art the Christ of God." Immediately, however, Jesus leads down their minds from these celestial heights to the lowest depths of degradation, dishonour, and death, as He says, "The Son of man must suffer many things, and be rejected of the elders, chief priests, and scribes, and be killed, and the third day be raised up." Those words shattered their bright dream at once. Like some fearful nightmare, the foreshadow of the cross fell upon their hearts, filling them with fear and gloom, and striking down hope, and courage, yea, even faith itself. It would almost seem as if the disciples were unnerved, paralyzed by the blow, and as if an atrophy had stolen over their hearts and lips alike; for the next six days are one void of silence, without word or deed, as far as the records show. How shall their lost hope be recalled, or courage be revived? How shall they be taught that death does not end all--that the enigma was true of Himself, as well as of them, that He shall find His life by losing it? The Transfiguration is the answer.

Taking with Him Peter, John, and James--the three who shall yet be witnesses of His agony-- Jesus retires to the mountain height, probably intending, as our Evangelist indicates, to spend the night in prayer. Keeping the midnight watch was nothing new to these disciples; it was their frequent experience upon the Galilean lake; but now, left to the quiet of their own thoughts, and with none of the excitements of the spoil about them, they yield to the cravings of nature and fall asleep. Awaking, they find their Master still engaged in prayer, all oblivious of earthly hours, and as they watch He is transfigured before them. The fashion, or appearance, of His countenance, as St. Luke tersely puts it, "became another," all suffused with a heavenly radiance, while His very garments became lustrous with a whiteness which was beyond the fuller's art and beyond the whiteness of the snow, and all iridescent, flashing and sparkling as if set with stars. Suddenly, ere their eyes have grown accustomed to the new splendours, two celestial visitants appear, wearing the glorious body of the heavenly life and conversing with Jesus.

Such was the scene upon the "holy mount," which the Apostles could never forget, and which St. Peter recalls with a lingering wonder and delight in the far-off after-years (2 Pet. i. 18). Can we push aside the outward draperies, and read the Divine thought and purpose that are hidden within? We think we may. And--

1. We see the place and meaning of the Transfiguration in the life of Jesus. Hitherto the humanity of Jesus had been naturally and perfectly human; for though heavenly signs have, as at the Advent and the Baptism, borne witness to its super-humanity, these signs have been temporary and external, shining or alighting upon it from without. Now, however, the sign is from within. The brightness of the outer flesh is but the outshining of the inner glory. And what was that glory but the "glory of the Lord," a manifestation of the Deity, that fulness of the Godhead which dwelt within? The faces of other sons of men have shone, as when Moses stepped downwards from the mount, or as Stephen looked upwards to the opened heavens; but it was the shining of a reflected glory, like the sunlight upon the moon. But when the humanity of Jesus was thus transfigured it was a native glory, the inward radiance of the soul stealing through, and lighting up, the enveloping globe of human flesh. It is easy to see why this celestial appearance should not be the normal manifestation of the Christ; for had it been, He would no longer have been the "Son of man." Between Himself and the humanity He had come to redeem would have been a gulf wide and profound, while the Fatherhood of God would have been a truth lying back in the vistas of the unknown, a truth unfelt; for men only reach up to that Fatherhood through the Brotherhood of Christ. But if we ask why now, just for once, there should be this transfiguring of the Person of Jesus, the answer is not so evident. Godet has a suggestion which is as natural as it is beautiful. He represents the Transfiguration as the natural issue of a perfect, a sinless his, a life in which death should have no place, as it would have had no place in the life of unfallen man. Innocence, holiness, glory--these would have been the successive steps connecting earth with heaven, an ever-upward path, across which death would not even have cast a shadow. Such would have been the path opened to the first Adam, had not sin intervened, bringing death as its wage and penalty. And now, as the Second Adam takes the place of the first, moving steadily along the path of obedience from which the first Adam swerved, should we not naturally look for that life to end in some translation or transfiguration, the body of the earthly life blossoming into the body of the heavenly? and where else so appropriately as here, upon the "holy mount," when the spirits of the perfected come forth to meet Him, and the chariot of cloud is ready to convey Him to the heavens which are so near? It is thus something more than conjecture--it is a probability--that had the life of Jesus been by itself, detached from mankind in general, the Transfiguration had been the mode and the beginning of the glorification. The way to the heavens, from which He was self-exiled, was open to Him from the mount of glory, but He preferred to pass up by the mount of passion and of sacrifice. The burden of the world's redemption is upon Him, and that eternal purpose leads Him down from the Transfiguration glories, and onwards to a cross and grave. He chooses to die, with and for man, rather than to live and reign without man.

But not only does the "holy mount" throw its light on what would have been the path of unfallen man, it gives us in prophecy a vision of the resurrection life. Compare the picture of the transfigured Christ, as drawn by the Synoptists, with the picture, drawn by John himself, of the Christ of the Exaltation, and how strikingly similar they are! (Rev. i. 13-17). In both descriptions we have an affluence of metaphor and simile, which affluence was itself but the stammering of our weak human speech, as it seeks to tell the unutterable. In both we have a whiteness like the snow, while to portray the countenance St. John repeats almost verbatim St. Matthew's words, "His face did shine as the sun." Evidently the Christ of the Transfiguration and the Christ of the Exaltation are one and the same Person; and why do we blame Peter for speaking in such random, delirious words upon the mount, when John, by the glory of that same vision, in Patmos, is stricken to the ground as if dead, not able to speak at all? When Peter spoke, somewhat incoherently, about the "three tabernacles," it was not, as some aver, the random speech of one who was but half awake, but of one whose reason was dazzled and confused with the blinding glory. And so the Transfiguration anticipates the Glorification, investing the sacred Person with those same robes of light and royalty He had laid aside for a time, but which He will shortly assume again--the habiliments of an eternal re-enthronement.

2. Again, the holy mount shows us the place of death in the life of man. We read, "There talked with Him two men, which were Moses and Elijah;" and as if the Evangelist would emphasize the fact that it was no apparition, existing only in their heated imagination, he repeats the statement (ver. 35) that they were "two men." Strange gathering--Moses, Elias, and Christ!--the Law in the person of Moses, the Prophets in the person of Elias, both doing homage to the Christ, who was Himself the fulfilment of prophecy and law. But what the Evangelist seems to note particularly is the humanness of the two celestials. Though the earthly life of each ended in an abrupt, unearthly way, the one having a translation, the other a Divine interment (whatever that may mean), they have both been residents of the heavenly world for centuries. But as they appear to-day "in glory," that is, with the glorified body of the heavenly life, outwardly, visibly, their bodies are still human. There is nothing about their form and build that is grotesque, or even unearthly. They have not even the traditional but fictitious wings with which poetry is wont to set on the inhabitants of the sky.

They are still "men," with bodies resembling, both in size and form, the old body of earth. But if the appearance of these "men" reminds us of earth, if we wait awhile, we see that their natures are very unearthly, not unnatural so much as supernatural. They glide down through the air with the ease of a bird and the swiftness of light, and when the interview ends, and they go their separate ways, these heavenly "men" gather up their robes and vanish, strangely and suddenly as they came. And yet they can make use of earthly supports, even the grosser forms of matter, planting their feet upon the grass as naturally as when Moses climbed up Pisgah or as Elijah stood in Horeb's cave.

And not only do the bodies of these celestials retain still the image of the earthly life, but the bent of their minds is the same, the set and drift of their thoughts following the old directions. The earthly lives of Moses and Elias had been spent in different lands, in different times; five hundred eventful years pushed them far apart; but their mission had been one. Both were prophets of the Highest, the one bringing God's law down to the people, the other leading a lapsed people back and up to God's law. Yes, and they are prophets still, but with a nearer vision now. No longer do they gaze through the crimson lenses of the sacrificial blood, beholding the Promised One afar off. They have read the Divine thought and purpose of redemption; they are initiated into its mysteries; and now that the cross is close at hand, they come to bring to the world's Saviour their heavenly greetings, and to invest Him, by anticipation, with robes of glory, soon to be His for evermore.

Such is the apocalypse of the holy mount. The veil which hides from our dull eye of sense the hereafter was lifted up. The heavens were opened to them, no longer far away beyond the cold stars, but near them, touching them on every side. They saw the saints of other days interesting themselves in earthly events--in one event at least, and speaking of that death which they mourned and feared, calmly, as a thing expected and desired, but calling it by its new and softened name, a "departure," an "exodus." And as they see the past centuries saluting Him whom they have learned to call the Christ, "the Son of God," as the truth of immortality is borne in upon them, not as a vague conception of the mind, but by oral and ocular demonstration, would they not see the shadow of the coming death in a different light? would not the painful pressure upon their spirits be eased somewhat, if not, indeed, entirely removed? and--

> "The Apostle's heart of rock
> Be nerved against temptation's shock"?

Would they not more patiently endure, now that they had become apostles of the Invisible, seers of the Unseen?

But if the glory of the holy mount sets in a fairer light the cross and grave of Christ, may we not throw from the mirror of our thought some of its light upon our lowlier graves? What is death, after all, but the transition into life? Retaining its earthly accent, we call it a "decease;" but that is true only of the corporeal nature, that body of "flesh and blood" which cannot inherit the higher kingdom of glory to which we pass. There is no break in the continuity of the soul's existence, not even one parenthetic hour. When He who was the Resurrection and the Life said, "To-day shalt thou be with Me in paradise," that word passed on a forgiven soul directly to a state of conscious blessedness. From "the azure deep of air" does the eagle look regretfully upon the eyrie of its crag, where it lay in its unfledged weakness? or does it mourn the broken shell from which its young life emerged? And why should we mourn, or weep with unrestrained tears, when the shell is broken that the freed spirit may soar up to the regions of the blessed, and range the eternities of God? Paganism closed the story of human life with an interrogation-point, and sought to fill up with guesses the blank she did not know. Christianity speaks with clearer voice; hers is "a sure and certain hope," for He who "hath abolished death" hath "brought life and immortality to light." Earth's exodus is heaven's genesis, and what we call the end celestials call the beginning.

And not only does the mount speak of the certainties of the after-life, it gives, in a binocular vision, the likeness of the resurrection body, answering, in part, the standing question, "How are the dead raised up?" The body of the heavenly life must have some correspondence with, and resemblance to, the body of our earthly life. It will, in a sense, grow out of it. It will not be something entirely new, but the old refined, spiritualized, the dross and earthliness all removed, the marks of care, and pain, and sin all wiped out. And more, the Transfiguration mount gives us indubitable proof that heaven and earth lie, virtually, close together, and that the so-called "departed" are not entirely severed from earthly things; they can still read the shadows upon earthly dials, and hear the strike of earthly hours. They are not so absorbed and lost in the new glories as to take no note of earthly events; nor are they restrained from visiting, at permitted times, the earth they have not wholly left; for as heaven was theirs, when on earth, in hope and anticipation, so now, in heaven, earth is theirs in thought and memory. They have still interests here, associations they cannot forget, friends who are still beloved, and harvests of influence they still may reap. With the absurdities and follies of so-called Spiritualism we have no sort of sympathy--they are the vagaries of weak minds; but even their eccentricities and excesses shall not be allowed to rob us of what is a truly Christian hope, that they who cared for us on earth care for us still, and that they who loved and prayed for us below love us none the less, and pray for us none the less frequently, now that the conflict with them is over, and the eternal rest begun. And why may not their spirits touch ours, influencing our mind and heart, even when we are not conscious whence those influences come? for are they not, with the angels, "ministering spirits, sent forth to do service for the sake of them that shall inherit salvation?" The Mount of Transfiguration does indeed stand "apart," for on its summit the paths of the celestials and of the terrestrials meet and merge; and it is "high" indeed, for it touches heaven.

3. Again, the holy mount shows us the place of death in the life of Jesus. How long the vision lasted we cannot tell, but in all probability the interview was but brief. What supreme moments they were! and what a rush of tumultuous thoughts, we may suppose, would fill the minds of the two saints, as they stand again on the familiar earth! But listen! They speak no word to revive the old-time memories; they bring no tidings of the heavenly world; they do not even ask, as they well might, the thousand questions concerning His life and ministry. They think, they speak, of one thing only, the "decease which He was about to accomplish at Jerusalem." Here, then, we see the drift of heavenly minds, and here we learn a truth which is wonderfully true, that the death of Jesus, the cross of Jesus, was the one central thought of heaven, as it is the one central hope of earth. But how can it be such if the life of Jesus is all we need, and if the death is but an ordinary death, an appendix, necessary indeed, but unimportant? Such is the belief of some, but such certainly is not the teaching of this narrative, nor of the other Scriptures. Heaven sets the cross of Jesus "in the midst," the one central fact of history. He was born that He might die; He lived that He might die. All the lines of His human life converge upon Calvary, as He Himself said, "For unto this hour came I into the world." And why is that death so all-important, bending towards its cross all the lines of Scripture, as it now monopolizes the speech of these two celestials? Why? There is but one answer which is satisfactory, the answer St. Peter himself gives: "His own Self bare our sins in His body upon the tree, that we, having died unto sins, might live unto righteousness" (1 Pet. ii. 24). And so the Mount of Transfiguration looks towards the Mount of Sacrifice. It lights up Calvary, and lays a wreath of glory upon the cross.

We need not speak again of Peter's random words, as he seeks to detain the celestial visitants. He would fain prolong what to him is a Feast of Tabernacles, and he suggests the building of three booths upon the mountain slope--"one for Thee," putting his Lord first, "and one for Moses, and one for Elias." He makes no mention of himself or of his companions. He is content to remain outside, so that he may only be near, as it were on the fringe of the transfiguring glories. But what a strange request! what wandering, delirious words, almost enough to make celestials smile! Well might the Evangelist excuse Peter's random words by saying, "Not knowing what he said." But if Peter gets no answer to his request, and if he is not permitted to build the tabernacles, Heaven spreads over the group its canopy of cloud, that Shekinah-cloud whose very shadow was brightness; while once again, as at the Baptism, a Voice speaks out of the cloud, the voice of the Father: "This is My Son, My Chosen; hear ye Him." And so the mountain pageant fades; for when the cloud has passed away Moses and Elias have disappeared, "Jesus only" is left with the three disciples. Then they retrace their steps down the mountain side, the three carrying in their heart a precious memory, the strains of a lingering music, which they only put into words when the Son of man is risen from the dead; while Jesus turns, not reluctantly, from the opened door and the welcome of Heaven, to make an atonement upon Calvary, and through the veil of His rent flesh to make a way for sinful man even into the Holiest.

# CHAPTER XIX - THE GOOD SAMARITAN

Luke x. 25-37.

It would scarcely have accorded with the traditions of human nature had the teachers of religion looked favourably upon Jesus. Stepping, as He did, within their domain, without any human ordination or scholastic authority, they naturally resented the intrusion, and when the teaching of the new Rabbi so distinctly contravened their own interpretation of the law their curiosity deepened into jealousy, and curdled at last into a virulent hate. The ecclesiastical atmosphere was charged with electricity, but it only manifested itself at first in the harmless play of summer lightning, the cross-fire of half-earnest and half-captious questions; later it was the forked lightning that struck Him down into a grave.

We have no means of localizing, either in point of time or place, the incident here recorded by our Evangelist, and which, by the way, only St. Luke mentions. It stands by itself, bearing in its dependent parable of the Good Samaritan an exquisite and perfect flower, from whose deep cup has dropped the very nectar of the gods.

It was probably during one of His public discourses that a "certain lawyer," or scribe--for the two titles are used interchangeably--"stood up and tempted Him." He sought to prove Him by questions, as the word means here, hoping to entrap Jesus amid the vagaries of Rabbinical tradition. "Teacher," said he, hiding his sinister motive behind a veil of courtesy and apparent candour, "what shall I do to inherit eternal life?" Had the question been sincere, Jesus would probably have given a direct answer; but reading the under-current of his thought, which moved transversely to the surface-current of his speech, Jesus simply answered his question by asking another: "What is written in the Law? How readest thou?" With a readiness which implied a perfect familiarity with the Law, he replied, "Thou shalt love the Lord thy God with all thy heart, and with all thy soul, and with all thy strength, and with all thy mind; and thy neighbour as thyself." Some expositors have thought that the Evangelist here gives the summary of what was a lengthened conversation, and that Jesus Himself led the mind of the lawyer to join together these detached portions of Scripture--one from Deuteronomy vi. 5, and the other from Leviticus xix. 18. It is true there is a striking resemblance between the answer of the lawyer and the answer Jesus Himself gave subsequently to a similar question (Mark xii. 30, 31); but there is no necessity for us to apologize for the resemblance, as if it were improbable and unnatural. The fact is, as the narrative of Mark xii. plainly indicates, that these two sentences were held in general consent as the epitome of the Law, its first and its second commandment. Even the scribe assents to this as an axiomatic truth he has no wish to challenge. It will be observed that a fourth term is added to the three of the original, possibly on account of the Septuagint rendering, which translated the Hebrew "heart" by "mind." Godet suggests that since the term "heart" is the most general term, denoting "in Scripture the central focus from which all the rays of the moral life go forth," that it stands in apposition to the other three, the one in its three particulars. This, which is the most natural interpretation, would refer the "mind" to the intellectual faculties, the "soul" to the emotional faculties, the sensibilities, and the "might" to the will, which rules all force; while by the "heart" is meant the unit, the "centred self," into which the others merge, and of which they form a part.

Jesus commended him for his answer: "Thou hast answered right: this do, and thou shalt live"--words which brushed away completely the Hebraic figment of inherited life. That life was not something that should be reached by processes of loving. The life should precede the love, and should give birth to it: the love should grow out of the life, its blossoming flower.

Having the tables so turned upon himself, and wishing to "justify," or to put himself right, the stranger asks still another question: "And who is my neighbour?" doubtless hoping to cover his retreat in the smoke of a burning question. To our minds, made familiar with the thought of humanity, it seems as if a question so simple scarcely deserved such an elaborate answer as Jesus gave to it. But the thought of humanity had not yet possessed the world; indeed, it had only just come to earth, to be spoken by, and incarnate in, Him who was the Son of man. To the Jew the question of the lawyer was a most important one. The word "neighbour" could be spoken in a breath; but unwind that word, and it measures off the whole of our earthly life, it covers all our practical, every-day duties. It ran through the pages of the Law, the ark in which the Golden Rule was hidden; or like a silent angel, it flashed its sword across life's forbidden paths. But if the Jew could not erase this broad word from the pages of the Law, he could narrow and emasculate its meaning by an interpretation of his own. And this they had done, making this Divine word almost of none effect by their tradition. To the Jewish mind "neighbour" was simply "Jew" spelt large. The only neighbourhood they recognized was the narrow neighbourhood of Hebrew speech and Hebrew sympathies. The Hebrew mind was isolated as their land, and all who could not frame their shibboleths were barbarians, Gentiles, whom they were at perfect liberty to spoil, as with anathemas and swords they chased them over their Jordans. Jesus, however, is on the alert; and how wisely He answers! He does not declaim against the narrowness of Hebrew thought; He utters no denunciatory word against their proud and false exclusiveness. He quietly unfolds the word, spreading it out into an exquisite parable, that all coming times may see how beautiful, how Divine the word "neighbour" is.

He said, "A certain man was going down from Jerusalem to Jericho; and he fell among robbers, which both stripped him, and beat him, and departed, leaving him half dead." The parables of Jesus, though drawn from real life, had no local colouring. They grouped themselves around some well-known fact of nature, or some general custom of social life; and so their spirit was national or cosmopolitan, rather than local. Here, however, Jesus departs from His usual manner, giving to His parable a local habitation. It is the road which led steeply down from Jerusalem to Jericho, and which for centuries has been so infested with robbers or bandits as to earn for itself the darkly ominous name of "the Bloody Way." Possibly that name itself is an outgrowth from the parable; but whether so or not, it is scarcely to be supposed that it had so evil a character in the days of Christ. As Jericho then was a populous city, and intimately connected with Jerusalem in its social and business life, the road would be much frequented. Indeed, the parable indicates as much; for Jesus, whose words were never untrue to nature or to history, represents His three travellers as all journeying singly; while the khan or "inn" shows, in its reflection, a constant stream of travel. Our anonymous traveller, however, does not find it so safe as he had anticipated. Attacked, in one of its dusky ravines, by a band of brigands, they strip him of his clothing, with whatever the girdle-purse might contain, and beating him out of sheer devilry, they leave him by the road-side, unable to walk, unable even to rise, a living-dying man.

"And by chance, a certain priest was going down that way; and when he saw him he passed by on the other side. And in like manner a Levite also, when he came to the place and saw him, passed by on the other side." As in a tableaux vivants, Jesus shows us the two ecclesiastics, who come in sight in the happy, coincidental way that Romance so delights in. They had probably just completed their "course" of Temple service, and were now going down to Jericho, which was a favourite residence of the priests, for the somewhat long interval their sacred duties allowed them. They had, therefore, no pressure of business upon them; indeed, the verb would almost imply that the priest was walking leisurely along. But they bring no help to the wounded man. Directly they see him, instead of being drawn to him by the attractions of sympathy, something, either the shock or the fright, acts upon them as a centrifugal force, and sends them describing an arc of a circle around that centre of groans and blood. At any rate they "passed by on the other side," leaving behind them neither deed nor word of mercy, but leaving behind them a shadow of themselves which, while time itself lasts, will be vivid, cold, and repelling. It is just possible, however, that they do not deserve all the unmeasured censure the critics and the centuries have given, and are still likely to give. It is very easy for us to condemn their action as selfish, heartless; but let us put ourselves in their place, alone in the lonely pass, with this proof of an imminent danger sprung suddenly upon us, and it is possible that we ourselves should not have been quite so brave as by our safe firesides we imagine ourselves to be. The fact is it needed something more than sympathy to make them turn aside and befriend the wounded man; it needed physical courage, and that of the highest kind, and this wanting, sympathy itself would not be sufficient. The heart might long to help, even when the feet were hastening away. A sudden inrush of fear, even of vague alarm, will sometimes drive us contrary to the drift of our sympathies, just as our feet are lifted and we ourselves carried onwards by a surging crowd.

Whether this be a correct interpretation of their conduct or not, it certainly harmonizes with the general attitude of Jesus towards the priesthood. The chief priests were always and bitterly hostile, but we have reasonable ground for supposing that the priests, as a body, looked favouringly upon Jesus. The bolts of terrible "woes" are hurled against Pharisees and scribes, yet Jesus does not condemn the priests in a single word; while in that aftermath of the Pentecost the Temple courts yielded the richest harvests, as "a great company of the priests were obedient to the faith." If, then, Jesus now holds up the priesthood to execration, setting these ecclesiastics in the pillory of His parable, that the coming centuries may throw sharp words at them, it is certainly an exceptional mood. The sweet silence has curdled into acrid speech. But even here Jesus does not condemn, except, as it would seem, by implication, the conduct of the priest and Levite. They come into the parable rather as accessories, and Jesus makes use of them as a foil, to throw out into bolder relief the central figure, which is the Samaritan, and so to emphasize His central truth, which is the real answer to the lawyer's question, that "neighbour" is too broad, and too human, a word to be cut off and eliminated by any boundaries of race.

But in thus casting a mantle of charity around our priest and Levite, we must admit that the character is sometimes true even down to recent days. Ecclesiasticism and religion, alas! are not always synonyms. Revolted Israel sins and sacrifices by turns, and seeking to keep the balance in equal poise, she puts over against her multitude of sins her multitude of sacrifices. Religiousness may be at times but a cloak for moral laxity, and to some rite is more than right. There are those, alas! to-day, who wear the livery of the Temple, to whom religion is a routine mechanism of dead things, rather than the commerce of living hearts, who open with hireling hand the Temple gates, who chant with hireling lips how "His mercy endureth for ever," and then step down from their sacred Jerusalem, to toss justice and mercy to the winds, as they defraud the widow and oppress the poor.

"But a certain Samaritan, as he journeyed, came where he was: and when he saw him, he was moved with compassion, and came to him, and bound up his wounds, pouring on them oil and wine; and he set him on his own beast, and brought him to an inn, and took care of him." At first sight it would appear as if Jesus had weakened the narrative by a topographical inaccuracy, as if He had gone out of His way to place a Samaritan on the road to Jericho, which was altogether out of the line of Samaritan travel. But it is a deliberate purpose on the part of Jesus, and not a lapsus linguæ, that introduces this Samaritan; for this is the gist of the whole parable. The man who had fallen among the robbers was doubtless a Jew; for had it been otherwise, the fact would have been stated. Now there was no question as to whether the word "neighbour" embraced their fellow-countrymen; the question was whether it passed beyond their national bounds, opening up lines of duty across the outlying world. It is therefore almost a necessity that the one who teaches this lesson should be himself an alien, a foreigner, and Jesus chooses the Samaritan as being of a race against which Jewish antipathies were especially strong, but for which He Himself had a special regard and warmest sympathy. Though occupying adjacent territory, the Jews and the Samaritans practically were far apart, antipodal races we might almost call them. Between them lay a wide and deep chasm that trade even could not bridge, and across which the courtesies and sympathies of life never passed. "The Jews have no dealings with the Samaritans," said the flippant woman of Samaria, as she voiced a jealousy and hatred which were as mutual as they were deep. But here, in this ideal Samaritan, is a noble exception. Though belonging to a lowly and obscure race, his thoughts are high. The ear of his soul has so caught the rhythm of Divine harmonies that it does not hear longer the little lisping shibboleths of earthly speech; and while the sympathies of smaller hearts flow like a stream down in their well-defined and accustomed channel, seldom knowing any overflow, save in some rare freshet of impulse and of feeling, the sympathies of the Samaritan moved outward like the currents of the wind, sweeping across all chasms and over all mountain heights of division, bearing their clouds of blessing anywhither as the need required. It makes no difference to him that the fallen man is of an alien race. He is a man, and that is enough; and he is down, and must be raised; he is in need, and must be helped. The priest and Levite thought first and most of themselves, and giving to the man but a brief and scared look, they passed on with a quickened pace. Not so with the Samaritan; he loses all thought of himself, and is perfectly oblivious to the danger he himself may be running. Upon his great soul he feels the pressure of this "must;" it runs along the tightened muscles of his arm, as he checks his steed. He himself comes down, dismounting, that he may help the man to rise. He opens his flask and puts his wine to the lips, that their groans may cease, or that they may be soothed down into inarticulate speech. The oil he has brought for his own food he pours upon the wounds, and when the man has sufficiently recovered he lifts him upon his own beast and takes him to the inn. Nor is this enough for his great heart, but continuing his journey on the morrow, he first arranges with his host that the man shall be well cared for, giving him two pence, which was the two days' wages of a labouring man, at the same time telling him that he must not limit his attentions to the sum he pays in advance, but that if anything more should be needed he would pay the balance on his return. We do not read whether it was needed or not, for the Samaritan, mounting his steed, passes out of our hearing and out of our sight. Not quite out of our hearing, however, for Heaven has caught his gentle, loving words, and hidden them within this parable, that all coming times may listen to their music; nor out of our sight either, for his photograph was caught in the sunlight of the Master's speech; and as we turn over the pages of Inspiration there is no picture more beautiful than that of the nameless Samaritan, whom all the world calls "the Good," the man who knew so much better than his age what humanity and mercy meant.

In the new light the lawyer can answer his own question now, and he does; for when Jesus asks, "Which of these three, thinkest thou, proved neighbour unto him that fell among the robbers?"

he replies, with no hesitation, but with a lingering prejudice that does not care to pronounce the, to him, outlandish name, "He that showed mercy on him." The lesson is learned, the lesson of humanity, for the whole parable is but an amplification of the Golden Rule, and Jesus dismisses the subject and the scholar with the personal application, which is but a corollary of the proposition He has demonstrated, "Go thou and do likewise." Go and do to others as you would have them do to you, were the circumstances reversed and your places changed. Read off your duty, not from your own low standpoint merely, but in a binocular vision, as you put yourself in his place; so will you find that the line of duty and the line of beauty are one.

The practical lessons of the parable are easy to trace, as they are of universal application. The first, lesson it teaches is the lesson of humanity, the neighbourhood and brotherhood of man. It is a convenience, and perhaps a necessity, of human life, that the great mass of humanity should be broken up into fragments, sections, with differing customs, languages, and names. It gives to the world the stimulus of competition and helpful rivalries. But these distinctions are superficial, temporary, and beneath this diversity of speech and thought there is the deeper unity of soul. We emphasize our differences; we pride ourselves upon them; but how little does Heaven make of them! Heaven does not even see them. Our national boundaries may climb up over the Alps, but they cannot touch the sky. Those skies look down and smile on all alike, divinely impartial in their gifts of beauty and of light. And how little of the provincial, or even national, there was about Jesus! Though He kept Himself almost entirely within the borders of the Holy Land, never going far from His central pivot, which was Jerusalem, and its cross, yet He belonged to the world, as the world belonged to Him. He called Himself the Son of man, at once humanity's flower, and humanity's Son and Saviour. And as over the cradle of the Son of man the far east and the far west together leaned, so around His cross was the meeting-place of the races. The three chief languages inscribed upon it proclaimed His royalty, while the cross itself, on which the Sacrifice for humanity was to be offered, was itself the gift of humanity at large, as Asia provided it, and Europe prepared it, and Africa, in the person of the Cyrenean, bore it. In the mind of Jesus, as in the purpose of God, humanity was not a group of fractions, but a unit one and indivisible, made of one blood, and by one Blood redeemed. In the heart of Jesus there was the "enthusiasm of humanity," all-absorbing and complete, and that enthusiasm takes possession of us, a new force generated in our lives, as we approach in spirit the great Ideal Man.

The second lesson of the parable is the lesson of mercy, the beauty of self-sacrifice. It was because the Samaritan forgot himself that all the world has remembered and applauded him. It is because of his stoop of self-renouncing love that his character is so exalted, his memory so dear, and that his very name, which is a title without a name, floats down the ages like a sweet song. "Go and do thou likewise" is the Master's word to us. Discipline your heart that you may see in man everywhere a brother, whose keeper you are. Let fraternity be, not a theory only, but a realized fact, and then a factor of your life. Train your eye to watch for others' needs, to read another's woe. Train your soul to sympathy, and your hand to helpfulness; for in our world there is room enough for both. Bethesda's porches stretch far as our eye can reach, all crowded, too, with the sorrowing, the sick, and the sad, thick enough indeed, but not so close as that an angel's foot may not step between them, and not so sad but an angel's voice may soothe and cheer. He who lifts another's load, who soothes another's smart, who brightens a life that else would be dark, who puts a music within a brother's soul, though it be only for a passing moment, wakes even a sweeter music within his own, for he enters on earth into his Master's joy, the joy of a redeeming, self-sacrificing love.

## CHAPTER XX – THE TWO SISTERS

*Luke x. 38-42.*

At first sight it appears as if our Evangelist had departed from the orderly arrangement of which he speaks in his prelude, in thus linking this domestic scene of Judæa with His northern Galilean journey, and to the casual glance this home-flower does certainly seem an exotic in this garden of the Lord. The strangeness, the out-of-placeness, however, vanishes entirely upon a nearer, closer view. If, as is probable, the parable of the Good Samaritan was spoken during that northward journey, its scene lies away in Judæa, in the dangerous road that sweeps down from Jerusalem to Jericho. Now, this road to Jericho lay through the village of Bethany, and in the Evangelist's mind the two places are intimately connected, as we see (chap. xix. vv. 1, 29); so that the idyll of Bethany would follow the parable of the Good Samaritan with a certain naturalness, the one recalling the other by the simple association of ideas. Then, too, it harmonizes so thoroughly with its context, as it comes between a parable on works and a chapter on prayer. In the one, man is the doer, heart and hand going out in the beautiful ministries of love; in the other, man is the receiver, waiting upon God, opening hand and heart for the inflow of Divine grace. In one it is Love in action that we see; in the other it is Love at rest, at rest from activities of her own, in quest of further good. This is exactly the picture our Evangelist draws of the two sisters, and which might have served as a parable had it not been so plainly taken from real life. Perhaps, too, another consideration influenced the Evangelist, and one that is suggested by the studied vagueness of the narrative. He gives no clue as to where the little incident occurred, for the "certain village" might be equally appropriate in Samaria or Judæa; while the two names, Martha and Mary, apart from the corroboration of St. John's Gospel, would not enable us to localize the scene. It is evident that St. Luke wished to throw around them a sort of incognito, probably because they were still living when he wrote, and too great publicity might subject them to inconvenience, or even to something more. And so St. Luke considerately masks the picture, shutting off the background of locality, while St. John, who writes at a later date, when Jerusalem has fallen, and who is under no such obligation of reserve, fixes the scene precisely; for there can be no doubt that the Mary and Martha of his Gospel, of Bethany, are the Martha and Mary of St. Luke; their very characters, as well as names, are identical.

It was in one of His journeys to the south, though we have no means of telling which, that He came to Bethany, a small village on the eastern slope of Olivet, and about three-quarters of an hour from Jerusalem. There are several indications in the Gospels that this was a favourite resort of Jesus during His Judæan ministry (Matt. xxi. 1; John viii. 1); and it is somewhat singular that the only nights that we read He spent in Jerusalem were the night in the garden and the two nights He slept in its grave. He preferred the quiet haven of Bethany; and though we cannot with absolute certainty recognize the village home where Jesus had such frequent welcome, yet throwing the side-light of John xi. 5 upon the haze, it seems in part to lift; for the deep affection Jesus had for the three implies a close and ripened intimacy.

St. John, in his allusions to the family, makes Mary prominent, giving precedence to her name, as he calls Bethany "the village of Mary and her sister Martha" (John xi. 1). St. Luke, however, makes Martha the central figure of his picture, while Mary is set back in the shade, or rather in the sunshine of that Presence which was and is the Light of the world. It was, "Martha received Him into her house." She was the recognized head of the family, "the lady" in fact, as well as by the implication of her name, which was the native equivalent of "lady." It was she who gave the invitation to the Master, and on her devolved all the care of the entertainment, the preparation of the feast, and the reception of the guests; for though the change of pronoun in ver. 38 from "they" to "Him" would lead us to suppose that the disciples had gone another way, and were not with Him now, still the "much serving" would show that it was a special occasion, and that others had been invited to meet Jesus.

It is a significant coincidence that St. John, speaking (xii. 2) of another supper at Bethany, in the house of Simon, states that Martha "served," using the same word that Jesus addressed to her in the narrative of St. Luke. Evidently Martha was a "server." This was her forte, so much so that her services were in requisition outside her own house. Hers was a culinary skill, and she delighted with her sleight of hand to effect all sorts of transformations, as, conjuring with her fire, she called forth the pleasures and harmonies of taste. In this case, however, she overdid it; she went beyond her strength. Perhaps her guests outnumbered her invitations, or something unforeseen had upset her plans, so that some of the viands were belated. At any rate, she was cumbered, distracted, "put about" as our modern colloquialism would have it. Perhaps we might say she was "put out" as well, for we can certainly detect a trace of irritability both in her manner and in her speech. She breaks in suddenly among the guests (the aorist participle gives the rustle of a quick movement), and in the hearing of them all she says to Jesus, "Lord, dost Thou not care that my sister did leave me to serve alone? bid her therefore that she help me." Her tone is sharp, querulous, and her words send a deep chill across the table, as when a sea-fret drifts coldly inland. If Mary was in the wrong thus to sit at the feet of Jesus, Martha certainly was not in the right. There was no occasion to give this public reprimand, this round-hand rebuke. She might have come and secretly called her, as she did afterwards, on the day of their sorrow, and probably Mary would have risen as quickly now as then. But Martha is overweighted, ruffled; her feelings get the better of her judgment, and she speaks, out of the impatience of her heart, words she never would have spoken had she but known that Inspiration would keep their echoes reverberating down all the years of time. And besides, her words were somewhat lacking in respect to the Master. True, she addresses Him as "Lord;" but having done this, she goes off into an interrogative with an implied censure in it, and closes with an imperative, which, to say the least, was not becoming, while all through an undue emphasis is laid upon the first personal pronoun, the "me" of her aggrieved self.

Turning to the other sister, we find a striking contrast, for Mary, as our Evangelist puts it, "also sat at the Lord's feet, and heard His word." This does not imply any forwardness on her part, or any desire to make herself conspicuous; the whole drift of her nature was in the opposite direction. Sitting "at His feet" now that they were reclining at the table, meant sitting behind Him, alone amid the company, and screened from their too-curious gaze by Him who drew all eyes to Himself. Nor does she break through her womanly reserve to take part in the conversation; she simply "heard His word;" or "she kept listening," as the imperfect tense denotes. She put herself in the listening attitude, content to be in the shadow, outside the charmed circle, if she only might hear Him speak, whose words fell like a rain of music upon her soul. Her sister chided her for this, and the large family of modern Marthas--for feminine sentiment is almost entirely on Martha's side--blame her severely, for what they call the selfishness of her conduct, seeking her own enjoyment, even though others must pay the price of it. But was Mary so utterly selfish? and did she sacrifice duty to gratify her inclination? Not at all, and certainly not to the extent our Marthas would have us believe. Mary had assisted in the preparations and the reception, as the "also" of ver. 39 shows; while Martha's own words, "My sister did leave me to serve alone," themselves imply that Mary had shared the labours of the entertainment before taking her place at the feet of Jesus. The probability is that she had completed her task; and now that He who spake as never man spake before was conversing with the guests, she could not forego the privilege of listening to the voice she might not hear again.

It is to Jesus, however, that we must go with our rivalry of claims. He is our Court of Equity. His estimate of character was never at fault. He looked at the essences of things, the soul of things, and not to the outward wrappings of circumstance, and He read that palimpsest of motive, the underlying thought, more easily than others could read the outward act. And certainly Jesus had no apology for selfishness; His whole life was one war against it, and against sin, which is but selfishness ripened. But how does Jesus adjust this sisterly difference? Does He dismiss the listener, and send her back to an unfinished task? Does He pass on to her Martha's warm reproof? Not at all; but He gently reproves the elder sister. "Martha, Martha," He said, as if her mind had wandered, and the iteration was necessary to call her to herself, "thou art anxious and troubled about many things: but one thing is needful: for Mary hath chosen the good part, which shall not be taken away from her."

It is easy to see from this where Jesus thought the blame should rest. It was Martha who had taken too much upon herself. Her generous heart had gone beyond her strength, and far beyond the need. Wishing to do honour to her Guest, studying to please Him, she had been over-lavish in her entertainment, until she had become worried--anxious, troubled, as Jesus said, the former word referring to the inner disquiet, the unrest of soul, and the latter to the outward perturbation, the tremor of the nerves, and the cloudiness that looked from her eyes. The fact was that Martha had misread the tastes of her Guest. She thought to please Him by the abundance of her provision, the largeness of her hospitality; but for these lower pleasures of sense and of taste Jesus cared little. He had meat to eat that others knew not of, and to do the will of Him that sent Him was to Jesus more than any ambrosia or nectar of the gods. The more simple the repast, the more it pleased Him, whose thoughts were high in the heavenly places, even while His feet and the mortal body He wore touched lightly the earth. And so while Martha's motive was pure, her judgment was mistaken, and her eager heart tempted her to works of supererogation, to an excess of care which was anxiety, the fret and fever of the soul. Had she been content with a modest service, such as would have pleased her Guest, she too might have found time to sit at His feet, and to have found there an Elim of rest and a Mount of Beatitudes.

But while Jesus has a kind rebuke for Martha, He has only words of commendation for her sister, whom she has been so openly and sharply upbraiding. "Mary," He said, speaking the name Martha had not uttered, "hath chosen the good part, which shall not be taken away from her." He answers Martha in her own language, her native tongue; for in speaking of Mary's choice as the "good part," it is a culinary phrase, the parlance of the kitchen or the table, meaning the choice bit. The phrase is in apposition with the one thing which is needful, which itself is the antithesis to the "many things" of Martha's care. What the "one thing" is of which Jesus speaks we cannot say with certainty, and almost numberless have been the interpretations given to it. But without going into them, can we not find the truest interpretation in the Lord's own words? We think we may, for in the Sermon on the Mount we have an exact parallel to the narrative. He finds people burdened, anxious about the things of this life, wearying themselves with the interminable questions, "What shall we eat? or What shall we drink?" as if life had no quest higher and vaster than these. And Jesus rebukes this spirit of anxiety, exorcising it by an appeal to the lilies and the grass of the field; and summing up His condemnation of anxiety, He adds the injunction, "Seek ye His kingdom, and these things shall be added unto you" (xii. 31). Here, again, we have the "many things" of human care and strife contrasted with the "one thing" which is of supremest moment. First, the kingdom; this in the mind of Jesus was the summum bonum, the highest good of man, compared with which the "many things" for which men strive and toil are but the dust of the balances. And this was the choice of Mary. She sought the kingdom of God, sitting at the feet of Him who proclaimed it, and who was, though she knew it not as yet, Himself the King. Martha too sought the kingdom, but her distracted mind showed that that was not her only, perhaps not her chief quest. Earthly things weighed too heavily upon her mind and heart, and through their dust the heavenly things became somewhat obscured. Mary's heart was set heavenward. She was the listener, eager to know the will of God, that she might do it. Martha was so busied with her own activities that she could not give her thoughts to Christ; Mary ceased from her works, that so she might enter into His rest, setting the world behind her, that her undivided gaze might be upon Him who was truly her Lord. And so Jesus loved Martha, yet pitied and chided her, while He loved and commended Mary.

Nor was the "good part" ever taken from her, for again and again we find her returning to the feet of Jesus. In the day of their great sorrow, as soon as she heard that the Master had come and called her, she arose quickly, and coming to Jesus, though it was the bare, dusty ground, she fell at His feet, seeking strength and help where she before had sought light and truth. And once more: when the shadow of the cross came vividly near, when Simon gave the feast which Martha served, Mary sought those feet again, to pour upon them the precious and fragrant nard, the sweet odours of which filled all the house, as they have since filled all the world. Yes, Mary did not sit at the feet of Jesus in vain; she had learned to know Christ as few of the disciples did; for when Jesus said, "She has done it for My burying," He intends us to infer that Mary feels, stealing over her retiring but loving soul, the cold and awful shadow of the cross. Her broken alabaster and its poured-out spikenard are her unspoken ode to the Redeemer, her pre-dated homage to the Crucified.

And so we find in Mary the truest type of service. Hers was not always the passive attitude, receiving and never giving, absorbing and not diffusing. There was the service before the session; her hands had prepared and wrought for Christ before she placed herself at His feet, and the sacrifice followed, as she brought her costly gift, to the astonishment of all the rest, her sweet and healing balm for the wounds which were soon to follow.

The life that is all receptive, that has no active ministries of love, no waiting upon Christ in the person of His followers, is an unnatural, an unhealthy life, a piece of morbid selfishness which neither pleases God nor blesses man. On the other hand, the life that is always busy, that is in a constant swirl of outward duties, flying here and there like the stormy petrel over the unresting waves, will soon weary or wear itself out, or it will grow into an automaton, a mechanism without a soul. Receiving, giving, praying, working--these are the alternate chords on which the music of our lives should be struck. Heavenward, earthward, should be the alternate looks--heavenward in our waiting upon God, and earthward in our service for man. That life shines the most and is seen the farthest which reflects most of the heavenly light; and he serves Christ the best who now sits humbly and prayerfully at His feet, and then goes forth to be a "living echo" of His voice, breaking for Him the alabaster of a self-sacrificing love. As one has beautifully expressed it, "The effective life and the receptive life are one. No sweep of arm that does some work for God but harvests also some more of the truth of God and sweeps it into the treasury of the life."[3]

But if Mary gives us a type of the truest and best service, Martha shows us a kind of service which is only too common. She gave to Jesus a right loving welcome, and was delighted with the privilege of ministering to His wants; but the coming of Jesus brought her, not peace, but distraction--not rest, but worry. Her very service ruffled and irritated her, until mind and heart were like the tempestuous lake ere the spell of the Divine "Peace" fell upon it. And all the time the Christ was near, who could bear each burden, and still all the disquiet of the soul! But Martha was all absorbed in the thought of what she could do for Him, and she forgot how much more He could do for her, giving to her chafed spirit quietness and rest, even amid her toil. The Divine Peace was near her, within her home, but the hurryings of her restless will and her manifold activities effectually excluded that peace from her heart.

And how many who call themselves Christians are true Marthas, serving Christ, but feeling the yoke to chafe, and the burden to weight them! perhaps preaching to others the Gospel of rest and peace, and themselves knowing little of its experience and blessedness--like the camels of the desert, which carry their treasures of corn and sweet spices to others, and themselves feed on the bitter and prickly herbs. Ah, you are too much upon your feet! Cease for awhile from your own works, and let God work in you. Wait in His presence. Let His words take hold of you, and His love enthuse you; so will you find rest amid your toil, calmness amid the strife, and you will prove that the fret and the fever of life will all disappear at the touch of the living Christ.

## Footnotes:

3. Phillips Brooks.

# CHAPTER XXI – LOST AND FOUND

*Luke xv.*

In this chapter we see how the waves of influence, moving outward from their Divine centre, touch the outermost fringe of humanity, sending the pulsations of new excitements and new hopes through classes Religion and Society both had banned. "Now all the publicans and sinners were drawing near unto Him, for to hear Him." It was evidently a movement widespread and deep. The hostility of Pharisees and scribes would naturally give to these outcasts a certain bias in His favour, causing their hearts to lean towards him, while His words of hope fell upon their lives like the breaking of a new dawn. Nor did Jesus forbid their approach. Instead of looking upon it as an intrusion, an impertinence, the attraction was mutual. Instead of receiving them with a cold and scant courtesy, He welcomed them, receiving them gladly, as the verb of the Pharisees' murmur implies. He even mingled with them in social intercourse, with an acceptance, if not an interchange, of hospitality. To the Pharisaic mind, however, this was a flagrant lapse, a breach of the proprieties which was unpardonable and half criminal, and they gave vent to their disapprobation and disgust in the loud and scornful murmur, "This man receiveth sinners, and eateth with them." It is from this hard sentence of withering contempt, as from a prickly and bitter calyx, we have the trifoliate parables of the Lost Sheep, the Lost Coin, and the Lost Man, the last of which is perhaps the crown and flower of all the parables. With minor differences, the three parables are really one, emphasizing, as they reiterate, the one truth how Heaven seeks after the lost of earth, and how it rejoices when the lost is found.

The first parable is pastoral: "What man of you," asks Jesus, using the Tu quoque retort, "having a hundred sheep, and having lost one of them, doth not leave the ninety and nine in the wilderness, and go after that which is lost, until he find it?" It is one of those questions which only need to be asked to be answered, an interrogative which is axiomatic and self-evident. Jesus tries to set his detractors in His place, that they may think His thoughts, feel His feelings, as they look out on the world from His standpoint; but since they cannot follow Him to these redemptive heights, He comes down to the lower level of their vision. "Suppose you have a hundred sheep, and one of them, getting separated from the rest, goes astray, what do you do? Dismissing it from your thought, do you leave it to its fate, the certain slaughter that awaits it from the wild beasts? or do you seek to minimize your loss, working it out by the rule of proportion as you ask, 'What is one to ninety-nine?' then writing off the lost one, not as a unit, but as a common fraction? No; such a supposition is incredible and impossible. You would go in search of the lost directly. Turning your back upon the ninety and nine, and turning your thoughts from them too, you would leave them in their mountain pasture,[4] as you sought the lost one. Calling it by its name, you would climb the terraced hills, and awake the echoes of the wadies, until the flinty heart of the mountain had felt the sympathy of your sorrow, repeating with you the lost wanderer's name. And when at last you found it you would not chide or punish it; you would not even force it to retrace its steps across the weary distance, but taking compassion on its weakness, you would lift it upon your shoulders and bear it rejoicing home. Then forgetful of your own weariness, fatigue and anxiety swallowed up in the new-found joy, you would go round to your neighbours, to break the good news to them, and so all would rejoice together."

Such is the picture, warm in colour and instinct with life, Jesus sketches in a few well-chosen words. He delicately conceals all reference to Himself; but even the chromatic vision of the Pharisees would plainly perceive how complete was its justification of His own conduct, in mingling thus with the erring and the lost; while to us the parable is but a veil of words, through which we discern the form and features of the "Good Shepherd," who gave even His life for the sheep, seeking that He might save that which was lost.

The second, which is a twin parable, is from domestic life. As in the parables of the kingdom, Jesus sets beside the man with the mustard-seed the woman with her leaven, so here He makes the same distinction, clothing the Truth both in a masculine and a feminine dress. He asks again, "Or what woman" (He does not say "of you," for if women were present amongst His hearers they would be in the background) "having ten pieces of silver, if she lose one piece, doth not light a lamp, and sweep the house, and seek diligently until she find it? And when she hath found it, she calleth together her friends and neighbours, saying, Rejoice with me, for I have found the piece which I had lost." Much objection has been taken to this parable for its supposed want of naturalness and reality. "Is it likely," our objectors say, "that the loss of a small coin like a drachma, whose value was about sevenpence-halfpenny, could be the occasion of so much concern, and that its recovery should be enough to call forth the congratulations of all the village matrons? Surely that is not parable, but hyperbole." But things have a real as well as an intrinsic value, and what to others would be common and cheap, to its possessor might be a treasure beyond reckoning, with all the added values of association and sentiment. So the ten drachmas of the woman might have a history; they might have been a family heirloom, moving quietly down the generations, with whole poems, ay, and even tragedies, hidden within them. Or we can conceive of a poverty so dire and strait that even one small coin in the emergent circumstance might grow into a value far beyond its intrinsic worth. But the parable does not need all these suppositions to steady it and keep it from falling to the ground. When rightly understood it becomes singularly natural, the truth of truth, if such an essence can be distilled in human speech. The probable interpretation is that the ten drachmas were the ten coins worn as a frontlet by the women of the east. This frontlet was given by the bridegroom to the bride at the time of marriage, and like the ring of western life, it was invested with a kind of sanctity. It must be worn on all public occasions, and guarded with a jealous, sacred care; for should one of its pieces be lost, it would be regarded as an indication that the possessor had not only been careless, but also that she had been unfaithful to her marriage vow. Throwing, then, this light of eastern custom upon the parable, how vivid and lifelike it becomes! With what intense eagerness would she seek for the missing coin! Lighting her lamp--for the house would be but dimly lighted with its open door and its small unglazed window--how carefully and almost tremblingly she would peer along its shelves, and sweep out the corners of her few rooms! and how great would be her joy as she saw it glistening in the dust! Her whole soul would go out after it, as if it were a living, sentient thing. She would clasp it in her hand, and even press it to her lips; for has it not taken a heavy care and sorrow from her heart? That one coin rising from the dust has been to her like the rising of another sun, filling her home with light and her life with melody; and what wonder that she hastens to communicate her joy, as, standing by her door, after the eastern wont, she holds up the missing treasure, and calls on her neighbours and friends (the substantives are feminine now) to rejoice with her.

The third parable carries the thought still higher, forming the crown of the ascending series. Not only is there a mathematical progression, as the lost fraction increases from one-hundredth to one-tenth, and then to one-half of the whole, but the intrinsic value of the loss rises in a corresponding series. In the first it was a lost sheep, a loss which might soon be replaced, and which would soon be forgotten; in the second it was a lost coin, which, as we have seen, meant the loss of what was more valuable than gold, even honour and character; while in the third it is a lost child. We call it the parable of the Prodigal Son; it might with equal propriety be called the Parable of the Bereaved Father, for the whole story crystallizes about that name, repeating it, in one form or another, no less than twelve times.

"A certain man," so begins this parabolic Paternoster, "had two sons." Tired of the restraints of home and the surveillance of the father's eye, the younger of them determined to see the world for himself, in order, as the sequel shows, that he might have a free hand, and give loose reins to his passions. With a cold, impertinent bluntness, he says to the father, whose death he thus anticipates, "Father, give me the portion of thy substance that falleth to me," a command whose sharp, imperative tone shows but too plainly the proud, masterful spirit of the youth. He respects neither age nor law; for though the paternal estate could be divided during the father's life, no son, much less the younger, had any right to demand it. The father grants the request, dividing "unto them," as it reads, "his living;" for the same line which marks off the portion of the younger marks out too that of the elder son, though he holds his portion as yet only in promise. Not many days after--for having found its wings, the foolish bird is in haste to fly--the youth gathers all together, and then takes his journey into a far country. The down grades of life are generally steep and short, and so one sentence is enough to describe this descensus Averni, down which the youth plunges so insanely: "He wasted his substance with riotous living," scattering it, as the verb means, throwing it away after low, illicit pleasures. "And when he had spent all"--the "all" he had scrambled for and gathered a short while before--"there arose a mighty famine in that country; and he began to be in want;" and so great were his straits, so remorseless the pangs of hunger, that he was glad to attach himself to a citizen of that country as swineherd, living out in the fields with his drove, like the swineherds of Gadara. But such was the pressure of the famine that his mere pittance could not cope with famine prices, and again and again he hungered to have his fill of the carob-pods, which were dealt out stately and sparingly to the swine. But no man gave even these to him; he was forgotten, as one already dead.

Such is the picture Jesus draws of the lost man, a picture of abject misery and degradation.

*The Expositor's Bible: The Gospel According to St. Luke*

When the sheep wandered it strayed unwittingly, blindly, getting farther from its fellows and its fold even when bleating vainly for them. When the drachma was lost it did not lose itself, nor had it any consciousness that it had dropped out of its proper environment. But in the case of the lost man it was altogether different. Here it is a wilful perversity, which breaks through the restraints of home, tramples upon its endearments, and throws up a blighted life, scarred and pealed amid the husks and swine of a far country. And it is this element of perversity, self-will, which explains, as indeed it necessitates, another marked difference in the parables. When the sheep and the drachma were lost there was an eager search, as the shepherd followed the wanderer over the mountain gullies, and the woman with broom and lamp went after the lost coin. But when the youth is lost, flinging himself away, the father does not follow him, except in thought, and love, and prayer. He sits "still in the house," nursing a bitter grief, and the work on the farm goes on just as usual, for the service of the younger brother would probably be not much missed. And why does not the father summon his servants, bidding them go after the lost child, bringing him home, if necessary, by force? Simply because such a finding would be no finding. They might indeed carry the wanderer home, setting down his feet by the familiar door; but of what use is that if his heart is still wayward and his will rebellious? Home would not be home to him; and with his heart in the far country, he would walk even in his father's fields and in his father's house as an alien, a foreigner. And so all embassies, all messages would be in vain; and even a father's love can do no more than wait, patiently and prayerfully, in hopes that a better spirit may yet come over him, and that some rebound of feeling may bring him home, a humbled penitent. The change comes at length, and the slow morning dawns.

When the photographer wishes to develop the picture that is hidden in the film of the sensitive plate he carries it to a darkened room, and bathed in the developing solution the latent image gradually appears, even to the minutest details. It was so here; for when in his extremest need, with the pinch of a fearful hunger upon him, and the felt darkness of a painful isolation surrounding him, there came into the prodigal's soul a sweet picture of the far-away home, the home which might still have been his but for his wantonness, but which is his now only in memory. It is true his first thoughts of that home were not very lofty; they only crouched with the dogs under the father's table, or hovered around the plentiful board of the servants, attracted by the "bread enough and to spare." But such is the natural association of ideas; the carob-pods of the swine naturally suggest the bread of the servants, while this in turn opens up all the chambers of the father's house, reviving its half-faded images of happiness and love, and awaking all the sweet memories that sin had stifled and silenced. That it was so here, the lower leading up to the higher thought, is evident from the young man's soliloquy: "I will arise and go to my father, and will say unto him, Father, I have sinned against Heaven and in thy sight: I am no more worthy to be called thy son: make me as one of thy hired servants." The hunger for the servants' bread is all forgotten now, swallowed up in the hunger of the soul, as it pines for the father's presence and for the father's smile, longing for the lost Eden. The very name "father" strikes with a strange music upon his awakened and penitent soul, making him for the time half-oblivious to his present wretchedness; and as Memory recalls a bright but vanished past, Hope peoples the dark sky with a heavenly host, who sing a new Advent, the dawn of a heavenly day. An Advent? Perhaps it was an Easter rather, with a "resurrection from earth to things above," an Easter whose anthem, in songs without end, was, "I will arise and go to my father," that Resurgam of a new and holier life.

No sooner is the "I will" spoken than there is a reversing of all the wheels. The hands follow whither the heart has gone; the feet shake off the dust of the far country, retracing the steps they measured so foolishly and lightly before; while the eyes, washed by their bitter tears--

*"Not backward are their glances bent,
But onward to the Father's house."*

"And he arose and came to his father." He came to himself first; and having found that better self, he became conscious of the void he had not felt before. For the first time he realizes how much the father is to him, and how terrible the bereavement and loss he inflicted upon himself when he put between that father and himself the desert of an awful distance. And as the bright memories of other days flash up within his soul, like the converging rays of a borealis, they all turn towards and centre in the father. Servants, home, and loaves of bread alike speak of him whose very shadow is brightness to the self-orphaned child. He yearns for the father's presence with a strange and intense yearning; and could that presence be his again, even if he were nothing more than a servant, with but casual interviews, hearing his voice but in its commanding tones, he would be content and happy.

And so he comes and seeks the father; will the father relent and receive him? Can he overlook and forgive the waywardness and wantonness which have embittered his old age? Can he receive him back even as a servant, a child who has scorned his authority, slighted his love, and squandered his substance in riotous living? Does the father say, "He has made his own bed, and he must lie upon it; he has had his portion, even to the swept-up crumbs, and there is nothing left for him now"? No, for there is something left, a treasure which he might scorn, indeed, but which he could not throw away, even a heritage of love. And what a picture the parable draws of the love that hopeth and endureth all things! "But while he was yet afar off, his father saw him, and was moved with compassion, and ran, and fell on his neck, and kissed him." As the moon in her revolutions lifts up the tides, drawing the deep oceans to herself, so do the unsounded depths of the father's heart turn towards the prodigal whose life has set, dropping out of sight behind wildernesses of darkness. Thought, prayer, pity, compassion, love flow out towards the attraction they can no longer see. Nay, it seems as if the father's vision were transfixed riveted to the spot where the form of his erring lad vanished out of sight; for no sooner has the youth come within sight of the home, than the father's eyes, made telescopic with love, discern him, and as if by intuition, recognize him, even though his attire be mean and tattered, and his step has no longer the lightness of innocence nor the firmness of integrity. It is, it is his child, the erring but now repenting child, and the pent-up emotions of the father's soul rush out as in a tumultuous freshet to meet him. He even "ran" to meet him, all forgetful of the dignity of years, and throwing himself upon his neck, he kissed him, not either with the cold kiss of courtesy, but with the warm, fervent kiss of love, as the intensive prefix of the verb implies.

So far this scene of reconciliation has been as a dumb show. The storm of emotion so interrupted the electric flow of quiet thought and speech that no word was spoken in the mutual embrace. When, however, the power of speech returns the youth is the first to break the silence. "Father," he said, repeating the words of his mental resolve when in the far country, "I have sinned against Heaven, and in thy sight: I am no more worthy to be called thy son." It is no longer the sense of physical need, but the deeper sense of guilt, that now presses upon his soul. The moral nature, which by the anodynes of sin had been thrown into a state of coma, awakes to a vivid consciousness, and in the new awakening, in the broadening light of the new dawn, he sees one thing only, and that is his sin, a sin which has thrown its blackness over the wasted years, which has embittered a father's heart, and which cast its shadow even into heaven itself. Nor is it the conviction of sin only; there is a full and frank confession of it, with no attempt at palliation or excuse. He does not seek to gloss it over, but smiting his breast with bitter reproaches, he confesses his sin with "a humble, lowly, penitent, and obedient heart," hoping for the mercy and forgiveness he is conscious he does not deserve. Nor does he hope in vain. Even before the confession is completed, the absolution is spoken, virtually at least; for without allowing the youth to finish his sentence, in which he offers to renounce his sonship and to accept a menial position, the father calls to the servants, "Bring forth quickly the best robe, and put it on him; and put a ring on his hand, and shoes on his feet: and bring the fatted calf, and kill it, and let us eat and make merry." In this peal of imperatives we detect the rapid beating of the father's heart, the loving, eager haste to wipe out all the sad marks that sin has left. In the luminous atmosphere of the father's love the youth is no more the prodigal; he is as one transfigured; and now that the chrysalis has left the mire, and crept up into the sunlight, it must have a dress befitting its new summer life, wings of gauze, and robes of rainbow hues. The best, or "the first robe" as it is in the Greek, must be brought out for him; a signet-ring, the pledge of authority, must be put upon his hand; shoes, the badge of freedom, must be found for the tired and bared feet; while for the merry-making which is extemporized, the domestic festa which is the crown of these rejoicings, the fatted calf, which was in reserve for some high festival, must be killed. And all this is spoken in a breath, in a sort of bewilderment, the ecstasy of an excessive joy; and forgetting that the simple command is enough for servants, the master must needs tell out his joy to them: "For this my son was dead, and is alive again; he was lost, and is found."

If the three parables were all through coincident, the parable of the Prodigal Son should close at this point, the curtain dropping over the festive scene, where songs, and music, and the rhythm of the dance are the outward and weak expressions of the father's joy over the son who comes back from the far country, as one alive from the dead. But Jesus has another purpose; He must not only plead the cause of the outcast and the low, setting open for them the door of mercy and of hope; He must also rebuke and silence the unreasoning murmur of the Pharisees and scribes--which He does in the picture of the Elder Brother. Coming from the field, the heir is surprised to find the whole house given up to an impromptu feast. He hears the sounds of merriment and music, but its strains fall strange and harsh upon his ear. What can it mean? Why was he not consulted? Why should his father thus take occasion of his absence in the fields to invite his friends and neighbours? The proud spirit chafes under the slight, and calling one of the servants, he asks what it all means. The answer is not reassuring, for it only perplexes and pains him the more: "Thy brother is come; and thy father hath killed the fatted calf, because he hath received him safe and sound"--an answer which does but deepen his displeasure, turning his sullenness to anger. "And would not go in." They may end the feast, as they began it, without him. The festive joy is something foreign to his nature; it awakes but feelings of repulsion, and all its music is to him a grating discord, a Miserere.

But let us not be too severe upon the elder brother. He was not perfect, by any means, but in any appraisement of his character there are certain veinings of worth and nobleness that must not be omitted. We have already seen how, in the division of the father's goods, when he divided unto them his living, while the younger took away his portion, and swiftly scattered it in riotous living, the elder brother took no advantage of the deed of gift. He did not dispossess the father, securing for himself the paternal estate. He put it back into his father's hands, content with the filial relation of dependence and obedience. The father's word was still his law. He was the dutiful son; and when he said, "These many years do I serve thee, and I never transgressed a commandment of thine," the boast was no exaggeration but the statement of a simple truth. Compared with the life of the prodigal, the life of the elder brother had been consistent, conscientious, and moral. Where, then, was his failure, his lack? It was just here, in the lack of heart, the absence of affection. He bore the name of a son, but he carried the heart of a servant. His nature was servile, rather than filial; and while his hands offered a service unremitting and precise, it was the cold service of an impassive mechanism. Instead of love passing out in living heart-throbs, suffusing all the life with its warmth, and clothing it in its own iridescent colouring, it was only a metallic mainspring called "duty." The father's presence is not the delight to him; he does not once mention that tender name in which the repenting one finds such a heaven; and when he draws the picture of his highest happiness, the feast of his earthly Walhalla, "my friends" are there, though the father is excluded. And so between the father and the elder brother, with all this seeming nearness, there was a distance of reserve, and where the voices of affection and of constant communion should have been heard there was too often a vacancy of silence. It takes a heart to read a heart; and since this was wanting in the elder brother, he could not know the heart of the father; he could not understand his wild joy. He had no patience with his younger brother; and had he received him back at all, it would have been with a haughty stiffness, and with a lowering in his looks, which should have been at once a rebuke for the past and a warning for the future. The father looked on his son's repentance; the elder brother did not regard the repentance at all; perhaps he had not heard of it, or perhaps he could not understand it; it was something that lay out of the plane of his consciousness. He saw the sin only, how the younger son had devoured his living with harlots; and so he was severe, exacting, bitter. He would have brought out the sackcloth, but nothing more; while as to the music and the fatted calf, they would appear to his loveless soul as an absurd anachronism.

But far removed as he is from the father's spirit, he is still his son; and though the father rejoices more over the younger than over the elder, as was but natural, he loves them both with an equal love. He cannot bear that there should be any estrangement now; and he even leaves the festive throng, and the son he has welcomed and robed, and going out, he begs, he entreats the elder brother to pass in, and to throw himself into the general joy. And when the elder son complains that, with all his years of obedient, dutiful service, he has never had even a kid, much less a fatted calf, on which to feast his friends, the father says, lovingly, but chidingly, "Son"--or "Child," rather, for it is a term of greater endearment than the "son" he had just used before--"thou art ever with me, and all that is mine is thine. But it was meet to make merry and be glad: for this thy brother was dead, and is alive again; and was lost, and is found." He plays upon the "child" as upon a harp, that he may drive away the evil spirits of jealousy and anger, and that even within the servant-heart he may awake some chords, if only the far-off echoes of a lost childhood. He reminds him how vastly different their two positions are. For him there has been no break in their intercourse; the father's house has been his home; he has had the free range of all: to the younger that home has been nothing but a distant memory, with a waste of dreary years between. He has been heir and lord of all; and so completely have father and son been identified, their separate personalities merged the one in the other, that the possessive pronouns, the "mine" and the "thine," are used interchangeably. The younger returns penniless, disinherited by his own misdeed. Nay, he has been as one dead; for what was the far country but a vault of slimy things, the sepulchre of a dead soul? "And should we not make merry and be glad, when thy brother" (it is the antithesis to "thy son" of ver. 30, a mutual "thy") "comes back to us as one raised from the dead?"

Whether the father's pleading prevailed, or not, we are not told. We can but hope it did, and that the elder brother, with his asperities all dissolved, and his jealousies removed, did pass within to share the general joy, and to embrace a lost brother. Then he too would know the sweetness of forgiveness, and taught by the erring but now forgiven one, he too would learn to spell out more correctly that deep word "father," the word he had stammered at, and perhaps misspelt before, as the fatherhood and the brotherhood became to him not ideas merely, but bright realities.

Gathering up now the lessons of the parables, they show us (1) the Divine grief over sin. In the first two this is the prominent thought, the sorrow of the loser. God is represented as losing that which is of worth to Him, something serviceable, and therefore valuable. In the third parable the same idea is suggested rather than stated; but the thought is carried farther, for now it is more than a loss, it is a bereavement the father suffers. The retreating form of the wanderer throws back its shadow across the father's home and heart, a shadow that congeals and stays, and that is darker than the shadow of Death itself. It is the Divine Grief, whose depths we cannot sound, and from whose mystery we must stand back, not one stone's cast, but many.

The parables show (2) the sad state of the sinner. In the case of the Lost Sheep and the Lost Coin we see his perfect helplessness to recover himself, and that he must remain lost, unless One higher than himself undertakes his cause, and "help is laid upon One that is mighty." It is the third parable, however, which especially emphasizes the downward course of sin and the deepening wretchedness of the sinner. The flowery path leads on to a valley of desolation. The way of transgressors is ever a downward path; and let an evil spirit possess a soul, it hurries him directly down the steep place, where, unless the flight be checked, a certain destruction awaits him. Sin degrades and isolates. Want, sorrow, penury, and pain are but a part of its viperous brood, and he who plays with sin, calling it freedom, will find his rod blossom with bitter fruit, or he will see it grow into a serpent with poison in its fangs.

The parables show (3) God's willingness and eagerness to save. The long and eager search after the lost sheep and the lost coin show, though but imperfectly, the supreme efforts God makes for man's salvation. He is not left to wander unrebuked and unsought. There is no forbidden path along which men insanely rush, but some bright angel stands beside it, warning back the sinner, it may be with a drawn sword, some "terror of the Lord," or it may be with a cross, the sacrifice of an infinite love. Though He could send His armies to destroy, He sends His messengers to win us back to obedience and to love--Conscience, Memory, Reason, the Word, the Spirit, and even the well-beloved Son. Nor is the great search discontinued, until it has proved to be in vain.

The parables show (4) the eager interest Heaven takes in man's salvation, and the deep joy there is among the angels over his repentance and recovery. And so the three parables close with a Jubilate. The shepherd rejoices over his recovered sheep more than over the ninety and nine which went not astray; the woman rejoices over the one coin found more than over the nine which were not lost. And this is perfectly natural. The joy of acquisition is more than the joy of possession; and as the crest of the waves is thrown up above the mean sea-level by the alternate depths of depression, so the very sorrow and grief over the loss and bereavement, now that the lost is found and the dead is alive, throw up the emotions beyond their mean level, up to the summits of an exuberant joy. And whether Jesus meant, by the ninety and nine just persons who needed no repentance the unfallen intelligences of heaven, or whether, as Godet thinks, He referred to those who under the Old Covenant were sincere doers of the Law, and who found their righteousness therein (Deut. vi. 25), it is still true, and a truth stamped with a Divine "Verily," that more than the joy of Heaven over these is its joy over the sinner that repented, the dead who now was alive, and the lost who now was found!

## Footnotes:

4. The word rendered "wilderness" means any land unenclosed.

## CHAPTER XXII – THE ETHICS OF THE GOSPEL

Whatever of truth there may be in the charge of "other-worldliness," as brought against the modern exponents of Christianity, such a charge could not even be whispered against its Divine Founder. It is just possible that the Church had been gazing too steadfastly up into heaven, and that she had not been studying the science of the "Humanities" as zealously as she ought, and as she has done since; but Jesus did not allow even heavenly things to obliterate or to blur the lines of earthly duty. We might have supposed that coming down from heaven, and familiar with its secrets, He would have much to say about the New World, its position in space, its society and manner of life. But no; Jesus says little about the life which is to come; it is the life which now is that engrosses His attention, and almost monopolizes His speech. Life with Him was not in the future tense; it was one living present, real, earnest, but fugitive. Indeed, that future was but the present projected over into eternity. And so Jesus, founding the kingdom of God on earth, and summoning all men into it, if he did not bring commandments written and lithographed, like Moses, yet He did lay down principles and rules of conduct, marking out, in all departments of human life, the straight and white lines of duty, the eternal "ought." It is true that Jesus Himself did not originate much in this department of Christian ethics, and probably for most of His sayings we can find a symphony struck from the pages of earlier, and perhaps heathen moralists; but in the wide realm of Right there can be no new law. Principles may be evolved, interpreted; they cannot be created. Right, like Truth, holds the "eternal years;" and through the millenniums before Christ, as through the millenniums after, Conscience, that "ethical intellect" which speaks to all men if they will but draw near to her Sinai and listen, spoke to some in clear, authoritative tones. But if Jesus did no more, He gathered up the "broken lights" of earth, the intermittent flashes which had played on the horizon before, into one steady electric beam, which lights up our human life outward to its farthest reach, and onward to its farthest goal.

In the mind of Jesus conduct was the outward and visible expression of some inner invisible force. As our earth moves round its elliptic in obedience to the subtle attractions of other outlying worlds, so the orbits of human lives, whether symmetrical or eccentric, are determined mainly by the two forces' Character and Circumstance. Conduct is character in motion; for men do what they themselves are, i.e. as far as circumstances will allow. And it is just at this point the ethical teaching of Jesus begins. He recognizes the imperium in imperio, that hidden world of thought, feeling, sentiment, and desire which, itself invisible, is the mould in which things visible are cast. And so Jesus, in His influence upon men, worked outward from within. He sought, not reform, but regeneration, moulding the life by changing the character; for, to use His own figure, how could the thorn produce grapes, or the thistle figs?

And so when Jesus was asked, "What shall I do that I may inherit eternal life?" He gave an answer which at first sight seemed to ignore the question entirely. He said no word about "doing," but threw the questioner back upon "being," asking what was written in the law: "Thou shalt love the Lord thy God with all thy heart, and with all thy soul, and with all thy strength, and with all thy mind; and thy neighbour as thyself" (x. 27). And as Jesus here makes Love the condition of eternal life, its sine qua non, so He makes it the one all-embracing duty, the fulfilling of the law. If a man love God supremely, and his neighbour as himself, he cannot do more; for all other commandments are included in these, the sub-sections of the greater law. Jesus thus sought to create a new force, hiding it within the heart, as the mainspring of duty, providing for that duty both aim and inspiration. We call it a "new" force, and such it was practically; for though it was, in a way, embedded in their law, it was mainly as a dead letter, so much so that when Jesus bade His disciples to "love one another" He called it a "new commandment." Here, then, we find what is at once the rule of conduct and its motive. In the new system of ethics, as taught and enforced by Jesus, and illustrated by His life, the Law of Love was to be supreme. It was to be to the moral world what gravitation is to the natural, a silent but mighty and all-pervasive force, throwing its spell upon the isolated actions of the common day, giving impulse and direction to the whole current of life, ruling alike the little eddies of thought and the wider sweeps of benevolent activities. To Jesus "the soul of improvement was the improvement of the soul." He laid His hand upon the heart's innermost shrine, building up that unseen temple four-square, like the city of the Apocalypse, and lighting up all its windows with the warm, iridescent light of love.

Henry Burton

With this, then, as the foundation-tone, running through all the spaces and along all the lines of life, the thoughts, desires, words, and acts must all harmonize with love; and if they do not, if they strike a note that is foreign to its key-tone, it breaks the harmony at once, throwing jars and discords into the music. Such a breach of the harmonic law would be called a mistake, but when it is a breach of Christ's moral law it is more than a mistake, it is a wrong.

Before passing to the outer life Jesus pauses, in this Gospel, to correct certain dissonances of mind and soul, of thought and feeling, which put us in a wrong attitude towards our fellows. First of all, He forbids us to sit in judgment upon others. He says, "Judge not, and ye shall not be judged: and condemn not, and ye shall not be condemned" (vi. 37). This does not mean that we close our eyes with a voluntary blindness, working our way through life like moles; nor does it mean that we keep our opinions in a state of flux, not allowing them to crystallize into thought, or to harden into the leaden alphabets of human speech. There is within us all a moral sense, a miniature Sinai, and we can no more suppress its thunders or sheath its lightnings than we can hush the breakers of the shore into silence, or suppress the play of the Northern Lights. But in that unconscious judgment we pass upon the actions of others, with our condemnation of the wrong, we pass our sentence upon the wrong-doer, mentally ejecting him from the courtesies and sympathies of life, and if we allow him to live at all, compelling him to live apart, as a moral incurable. And so, with our hatred of the sin, we learn to hate the sinner, and calling from him both our charities and our hopes, we hurl him down into some little Gehenna of our own. But it is exactly this feeling, this kind of judgment, the Law of Love condemns. We may "hate the sin, and yet the sinner love," keeping him still within the circle of our sympathies and our hopes. It is not meet that we should be merciless who have ourselves experienced so much of mercy; nor is it for us to hale others off to prison, or ruthlessly to exact the uttermost farthing, when we ourselves at the very best are erring and unfaithful servants, standing so much and so often in need of forgiveness.

But there is another "judging" that the command of Christ condemns, and that is the hasty and the false judgments we pass on the motives and lives of others. How apt we are to depreciate the worth of others who do not happen to belong to our circle! We look so intently for their faults and foibles that we become blind to their excellences. We forget that there is some good in every person, some that we can see if we only look, and we may be always sure that there is some we cannot see. We should not prejudge. We should not form our opinion upon an ex parte statement. We should not leave the heart too open to the flying germs of rumour, and we should discount heavily any damaging, disparaging statement. We should not allow ourselves to draw too many inferences, for he who is given to drawing inferences draws largely on his imagination. We should think slowly in our judgment of others, for he who leaps to conclusions generally takes his leap in the dark. We should learn to wait for the second thoughts, for they are often truer than the first. Nor is it wise to use too much "the spur of the moment;" it is a sharp weapon, and is apt to cut both ways. We should not interpret others' motives by our own feelings, nor should we "suppose" too much. Above all, we should be charitable, judging of others as we judge ourselves. Perhaps the beam that is in a brother's eye is but the magnified mote that is in our own. It is better to learn the art of appreciating than that of depreciating; for though the one is easy, and the other difficult, yet he who looks for the good, and exalts the good, will make the very wilderness to blossom and be glad; while he who depreciates everything outside his own little self impoverishes life, and makes the very garden of the Lord one arid, barren desert.

Again, Jesus condemns pride, as being a direct contravention of His Law of Love. Love rejoices in the possessions and gifts of others, nor would she care to add to her own if it must be at the cost of theirs. Love is an equalizer, levelling up the inequalities the accidents of life have made, and preferring to stand on some lower level with her fellows than to sit solitary on some lofty and cold Olympus. Pride, on the other hand, is a repelling, separating force. Scorning those who occupy the lower places, she is contented only on her Olympian summit, where she keeps herself warm with the fires of her self-adulation. The proud heart is the loveless heart, one huge inflation; if she carries others at all, it is only as a steadying ballast; she will not hesitate to throw them over and throw them down, as mere dust or sand, if their fall will help her to rise. Pride, like the eagle, builds her nest on high, bringing forth whole broods of loveless, preying passions, hatreds, jealousies, and hypocrisies. Pride sees no brotherhood in man; humanity to her means no more than so many serfs to wait upon her pleasure, or so many victims for her sacrifice! And how Jesus loved to prick these bubbles of airy nothings, showing up these vanities as the very essence of selfishness! He did not spare His words, even though they stung, when "He marked how they chose out the chief seats" at the friendly supper (xiv. 7); and one of His bitter "woes" He hurled at the Pharisees just because "they loved the chief seats in the synagogues," worshipping Self, when they pretended to worship God, so making the house of God itself an arena for the sport and play of their proud ambitions. "He that is least among you all," He said, when rebuking the disciples' lust for pre-eminence, "the same is great." And such is Heaven's law: humility is the cardinal virtue, the "strait" and low gate which opens into the very heart of the kingdom. Humility is the one and the only way of heavenly preferments and eternal promotions; for in the life to come there will be strange contrasts and inversions, as he that exalted himself is now humbled, and he that humbled himself is now exalted (xiv. 11).

Tracing now the lines of duty as they run across the outer life, we find them following the same directions. As the golden milestone of the Forum marked the centre of the empire, towards which its roads converged, and from which all distances were measured, so in the Christian commonwealth Jesus makes Love the capital, the central, controlling power; while at the focal point of all the duties He sets up His Golden Rule, which gives direction to all the paths of human conduct: "And as ye would that men should do to you, do ye also to them likewise" (vi. 31). In this general law we have what we might call the ethical compass, for it embraces within its circle the "whole duty of man" towards his fellow; and it only needs an adjusted conscience, like the delicately poised needle, and the line of the "ought" can be read off at once, even in those uncertain latitudes where no specific law is found. Are we in doubt as to what course of conduct to pursue, as to the kind of treatment we should accord to our fellow? we can always find the via recta by a short mental transposition. We have only to put ourselves in his place, and to imagine our relative positions reversed, and from the "would" of our supposed desires and hopes we read the "ought" of present duty. The Golden Rule is thus a practical exposition of the Second Commandment, investing our neighbour with the same luminous atmosphere we throw about ourselves, the atmosphere of a benevolent, beneficent love.

But beyond this general law Jesus gives us a prescript as to the treatment of enemies. He says, "Love your enemies, do good to them that hate you, bless them that curse you, pray for them that despitefully use you. To him that smiteth thee on the one cheek offer also the other: and from him that taketh away thy cloak withhold not thy coat also" (vi. 27-29). In considering these injunctions we must bear in mind that the word "enemy" in its New Testament meaning had not the wide and general signification it has to-day. It then stood in antithesis to the word "neighbour," as in Matt. v. 43; and as the word "neighbour" to the Jew included those, and those only, who were of the Hebrew race and faith, the word "enemy" referred to those outside, who were aliens from the commonwealth of Israel. To the Hebrew mind it stood as a synonym for "Gentile." In these words, then, we find, not a general and universal law, but the special instructions as to their course of conduct in dealing with the Gentiles, to whom they would shortly be sent. No matter what their treatment, they must bear it with an uncomplaining patience. Stripped, beaten, they must not resist, much less retaliate; they must not allow any vindictive feelings to possess them, nor must they take in their own hot hand the sword of a "sweet revenge." Nay, they must even bear a good-will towards their enemies, repaying their hate with love, their spite and enmity with prayers, and their curses with sincerest benedictions.

It will be observed that no mention is made of repentance or of restitution: without waiting for these, or even expecting them, they must be prepared to forgive and prepared to love their enemies, even while they are shamefully treating them. And what else, under the circumstances, could they have done? If they appealed to the secular power it would simply have been an appeal to a heathen court, from enemies to enemies. And as to waiting for repentance, their "enemies" are only treating them as enemies, aliens and foreigners, wronging them, it is true, but ignorantly, and not through any personal malice. They must forgive just for the same reason that Jesus forgave His Roman murderers, "for they know not what they do."

We cannot, therefore, take these injunctions, which evidently had a special and temporary application, as the literal rule of conduct towards those who are unfriendly or hostile to us. This, however, is plain, that even our enemies, whose enmity is directly personal rather than sectional or racial, are not to be excluded from the Law of Love. We must bear them neither hatred nor resentment; we must guard our hearts sacredly from all malevolent, vindictive feelings. We must not be our own avenger, taking vengeance upon our adversaries, as we let loose the barking Cerberus to track and run them down. All such feelings are contrary to the Law of Love, and so are contraband, entirely foreign to the heart that calls itself Christian. But with all this we are not to meet all sorts of injuries and wrongs without protest or resistance. We cannot condone a wrong without being accomplices in the wrong. To defend our property and life is just as much our duty as it was the wisdom and the duty of those to whom Jesus spoke to offer an uncomplaining cheek to the Gentile smiter. Not to do this is to encourage crime, and to put a premium upon evil. Nor is it inconsistent with a true love to seek to punish, by lawful means, the wrong-doer. Justice here is the highest type of mercy, and pains and penalties have a remedial virtue, taming the passions which had grown too wild, or straightening the conscience that had become warped.

And so Jesus, speaking of the "offences," the occasions of stumbling that would come, said, "If thy brother sin, rebuke him; and if he repent, forgive him" (xvii. 3). It is not the patient, silent acquiescence now. No, we must rebuke the brother who has sinned against us and wronged us. And if this is vain, we must tell it to the Church, as St. Matthew completes the injunction (xviii. 17); and if the offender will not hear the Church, he must be cast out, ejected from their fellowship, and becoming to their thought as a heathen or a publican. The wrong, though it is a brother who does it, must not be glossed over with the enamel of a euphemism; nor must it be hushed up, veiled by a silence. It must be brought to the light of day; it must be rebuked and punished; nor must it be forgiven until it is repented of. Let there be, however, a genuine repentance, and there must be on our part the prompt and complete forgiveness of the wrong. We must set it back out of our sight, amongst the forgotten things. And if the wrong be repeated, if the repentance be repeated, the forgiveness must be repeated too, not only for seven times seven offences, but for seventy times seven. Nor is it left to our option whether we forgive or no; it is a duty, absolute and imperative; we must forgive, as we ourselves hope to be forgiven.

Again, Jesus treats of the true use of wealth. He Himself assumed a voluntary poverty. Silver and gold had He none; indeed, the only coin that we read He handled was the borrowed Roman penny, with Cæsar's inscription upon it. But while Jesus Himself preferred poverty, choosing to live on the outflowing charities of those who felt it both a privilege and an honour to minister to Him of their substance, yet He did not condemn wealth. It was not a wrong per se. In the Old Testament it had been regarded as a sign of Heaven's special favour, and amongst the rich Jesus Himself found some of His warmest, truest friends--friends who came nobly to the front when some who had made louder professions had ignominiously fled. Nor did Jesus require the renunciation of wealth as the condition of discipleship. He did not advocate that fictitious égalité of the Commune. He sought rather to level up than to level down. It is true He did say to the ruler, "Sell all that thou hast, and distribute unto the poor;" but this was an exceptional case[5] and probably it was put before him as a test command, like the command to Abraham that he should sacrifice his son--which was not intended to be carried out literally, but only as far as the intention, the will. There was no such demand made from Nicodemus, and when Zacchæus testified that it had been his practice (the present tense would indicate a retrospective rather than a prospective rule) to give one-half of his income to the poor, Jesus does not find fault with his division, and demand the other half; He commends him, and passes him up, right over the excommunication of the rabbis, among the true sons of Abraham. Jesus did not pose as an assessor; He left men to divide their own inheritance. It was enough for Him if He could put within the soul this new force, the "moral dynamic" of love to God and man; then the outward relations would shape themselves, regulated as by some automatic action.

But with all this, Jesus recognized the peculiar temptations and dangers of wealth. He saw how riches tend to engross and monopolize the thought, diverting it from higher things, and so He classed riches with cares, pleasures, which choke the Word of life, and make it unfruitful. He saw how wealth tended to selfishness; that it acted as an astringent, closing up the valves of the heart, and thus shutting down the outflow of its sympathies. And so Jesus, whenever He spoke of wealth, spoke in words of warning: "How hardly shall they that have riches enter into the kingdom of God!" He said, when He saw how the rich ruler set wealth before faith and hope. And singularly enough, the only times Jesus, in His parables, lifts up the curtain of doom it is to tell of "certain rich" men--the one, whose soul swung selfishly between his banquets and his barns, and who, alas! had laid up no treasures in heaven; and the other, who exchanged his purple and fine linen for the folds of enveloping flames, and the sumptuous fare of earth for eternal want, the eternal hunger and thirst of the after-retribution!

What, then, is the true use of wealth? and how may we so hold it that it shall prove a blessing, and not a bane? In the first place, we must hold it in our hand, and not lay it up in the heart. We must possess it; it must not possess us. We may give our thought, moderately, to it, but our affections must not be allowed to centre upon it. We read that the Pharisees "were lovers of money" (xvi. 14), and that argentic passion was the root of all their evils. The love of money, like an opiate, little by little, steals over the whole frame, deadening the sensibility, perverting the judgment, and weakening the will, producing a kind of intoxication, in which the better reason is lost, and the confused speech can only articulate, with Shylock, "My ducats, my ducats!" The true way of holding wealth is to hold it in trust, recognizing God's ownership and our stewardship. Bank it up, give it no outlet, and your wealth becomes a stagnant pool, breeding malaria and burning fevers; but open the channel, give it an outlet, and it will bring life and music to a thousand lower vales, increasing the happiness of others, and increasing your own the more. And so Jesus strikes in with His frequent imperative, "Give"--"Give, and it shall be given unto you; good measure, pressed down, shaken together, running over, shall they give into your bosom" (vi. 38). And this is the true use of wealth, its consecration to the needs of humanity. And may we not say that here is its truest pleasure? He who has learned the art of generous giving, who makes his life one large-hearted benevolence, living for others and not for himself, has acquired an art that is beautiful and Divine, an art that turns the deserts into gardens of the Lord, and that peoples the sky overhead with unseen singing Ariels. Giving and living are heavenly synonyms, and he who giveth most liveth best.

But not from the words of Jesus alone do we read off the lines of our duty. He is in His own Person a Polar Star, to whom all the meridians of our round life turn, and from whom they emanate. His life is thus our law, His example our pattern. Do we wish to learn what are the duties of children to their parents? the thirty silent years of Nazareth speak in answer. They show us how the Boy Jesus is in subjection to His parents, giving to them a perfect obedience, a perfect trust, and a perfect love. They show us the Divine Youth, still shut in within that narrow circle, ministering to that circle, by hard manual toil becoming the stay of that fatherless home. Do we wish to learn our duties to the State? See how Jesus walked in a land across which the Roman eagle had cast its shadow! He did not preach a crusade against the barbarian invaders. He recognized in their presence and power the ordination of God--that they had been sent to chastise a lapsed Israel. And so Jesus spoke no word of denunciation, no fiery word, which might have proved the spark of a revolution. He took Himself away from the multitudes when they would by force make Him King. He spoke in respectful terms of the powers that were; He even justified the payment of tribute to Cæsar, acknowledging his lordship, while at the same time He spoke of the higher tribute to the great Over-Lord, even God. When upon His trial for life or death, before a Roman tribunal, He even stayed to apologize for Pilate's weakness, casting the heavier sin back on the hierarchy that had bought Him and delivered Him up; while upon the cross, amid its untold agonies, though His lips were glued by a fearful thirst, He opened them to breathe a last prayer for His Roman executioners: "Father, forgive them; for they know not what they do."

But was Jesus, then, an alien from His kinsmen according to the flesh? Was patriotism to Him an unknown force? Did He know nothing of love of country, that inspiration which has turned common men into heroes and martyrs, that love which oceans cannot quench, nor distance weaken, which throws an auroral brightness around the most sterile shores, and which makes the emigrant sick with a strange Heimweh? Did the Son of man, the ideal Man, know nothing at all of this? He did know it, and know it well. He identified Himself thoroughly with His people; He placed Himself under the law, observing its rites and ceremonies. After the Childhood-exile in Egypt, He scarcely passed out of the sacred bounds; no storms of rough persecution could dislodge the heavenly Dove, or send Him wheeling off from His native hills. And if He did not preach rebellion, He did preach that righteousness which gives to a nation its truest wealth and widest liberty. He did denounce the Pharisaic shams, the hollow hypocrisies, which had eaten away the nation's heart and strength. And how He loved Jerusalem, forgetting His own triumph in the vision of her humiliation, and weeping for the desolations which were coming sure and fast! This, the Holy City, was the centre to which He ever returned, and to which He gave His last bequest--His cross and His grave. Nay, when the cross is taken down, and the grave is vacant, He lingers to give His Apostles their commission; and when He bids them, "Go ye out into all the world," He adds, "beginning at Jerusalem." The Son of man is the Son of David still, and within His deep love for humanity at large was a peculiar love for His "own," as the ark itself was enshrined within the Holy of holies.

And so we might traverse the whole ethical domain, and we should find no duty which is not enforced or suggested by the words or the life of the great Teacher. As Dr. Dorner says, "There is only one morality; the original of it is in God; the copy of it is in the Man of God." Happy is He who sees this Polar Star, whose light shines clear and calm above the rush of human years and the ebbs and flows of human life! Happier still is he who shapes his course by it, who reads off all his bearings from its light! He who builds his life after the Divine model, reading the Christ-life into his own, will build up another city of God on earth, four-square and compact together, a city of peace, because a city of righteousness and a city of love.

## Footnotes:

5. This demand was made from the Apostles (xii. 33), but not from others beyond the Apostolic circle.

# CHAPTER XXIII – THE ESCHATOLOGY OF THE GOSPEL

Coifi, in his parable to the thanes and nobles of the North Humber country, likened the present life of man to the flight of a sparrow through one of their lighted halls, coming out of the night, and then disappearing in the dark winter whence it came; and he asked for Christianity a candid hearing, if perhaps she might tell the secrets of the beyond. And so indeed she does, lighting up the "dark winter" with a bright, though a partial apocalypse. It is not our purpose to enter into a general discussion of the subject; our task is simply to arrest the beams of inspired light hiding within this Gospel, and by a sort of spectrum analysis to read from them what they are permitted to reveal. And--

1. The Gospel teaches that the grave is not the end of life. It may seem as if we were stating but a truism in saying this; yet if a truism, it perhaps has not been allowed its due place in our thought, and its restatement may not be altogether a superfluous word. We cannot study the life of Jesus without noticing that His views of earth were not the views of men in general. To them this world was everything; to possess it, even in some infinitesimal quantity, was their supreme ambition; and though in their better, clearer moments they caught glimpses of worlds other than their own, yet to their distant vision they were as the twinkling stars of the azure, far off and cold, soon losing themselves in the haze of unreality, or setting in the shadows of the imposing earth. To Jesus earth was but a fragment of a vaster whole, a fragment whose substances were but the shadows of higher, heavenlier realities. Nor were these outlying spaces to His mind voids of silence, a "dark inane," without life or thought; they were peopled with intelligences whose personalities were as distinctly marked as is this human Ego, and whose movements, unweighted by the gyves of flesh, seemed subtle and swift as thought itself. With one of these worlds Jesus was perfectly familiar. With heaven, which was the abode of His Father and innumerable hosts of angels, He was in close and constant correspondence, and the frequent prayer, the frequent upward looks tell us how near and how intensely real the heavenly places were to Him. But in the mind of Jesus this empyrean of happiness and light had its antipodes of woe and darkness, a penal realm of fearful shadow, and which, borrowing the language of the city, He called the Gehenna of burning. Such were the two invisible realms, lying away from earth, yet closely touching it from opposite directions, and to one or other of which all the paths of human life turned, to find their goal and their self-chosen destiny.

And not only so, but the transition from the Seen to the Unseen was not to Jesus the abrupt and total change that it seems to man. To us the dividing-line is both dark and broad. It seems to us a transmigration to some new and strange world, where we must begin life de novo. To Jesus the line was narrow, like one of the imaginary meridians of earth, the "here" shading off into the "hereafter," while both were but the hemispheres of one round life. And so Jesus did not often speak of "death;" that was too human a word. He preferred the softer names of "sleep" or "exodus," thus making death the quickener of life, or likening it to a triumphal march from bondage to liberty. Nor was "the Valley of the Shadow" to Jesus a strange, unfamiliar place. He knew all its secrets, all its windings. It was His own territory, where His will was supreme. Again and again He throws a commanding voice across the valley, a voice which goes reverberating among the heights beyond, and instantly the departed spirit retraces its steps, to animate again the cold clay it had forsaken. "He is not the God of the dead, but of the living," said Jesus, as He claimed for Abraham, Isaac, and Jacob an existence altogether apart from the crumbling dust of Hebron; and as we see Moses and Elias coming to the Mount of Transfiguration, we see that the departed have not so far departed as to take no interest in earthly things, and as not to hear the strike of earthly hours. And how clearly this is seen in the resurrection life of Jesus, with which this Gospel closes! Death and the Grave have done their worst to Him, but how little is that worst! how insignificant the blank it makes in the Divine Life! The few hours in the grave were but a semibreve rest in the music of that Life; the Easter morning struck a fresh bar, and the music went on, in the higher spaces, it is true, but in the same key and in the same sweet strain. And just so is it with all human life; "the grave is not our goal." Conditions and circumstances will of necessity change, as the mortal puts on immortality, but the life itself will be one and the same life, here amid things visible and temporal, and there amid the invisible and eternal.

2. The Gospel shows in what respects the conditions of the after-life will be changed. In chapter xx. 27 we read how that the Sadducees came to Jesus, tempting Him. They were the cold materialists of the age, denying the existence of spirits, and so denying the resurrection. They put before Him an extreme, though not impossible case, of a woman who had been the wife, successively, of seven brethren; and they ask, with the ripple of an inward laugh in their question, "In the resurrection therefore whose wife of them shall she be?" Jesus answered, "The sons of this world marry, and are given in marriage: but they that are accounted worthy to attain to that world, and the resurrection from the dead, neither marry, nor are given in marriage: for neither can they die any more: for they are equal unto the angels; and are sons of God, being sons of the resurrection." It will be observed how Jesus plays with the word around which the Sadducean mind revolves. To them marriage was a key-word which locked up the gates of an after-life, and threw back the resurrection among the impossibilities and absurdities. But Jesus takes up their key-word, and turning it round and round in His speech, He makes it unlock and open the inner soul of these men, showing how, in spite of their intellectuality, the drift of their thoughts was but low and sensual. At the same time Jesus shows that their test-word is altogether mundane. It is made for earth alone; for having a nature of flesh and blood, it cannot enter into the higher kingdom of glory. Marriage has its place in the life whose termini are birth and death. It exists mainly for the perpetuation and increase of the human race. It has thus to do with the lower nature of man, the physical, the earthly; but in the world to come birth, marriage, death will be outdated, obsolete terms. Man then will be "equal unto the angels," the coarser nature which fitted him for earth being shaken off and left behind, amongst other mortalities.

And exactly the same truth is taught by the three posthumous appearances recorded in this Gospel. When they appeared upon the Mount of Transfiguration, Moses and Elias had been residents of the other world, the one for nine, the other for fourteen centuries. But while possessing the form, and perhaps the features of the old body of earth, the glorious body they wear now is under conditions and laws altogether different. How easy and aërial are its movements! Though it possesses no wings, it has the lightness and buoyancy of a bird, moving through space swiftly and silently as the light pulses through the ether. Or take the body of Christ's resurrection life. It has not yet become the glorified body of the heavenly life; it is in its transition state, between the two; yet how changed it is! Lifted above the needs and laws of our earth-bound nature, the risen Christ no longer lives among His own; He dwells apart, where we cannot tell. When He does appear He comes in upon them suddenly, giving no warning of His approach; and then, after the bright though brief apocalypse, He vanishes as mysteriously as He came, passing at the last on the clouds to heaven. There is thus some correspondence between the body of the old and that of the new life, though how far the resemblance extends we cannot tell; we can only fall back upon the Apostle's words, which to our human ear sound like a paradox, but which give us our only solution of the enigma, "It is raised a spiritual body" (i Cor. xv. 44). It is no longer the "natural body," but a supernatural one, with a spiritual instead of a material form, and under spiritual laws.

But taking the Apostle's words as our base-line, and measuring from them, we may throw our lines of sight across the hereafter, reading at least as much as this, that whatever may be the pleasures or the pains of the after-life, they will be of a spiritual, and not of a physical kind. It is just here that our vision sometimes gets blurred and indistinct, as all the descriptions of that after-life, even in Scripture, are given in earthly figures. And so we have built up before us a material heaven, with jasper walls, and gates of pearl, and gardens of perennial fruits, with crowns and other palace delights. But it is evident that these are but the earthly shadows of the heavenly realities, the darkened glasses of our earthly speech, which help our dull vision to gaze upon glories which the eye of our mortality hath not seen, and which its heart cannot conceive, except dimly, as a few "broken lights" pass through the dark lenses of these earthly figures. What new senses may be created we do not know, but if the body of the after-life is "a spiritual body," then its whole environment must be changed. Material substances can no longer affect it, either to cause pleasure or pain; and though we may not yet tell in what the delights of the one state, or the pains of the other will consist, we do know that they must be something other than literal palms and crowns, and other than material fires. These figures are but the stammerings of our earthly speech, as it tries to tell the unutterable.

3. Our Gospel teaches that character determines destiny. "A man's life," said Jesus, when rebuking covetousness (xii. 15), "consisteth not in the abundance of the things which he possesseth." These are not life's noblest aim, nor its truest wealth. They are but the accidents of life, the particles of floating dust, caught up by the stream; they will be left behind soon as the sediment, if not before, when they reach the barrier of the grave. A man's possessions do not constitute the true life; they do not make the real self, the man. Here it is not what a man has, but what a man is. And a man is just what his heart makes him. The outer life is but the blossoming of the inner soul,

and what we call character, in its objective meaning, is but the subtle and silent influence, the odour, as we might call it, fragrant or otherwise, which the soul unconsciously throws out. And even in this world character is more than circumstance, for it gives aim and direction to the whole life. Men do not always reach their goal in earthly things, but in the moral world each man goes to his "own place," the place he himself has chosen and sought; he is the arbiter of his own destiny.

And what we find to be a law of earth is the law of the kingdom of heaven, as Jesus was constantly affirming. The future life would simply be the present life, with eternity as its coefficient. Destiny itself would be but the harvest of earthly deeds, the hereafter being only the after-here. Jesus shows us how while on earth we may lay up "treasures in the heavens," making for ourselves "purses which wax not old," and thus becoming "rich toward God." He draws a vivid picture of "a certain rich man," whose one estimate of life was "the abundance of the things which he possessed," the size and affluence of his barns, and whose soul was required of him just when he was congratulating it on the years of guaranteed plenty, bidding it, "Take thine ease, eat, drink, and be merry (xii. 16-12)." He does not here trace for us the destiny of such a soul--He does this in another parable--but He pictures it as suddenly torn away, and eternally separated, from all it had possessed before, leaving it, perhaps, to be squandered thriftlessly, or consumed by the fires of lust; while, starved and shrivelled, the pauper soul is driven out from its earthly stewardship, to find, alas! no welcome in the "eternal tabernacles." In the appraisement of this world such a man would be deemed wise and happy, but to Heaven he is the "foolish one," committing the great, the eternal folly.

The same lesson is taught in the parables of the Housebuilders (vi. 47) and of the Talents (xix. 12). In each there comes the inevitable test, the down-rush of the flood and the reckoning of the lord, a test which leaves the obedient secure and happy, the faithful promoted to honour and rewards, passed up among the kings; but the disobedient, if not entombed in the ruins of their false hopes, yet all shelterless from the pitiless storm, and the unfaithful and slothful servant stripped of even the little he had, passed downwards into dishonour and shame.

In another parable, that of the Rich Man and Lazarus (xvi. 19-31) we have a light thrown upon our subject which is at once vivid and lurid. In a few graphic words He draws for us the picture of strange contrasts. The one is rich, dwelling in a palatial residence, whose imposing gateway looked down upon the vulgar crowd; clothed in garments of Tyrian purple and of Egyptian byssus, which only great wealth could purchase, and faring sumptuously every day. So, with perpetual banquets, the rich man lived his selfish, sensual life. With thought all centred upon himself, and that his lowest self, he has no thoughts or sympathies to spare for the outlying world. They do not even travel so far as to the poor beggar who is cast daily at his gate, in hopes that some of the shaken-out crumbs of the banquet may fall within his reach. Such is the contrast--the extreme of wealth, and the extreme of poverty; the one with troops of friends, the other friendless--for the verb shows that the hands which laid him down by the rich man's gate were not the gentle hands of affection, but the rough hands of duty or of a cold charity; the one clothed in splendid attire, the other not possessing enough even to cover his sores; the one gorged to repletion, the other shrunken and starved; the one the anonymous Epicurean, the other possessing a name indeed, but nought beside, but a name that had a Divinity hidden within it,[6] and which was an index to the soul that bore it. Such were the two characters Jesus portrayed; and then, lifting up the veil of shadows, He shows how the marked contrast reappears in the after-life, but with a strange inverting. Now the poor man is blessed, the rich in distress; the one is enfolded in Abraham's bosom, the other enveloped in flames; the one has all the delights of Paradise, the other begs for just a drop of water with which to cool the parched tongue.

It may be said that this is simply parable, set forth in language which must not be taken literally. So it is; but the parables of Jesus were not mere word-pictures; they field in solution essential truth. And when we have eliminated all this figurative colouring there is still left this residuary, elementary truth, that character determines destiny: that we cast into our future the shadow of our present selves; that the good will be blessed, and the evil unblessed, which means accursed; and that heaven and hell are tremendous realities, whose pleasures and whose pains lie alike deep beyond the sounding of our weak speech. When the rich man forgot his duties to humanity; when he banished God from his mansion, and proscribed mercy from his thoughts; when he left Heaven's foundling to the dogs, he was writing out his book of doom, passing sentence upon himself. The tree lies as it falls, and it falls as it leans; and where is there place for the unforgiven, the unregenerate, for the sensual and the selfish, the unjust and the unclean, but somewhere in the outer darkness they themselves have helped to make? To the sensual and the vile heaven itself would be a hell, its very joys curdling into pain, its streets, thronged with the multitudes of the redeemed, offering to the guilty and unrenewed soul but a solitude of silence and anguish; and even were there no final judgment, no solemn pronouncement of destiny, the evil could never blend with the good, the pure with the vile; they would gravitate, even as they do now, in opposite directions,

*The Expositor's Bible: The Gospel According to St. Luke*

each seeking its "own place." Wherever and whatever our final heaven may be, no one is an outcast but who casts himself out, a self-immolation, a suicide.

But is it destiny? it may be asked. May there not be an after-probation, so that character itself may be transformed? may not the "great gulf" itself disappear, or at last be bridged over, so that the repentant may pass out of its penal but purifying fires? Such, indeed, is the belief, or rather the hope, of some; but "the larger hope" as they are pleased to call it, as far as this Gospel is concerned, is a beautiful but illusive dream. He who was Himself the "Resurrection and the Life," and who holds in His own hands the keys of death and of Hades, gives no hint of such a posthumous palingenesis. He speaks again and again of a day of test and scrutiny, when actions will be weighed and characters assayed, and when men will be judged according to their works. Now it is at the "coming" of the Son of man, in the glory of His Father, and with a retinue of "holy angels;" now it is the returning of the lord, and the reckoning with his servants; while again it is at the end of the world, as the angel-reapers separate the wheat from the tares; or as He Himself, the great Judge, with His "Come ye," passes on the faithful to the heavenly kingdom, and at the same time, with His "Depart ye," drives from His presence the unfaithful and unforgiven into the outer darkness. Nor does Jesus say one word to suggest that the judgment is not final. The blasphemy against the Holy Ghost, whatever that may mean, shall not be forgiven (xii. 10), or, as St. Matthew expresses it, "neither in this world, nor in that which is to come." The unfaithful servant is "cut asunder" (xii. 46); the enemies who would not have their Lord to reign over them are slain (xix. 27); and when once the door is shut it is all in vain that those outside cry, "Lord, open to us!" They had an open door, but they slighted and scorned it, and now they must abide by their choice, outside the door, outside the kingdom, with the "workers of iniquity," where "there is weeping and gnashing of teeth" (xiii. 28).

Or if we turn again to the parable of the Rich Man, where is there room for the "larger hope"? where is the suggestion that these "pains of hell" may be lessened; and ultimately escaped altogether? We listen in vain for one syllable of hope. In vain he makes his appeal to "father Abraham;" in vain he entreats the good offices of Lazarus; in vain he asks for a momentary alleviation of his pain, in the boon of one drop of water: between him and help, yea, between him and hope, is a "great gulf fixed, ... that none may cross" (xvi. 26).

"That none may cross." Such are the words of Jesus, though here put in the mouth of Abraham; and if finality is not here, where can we find it? What may be the judgment passed upon those who, though erring, are ignorant, we cannot tell, though Jesus plainly indicates that the number of the stripes will vary, as they knew, or they did not know, the Lord's will; but for those who had the light, and turned from it, who saw the right, but did it not, who heard the Gospel of love, with its great salvation, and only rejected it--for these there is only an "outer darkness" of eternal hopelessness. And what is the outer darkness itself but the darkness of their own inner blindness, a blindness which was wilful and persistent?

Our Gospel thus teaches that death does not alter character, that character makes destiny, and that destiny once determined is unalterable and eternal. Or, to put it in the words of the angel to the seer, "He that is unrighteous, let him do unrighteousness still: and he that is filthy, let him be made filthy still: and he that is righteous, let him do righteousness still: and he that is holy, let him be made holy still" (Rev. xxii. 11).

## *Footnotes:*

6. The name "Lazarus" is derived from El-ezer, or "God helps."

*Henry Burton*

## CHAPTER XXIV - THE WATCH IN GETHSEMANE

Hitherto the life of Jesus has been comparatively free from sorrow and from pain. With the exception of the narrow strip of wilderness which fell between the Baptism and His inaugural miracle, the Divine Life has lain for the most part in the sunshine, above the fret and fever of anxious thought and care. True, He had enemies, whose hatred was persistent and virulent; the shafts of calumny fell around Him in one steady rain; His motives were constantly misconstrued, His words misunderstood; but with all this His life was peace. How could He have spoken of "rest" of soul, and have promised it to the weary and heavy-laden, if He Himself were a stranger to its experience? How could He have awoke such songs and shouts of gladness, or have strewn the lives of men with such unusual brightness, without having that brightness and music coming back in reflections and echoes within His own heart--that heart which was the fontal source of their new-found joys? And if many doubted, or even hated Him, there were many who admired and feared, and not a few who loved and adored Him, and who were glad to place at His disposal their entire substance, nay, their entire selves. But if His anointing thus far has been the anointing of gladness, there is a baptism of sorrow and anguish prepared for Him, and to that ordeal He now proceeds, first girding up His soul with the music of a thanksgiving psalm. Let us, too, arise and follow Him; but taking off our shoes, let us step softly and reverently into the mystery of the Divine sorrow; for though we must ever stand back from that mystery more than a "stone's cast," perhaps, if we keep mind and heart awake and alert, we may read something of its deep meaning.

The whole scene of Gethsemane is unique. Like the Mount of Transfiguration, the Garden of the Agony stands "apart" from all other paths, in a profound isolation. And in more senses than this these two august scenes are related and coincident. Indeed, we cannot fully understand the mystery of the Garden but as we allow the mystery of the Mount to explain it, in part at least, so threading the light of the one into the darkness of the other. On the Mount of Transfiguration the Divine Life, as we have seen, reached its culminating point, its perihelion as we may call it, where it touched the very heavens for one brief night, passing through its out-streaming glories and crossing the paths of celestials. In Gethsemane we have the antipodal fact; we see the Divine Life in its far aphelion, where it touches hell itself, moving round in an awful gloom, and crossing the paths of the "powers of darkness." And so our best outlook into Gethsemane is not from the Mount of Olives--though the two names are related, as the two places are adjacent, Gethsemane lying at the foot of Olivet--but from that more distant Mount of Transfiguration.

Leaving the "guest-chamber," where a Passover of a new order has been instituted, and the cup, with its fruit of the vine, has received a higher consecration, Jesus leads the broken band down the stairs, which still vibrate with the heavy tread of the traitor, and in the still, full moonlight they pass out of the city, the gates being open because of the Passover. Descending the steep ravine, and crossing the brook Kedron, they enter the enclosure of Gethsemane. Both St. Luke and St. John tell us that He was accustomed to resort thither--for, strangely enough, we do not read of Jesus spending so much as one night within the city walls--and so probably the garden belonged to one of His adherents, possibly to St. Mark. Bidding the eight remain near the entrance, and exhorting them to pray that they enter not into, or, as it means here, that they "yield not to," the temptation which is shortly to come upon them, Jesus takes Peter, James, and John farther into the garden. They were witnesses of His Transfiguration, when His face shone like the sun, and the spirits of the perfected came to do Him homage; they must now see a transfiguration of sorrow, as that face is furrowed by the sharp lines of pain, and half-masked by a veil of blood. From the narratives of St. Matthew and St. Mark it would appear as if Jesus now experienced a sudden change of feeling. In the guest-chamber He was calmly confident; and though we may detect in His words and symbolic acts a certain undertone of sadness, the salutation of one "about to die," yet there was no tremor, no fear. He spoke of His own death, which now was near at hand, as calmly as if the Mount of Sacrifice were but another mountain of spices; while to His disciples He spoke words of cheer and hope, putting around their hearts a soothing, healing balm, even before the dreadful wound is made. But now all this is changed: "He began to be greatly amazed and sore troubled" (St. Mark xiv. 33). The word we here render "amazed," as St. Mark uses it, has sometimes the element of fear within it, as when the women were "amazed," or "affrighted," by the vision of the angels (xvi. 5); and such, we are inclined to think, is its meaning here. It was not so much wonder as it was trepidation, and a certain dread, which now fell of a sudden upon the Master. Over that pure soul, which ever lay calm and serene as the bright heaven which stooped to embrace it, has broken a storm of conflicting winds, and dense, murky clouds, and all is disquiet and distress, where before was nothing but peace. "My soul is exceeding sorrowful, even unto death;" such is the strange confession of tremulous lips, as for once He opens the infinite depths of His heart, and shows the mortal grief which has suddenly fallen there. It is the first contact of the eclipse, as between Himself and the Father's smile another world is passing, the world of the "outer darkness," even hell, throwing down upon His soul a chilling, awful shadow.

Jesus understands its meaning. It is the signal for the final battle, the shadow of the "prince of this world," who, rallying all his forces, cometh to find "nothing in Me." Jesus accepts the challenge, and that He may meet the enemy single-handed, with no earthly supports, He bids the three, "Abide ye here, and watch with Me." "With Me," and not "for Me;" for what could avail to Him the vigilance of human eyes amid this felt darkness of the soul? It was not for Himself He bade them "watch," but for themselves, that waking and praying they might gain a strength which would be proof against temptation, the test which would be keenly severe, and which now was close at hand.

"And He was parted from them about a stone's cast." The verb implies a measure of constraint, as if, in the conflict of emotion, the longing for some human presence and human sympathy held Him back. And why not? Is not the very presence of a friend a solace in grief, even if no words are spoken? and does not the "aloneness" of a sorrow make the sorrow tenfold more bitter? Not like the "stricken deer that left the herd," the human heart, when wounded or sore pressed, yearns for sympathy, finding in the silent look or in the touch of a hand a grateful anodyne. But this wine-press He must tread alone, and of the people there must be none with Him; and so the three who are most favoured and most beloved are left back at a stone's cast from the physical suffering of Christ, while from His heart-agony they must stand back at an infinite distance.

It was while Jesus was praying upon the holy mount that the heavens were opened unto Him; and now, as another cloud envelopes Him, not of glory, but of a thick darkness, it finds Him in the same attitude of prayer. He at whose feet sinful man had knelt, all unrebuked, Himself now kneels, as He sends to heaven the earnest and almost bitter cry, "O My Father, if it be possible, let this cup pass from Me!" The three Evangelists differ in their wording of the Saviour's petition, showing that the spirit is more than the letter of prayer; that Heaven thinks more of the inner thought than of the outward drapery of words; but the thought of the three is identical, while all make prominent the central figure of the "cup."

The cups of Scripture are of divers patterns and of varied meanings. There was the cup of blessing, like that of the Psalmist (Psalm xxiii. 5), filled to the brim and running over with mercy. There was the "cup of salvation," that sacrament of the Old Testament which kept in memory one deliverance, that of Israel, while it prophesied of another, the "great salvation" which was to come. What, then, was the cup Jesus so feared to drink, and which He asked, so earnestly and repeatedly, that it might pass from Him? Was it the fear of death? Certainly not; for how could He be afraid of death, who had so triumphed over it, and who had proclaimed Himself the Resurrection and the Life? How could He fear death, when He knew so well "the seraph face that smiled beneath the frowning mask," and knew that it would end for ever all His sufferings and His pain? Death to Him was a familiar thought. He spoke of it freely, not either with the hard indifference of the Stoic, or with the palsied speech of one whose lips shake with an inward fear, but in calm, sweet accents, as any child of earth might speak of going home. Was this "cup," then, the death itself? and when He asked that it might pass away, was He suggesting that possibly some mode of atonement might be found other than the cross? We think not. Jesus knew full well that His earthly life would have, and could have, but one issue. Death would be its goal, as it was its object. Whether, as Holman Hunt represents, the cross threw its shadow back as far as the shop at Nazareth, we do not know, for the record is silent. But we do know that the shadow of death lay across the whole of His public life, for we find it appearing in His words. The cross was a dark and vivid certainty that He wished neither to forget nor to evade, for must not the Son of man be "lifted up," that He may draw all men to Himself? Must not the corn of wheat be hidden in its grave before it can become fruitful, throwing itself forward down the years in hundredfold multiplications? Yes; death to Jesus is the inevitable, and long before the Roman soldiers have pieced together the transverse beams Jesus had made His cross, fashioning it in His thought, and hiding it in His words. Nay, He has this very night instituted a new sacrament, in which, for all generations, the broken bread shall be the emblem of His bruised and broken body, and the wine, of His blood, the blood of the New Testament, which is shed for man. And does Jesus now seek, by reiterated prayers, to shift that cross from the Divine purpose, substituting in its place something less painful, less cruel? does He seek now to annul His own predictions, and to make His own sacrament void and meaningless? This cannot be; and so, whatever the "cup" may mean, we cannot take it as a synonym for His death.

What, then, is its meaning? The Psalmist had long before sung--

*"For in the hand of the Lord there is a cup, and the wine foameth;*
*It is full of mixture, and He poureth out of the same:*
*Surely the dregs thereof, all the wicked of the earth shall wring them out, and drink them"*
(Psalm lxxv. 8);

while St. John, speaking of the last woes (Rev. xiv. 10), tells how they who have the mark of the beast upon their foreheads "shall drink of the wine of the wrath of God, which is prepared unmixed in the cup of His anger." Here, then, is the "cup" which now is set before the Son of man, the very touch of which fills His soul with unutterable dread. It is the cup of God's anger, filled to the brim with its strange red wine, the wine of His wrath. Jesus comes to earth as the Representative Man, the Second Adam, in whom all shall be made alive. He voluntarily assumes the place of the transgressor, as St. Paul writes (2 Cor. v. 21), "Him who knew no sin He made to be sin on our behalf; that we might become the righteousness of God in Him," a passage which corresponds exactly with the prophetic idea of substitution, as given by Isaiah (liii. 5), "He was wounded for our transgressions, He was bruised for our iniquities: the chastisement of our peace was upon Him; and with His stripes we are healed." And so "the iniquity of us all" was laid on Him, the Holy One. In His own Person He must feel, in its concentrated forms, the smart and consequence of sin; and as His physical sufferings are the extremest pain even sin can produce, so Jesus must suffer, too, all the mental anguish, the agony of a soul bereft of God. And as Jesus, on the Transfiguration mount, passed up to the very gate of heaven, so lighting up with splendour and glory the lost path of unfallen man, so now, in the Garden, Jesus tracks the path of fallen man, right on to its fearful consummation, which is the "outer darkness" of hell itself. This vivid consciousness has been graciously withheld from Him hitherto; for the terrible pressure would simply have unfitted Him for His ministry of blessing; for how could He have been the "kindly Light," leading humanity homeward, heavenward, if that Light Himself were hidden in "encircling gloom," and lost in a felt darkness? But ere His mission is complete this is an experience that He must know. Identifying Himself with sin, He must feel its very farthest consequence, the awful solitude, and the unutterable anguish, of a soul now bereft of hope and forsaken of God. In the heathen fable Orpheus goes down, lyre in hand, to the Plutonic realm, to bring back again to life and love the lost Eurydice; but Jesus, in His vicarious sufferings, goes down to hell itself, that He may win back from their sins, and bear in triumph to the upper heavens, a lost humanity.

Rising from the ground, and going back to His three disciples, He finds them asleep. The Synoptists all seek to explain, and to apologize for, their unnatural slumber, St. Matthew and St. Mark telling us that their "eyes were heavy," while St. Luke states that their sleep was the result of their grief; for, happily, in the wonderful compensations of nature, intense grief does tend to induce somnolence. But while the Evangelists refer their slumber to natural causes, might there not be something more in it, some supernatural element? Sleep can be caused by natural means, and yet be an unnatural sleep, as when narcotics benumb the senses, or some mesmeric spell muffles the speech, and makes the soul for a time unconscious. And might it not have been some invisible touch which made their eyes so heavy? for it is an exact repetition of their attitude when on the holy mount, and in that sleep sorrow certainly had no part. When St. John saw the vision upon Patmos, he "fell at His feet as one dead;" and when Saul beheld the light, near Damascus, he fell to the ground. And how often we find the celestial vision connected with a trance-like state! and why may not the "trance" be an effect of the vision, just as well as its cause, or rather its circumstance? At any rate, the fact is plain, that supernatural visions tend to lock up the natural senses, the veil which is uplifted before the unseen world being wrapped around the eyes and the soul of the seer. And this, we are inclined to think, was a possible, partial cause for the slumber upon the mount and in the garden, a sleep which, under the circumstances, was strangely unnatural and almost unpardonable.

Addressing Himself directly to Peter, who had promised to follow His Lord unto death, but whose heart now strangely lagged behind, and calling him by his earlier name--for Jesus only once made use of the name He Himself had chosen; the "Rock" was at present in a state of flux, and had not yet settled down to its petrine character--He said, "What, Simon, could ye not watch with Me one hour? Watch and pray, that ye enter not into temptation." Then, for a moment forgetting His own sorrow, and putting Himself in their place, He makes the apology for them which their lips are afraid to utter: "The spirit indeed is willing, but the flesh is weak;" so compassionate is He over human weakness and infirmity, even while He is severity itself towards falsity and sin.

St. Luke records the narrative only in a condensed form, giving us the salient points, but not entering so fully into detail. It is from St. Matthew and St. Mark that we learn how Jesus went back a second time, and falling prostrate on the ground, prayed still in the self-same words, and how He returned to His disciples to find them again asleep; even the reproof of the Master has not been able to counterbalance the pressure of the supernatural heaviness. No word is spoken this time--at any rate the Evangelists have not repeated them for us--but how eloquent would be that look of disappointment and of grief! and how that rebuke would fall burning hot upon their heart, focussed in the lenses of His sad and tearful eyes! But the three are dazed, bewildered, and for once the ready tongue of Peter is speechless; "they wist not what to answer Him" (Mark xiv. 40).

Not yet, however, is the conflict ended. Three times did the tempter come to Him in the wilderness, and three times is the fierce battle to be waged in the garden, the last the sorest. It would almost seem as if the three assaults were descending steps of sorrow, each marking some lower deep in the dark mystery; for now the death-sorrow becomes an "agony" of spirit, a pressure from within so fearful as to arrest the flow of blood, forcing it through the opened pores in an awful sweat, until great drops, or "clots," of blood gathered upon His face, and then fell to the ground. Could there be possibly, even for the lost, an anguish more intense? and was not Jesus then, as man's Surety, wringing out and drinking the very last dregs of that cup of His anger which "the wicked of the earth," if unredeemed, had been doomed to drink? Verily He was, and the bloody sweat was a part, an earnest, of our atonement, sprinkling with its redemptive virtues the very ground which was "cursed" for man's sake (Gen. iii. 17). It was the pledge and the foregathered fruit of a death already virtually accomplished, in the absolute surrender of the Divine Son as man's sacrifice.

And so the thrice-uttered prayer of Jesus, even though He prayed the "more earnestly," was not granted. It was heard, and it was answered, but not in the specific way of the request. Like Paul's prayer for the removal of the thorn, and which, though not granted, was yet answered in the promise of the "sufficient" grace, so now the thrice-uttered prayer of Jesus does not remove the cup. It is there, and it is there for Him to drink, as He tastes for man both of the earthly death and of the bitterness of the after, the second death. But the answer came in the strengthening of His soul, and in the heavenly greetings the angel brought down to Him when the conflict was over. But in this reiterated prayer for the removal of the cup there was no conflict between Himself and the Father. The request itself was enveloped in submission, the contingent "if" which preceded it, and the "not My win, but Thine," which followed, completely enclosing it. The will of Jesus was ever adjusted to the will of the Father, working within it in an absolute precision, with no momentary breaks. But here the "if" implies uncertainty, doubt. Even Jesus is not quite sure as to what, in the special case, the Father's will may involve, and so, while He asks for the removal of the cup, this is the smaller request, inlaid within the larger, deeper prayer, that "not My will, but Thine, be done." Jesus did not seek to bend the Father's will, and make it conform to His desires, but He sought, whatever might be the cost, to configure His desires to that all-wise and all-loving Will.

So in our smaller lives there may be hours of distress and uncertainty. We may see, mingled for us, cups of sorrow, loss, or pain, which we fear to drink, and the shrinking flesh may seek to be exempted from the ordeal; but let us not too hastily ask that they may be put away, for fear we may dismiss some cup of blessing from our life. Let us seek rather for a perfect submission to the will of God, conforming all our desires and all our prayers to that will. So in that "perfect acquiescence" there will be for us a "perfect rest." Gethsemane itself will become bright and all musical with songs, and where the powers of darkness mocked us Heaven's angels will come, with their sweet ministry. Nay, the cup of sorrow and of pain, at which we trembled before, if we see how God's will has wrought and filled it, and we embrace that will, the cup of sorrow will be a transfigured cup, a golden chalice of the King, all filled to the brim, and running over, with the new wine of the kingdom.

## CHAPTER XXV – THE PASSION

*Luke xxii. 47-xxiii.*

While Jesus kept His sad watch in Gethsemane, treading the winepress alone, His enemies kept theirs in the city. The step of Judas, as he passed out into the night, went verberating within the house of the high priest, and onwards into the palace of Pilate himself, awaking a thousand echoes, as swift messengers flew hither and thither, bearing the hurried summons, calling the rulers and elders from their repose, and marshalling the Roman cohort. Hitherto the powers of darkness have been restrained, and though they have, again and again, attempted the life of Jesus, as if some occult spell were upon them, they could not accomplish their purpose. Far back in the Infancy Herod had sought to kill Him; but though his cold steel reaped a bloody swath in Ramah, it could not touch the Divine Child. The men of Nazareth had sought to hurl Him down the sheer precipice, but He escaped; Jesus had not come into the world to die at Nazareth, thrown off, as by an accident, from a Galilean cliff. He had come to "accomplish His decease," as the celestials put it upon the mount, "at Jerusalem," and that too, as He indicated plainly and frequently in His speech, upon a cross. Now, however, the hour of darkness has struck, and the fulness of the time has come. The cross and the Victim both are ready, and Heaven itself consents to the great sacrifice.

Strangely enough, the first overture of the "Passion music" is by one of the twelve--as our Evangelist names him, "Judas who was called Iscariot, being of the number of the twelve" (xxii. 3). It will be observed that St. Luke puts a parenthesis of forty verses between the actual betrayal and its preliminary stages, so throwing the conception of the plot back to an earlier date than the eve of the Last Supper, and the subsequent narrative is best read in the light of its programme. At first sight it would appear as if the part of the betrayer were superfluous, seeing that Jesus came almost daily into the Temple, where He spoke openly, without either reserve or fear. What need could there be for any intermediary to come between the chief priests and the Victim of their hate? Was not His person familiar to all the Temple officials? and could they not apprehend Him almost at any hour? Yes, but one thing stood in the way, and that was "the fear of the people." Jesus evidently had an influential following; the popular sympathies were on His side; and had the attack been made upon Him during the day, in the thronged streets of the city or in the Temple courts, there would have been, almost to a certainty, a popular rising on His behalf. The arrest must be made in the absence of the multitude (xxii. 6), which means that they must fall upon Him in one of His quiet hours, and in one of His quiet retreats; it must be a night attack, when the multitudes are asleep. Here, then, is room for the betrayer, who comes at the opportune moment, and offers himself for the despicable task, a task which has made the name of "Judas" a synonym for all that is treacherous and vile. How the base thought could ever have come into the mind of Judas it were hard to tell, but it certainly was not sprung upon him as a surprise. But men lean in the direction of their weakness, and when they fall it is generally on their weakest side, the side on which temptation is the strongest. It was so here. St. John writes him down in a single sentence: "He was a thief, and having the bag, took away what was put therein" (John xii. 6). His ruling passion was the love of money, and in the delirium of this fever his hot hands dashed to the ground and broke in pieces the tables of law and equity alike, striking at all the moralities. And between robbing his Master and betraying Him there was no great distance to traverse, especially when conscience lay in a numb stupor, drugged by opiates, these tinctures of silver.

Here, then, is a betrayer ready to their hand. He knows what hour is best, and how to conduct them to His secret retreats. And so Judas communed with the chief priests and captains, or he "talked it over with them" as the word means, the secret conference ending in a bargain, as they "covenanted" to give him money (xxii. 5). It was a hard and fast bargain; for the word "covenanted" has about it a metallic ring, and opening it out, it lets us see the wordy chaffering, as Judas abates his price to the offer of the high priests, the thirty pieces of silver, which was the market price of an ordinary slave. Not that Judas intended to be a participator in His death, as the sequel of his remorse shows. He probably thought and hoped that his Master would escape, slipping through the meshes they so cunningly had thrown about Him; but having done his part of the covenant, his reward would be sure, for the thirty pieces were already in his possession. Ah, he little dreamed how far-reaching his action would be! That silver key of his would set in motion the ponderous wheel which would not stop until his Master was its Victim, lying all crushed and bleeding beneath it! He only discovered his mistake when, alas! it was too late for remedy. Gladly would he have given back his thirty pieces, ay, and thirty times thirty, to have called back his treacherous "Hail," but he could not. That "Hail, Master," had gone beyond his recall, reverberating down the ages and up among the stars, while even its echoes, as they came back to him in painful memories, threw him out of the world an unloved and guilty suicide!

What with the cunning of the high priests and the cold calculations of Judas, whose mind was practised in weighing chances and providing for contingences, the plot is laid deeply and well. No detail is omitted: the band of soldiers, who shall put the stamp of officialism upon the procedure, while at the same time they cower the populace and repress any attempt at rescue; the swords and staves, should they have to resort to force; the lanterns and torches, with which to light up the dark hiding-places of the garden; the cords or chains, with which to bind their Prisoner; the kiss, which should be at once the sign of recognition and the signal for the arrest, all are prearranged and provided; while out of sight the high priests are keeping their midnight watch, ready for the mock trial, for which the suborned witnesses are even now rehearsing their parts. Could worldly prudence or malicious skill go farther?

Stealthily as the leopard approaches its victim, the motley crowd enter the garden, coming with muffled steps to take and lead away the Lamb of God. Only the glimmer of their torches gave notice of their approach, and even these burned dull in the intense moonlight. But Jesus needed no audible or visible warning, for He Himself knew just how events were drifting, reading the near future as plainly as the near past; and before they have come in sight He has awoke the three sleeping sentinels with a word which will effectually drive slumber from their eyelids: "Arise, let us be going: behold, he is at hand that betrayeth Me" (Matt. xxvi. 46).

It will be seen from this that Jesus could easily have eluded His pursuers had He cared to do so. Even without any appeal to His supernatural powers, He could have withdrawn Himself under cover of the night, and have left the human sleuth-hounds foiled of their prey and vainly baying at the moon. But instead of this, He makes no attempt at flight. He even seeks the glades of Gethsemane, when by simply going elsewhere He might have disconcerted their plot and brought their counsel to nought. And now He yields Himself up to His death, not passively merely, but with the entire and active concurrence of His will. He "offered Himself," as the writer of the Epistle to the Hebrews expresses it (Heb. ix. 14), a free-will Offering, a voluntary Sacrifice. He could, as He Himself said, have called legions of angels to His help; but He would not give the signal, though it were no more than one uplifted look. And so He does not refuse even the kiss of treachery; He suffers the hot lips of the traitor to burn His cheeks; and when others would have shaken off the viper into the fire, or have crushed it with the heel of a righteous indignation, Jesus receives patiently the stamp of infamy, His only word being a question of surprise, not at the treachery itself, but at its mode: "Betrayest thou the Son of man with a kiss?" And when for the moment, as St. John tells us, a strange awe fell upon the multitude, and they "went backward and fell to the ground," Jesus, as it were, called in the outshining glories, masking them with the tired and blood-stained humanity that He wore, so stilling the tremor that was upon His enemies, as He nerved the very hands that should take Him. And again, when they do bind Him, He offers no resistance; but when Peter's quick sword flashes from its scabbard, and takes off the right ear of Malchus, the servant of the high priest, and so one of the leaders in the arrest, Jesus asks for the use of His manacled hand-- for so we read the "Suffer ye thus far"--and touching the ear, heals it at once. He Himself is willing to be wounded even unto death, but His alone must be the wounds. His enemies must not share His pain, nor must His disciples pass with Him into this temple of His sufferings; and He even stays to ask for them a free parole: "Let these go their way."

But while for the disciples Jesus has but words of tender rebuke or of prayer, while for Malchus He has a word and a touch of mercy, and while even for Judas He has an endearing epithet, "friend," for the chief priests, captains, and elders He has severer words. They are the ringleaders, the plotters. All this commotion, this needless parade of hostile strength, these superfluous insults are but the foaming of their rabid frenzy, the blossoming of their malicious hate; and turning to them as they stand gloating in their supercilious scorn, He asks, "Are ye come out, as against a robber, with swords and staves? When I was daily with you in the Temple, ye stretched not forth your hands against Me: but this is your hour, and the power of darkness." True words, for they who should have been priests of Heaven are in league with hell, willing ministers of the powers of darkness. And this was indeed their hour, but the hour of their victory would prove the hour of their doom.

St. Luke, as do the other Synoptists, omits the preliminary trial before Annas, the ex-high priest (John xviii. 13), and leads us direct to the palace of Caiaphas, whither they conduct Jesus bound. Instead, however, of pursuing the main narrative, he lingers to gather up the side-lights of the palace-yard, as they cast a lurid light upon the character of Simon. Some time before, Jesus had forewarned him of a coming ordeal, and which He called a Satanic sifting; while only a few hours ago He had prophesied that this night, before the cock should crow twice, Peter would thrice deny Him--a singular prediction, and one which at the time seemed most unlikely, but which proved true to the very letter. After the encounter in the garden, Peter retires from our sight for awhile; but his flight was neither far nor long, for as the procession moves up towards the city Peter and John follow it as a rear-guard, on to the house of Annas, and now to the house of Caiaphas. We need not repeat the details of the story--how John passed him through the door into the inner court, and how he sat, or "stood," as St. John puts it, by the charcoal fire, warming himself with the officers and servants. The differing verbs only show the restlessness of the man, which was a life-long characteristic of Peter, but which would be doubly accentuated here, with suspecting eyes focussed upon him. Indeed, in the whole scene of the courtyard, as sketched for us in the varying but not discordant narratives of the Evangelists, we may detect the vibrations of constant movement and the ripple-marks of intense excitement.

When challenged the first time, by the maid who kept the door, Peter answered with a sharp, blunt negative: he was not a disciple; he did not even know Him. At the second challenge, by another maid, he replied with an absolute denial, but added to his denial the confirmation of an oath. At the third challenge, by one of the men standing near, he denied as before, but added to his denial both an oath and an anathema. It is rather unfortunate that our version renders it (Matt. xxvi. 74; Mark xiv. 71), "He began to curse and to swear;" for these words have a peculiarly ill savour, a taste of Billingsgate, which the original words have not. To our ear, "to curse and to swear" are the accomplishments of a loose and a foul tongue, which throws out its fires of passion in profanity, or in coarse obscenities, as it revels in immoralities of speech. The words in the New Testament, however, have a meaning altogether different. Here "to swear" means to take an oath, as in our courts of law, or rather to make an affirmation. Even God Himself is spoken of as swearing, as in the song of Zacharias (i. 73), where He is said to have remembered His holy covenant, "the oath which He sware unto Abraham our father." Indeed, this form of speech, the oath or affirmation, had come into too general use, as we may see from the paragraph upon oaths in the Sermon on the Mount (Matt. v. 33-37). Jesus here condemned it, it is true, for to Him who was Truth itself our word should be as our bond; but His reference to it shows how prevalent the custom was, even amongst strict legalists and moralists. When, then, Peter "swore," it does not mean that he suddenly became profane, but simply that he backed up his denial with a solemn affirmation. So, too, with the word "curse;" it has not our modern meaning. Literally rendered, it would be, "He put himself under an anathema," which "anathema" was the bond or penalty he was willing to pay if his words should not be true. In Acts xxiii. 12 we have the cognate word, where the "anathema" was, "They would neither eat nor drink till they had killed Paul." The curse thus was nothing immoral in itself; it was a form of speech even the purest might use, a sort of underlined affirmation.

But though the language of Peter was neither profane nor foul, though in his "oath" and in his "curse" there is nothing for which the purest taste need apologize, yet here was his sin, his grievous sin: he made use of the oath and the curse to back up a deliberate and cowardly lie, even as men to-day will kiss the book to make God's Word of truth a cover for perjury. How shall we explain the sad fall of this captain-disciple, who was first and foremost of the Twelve? Were these denials but the wild and wandering cries of some delirium? We find that Peter's lips did sometimes throw off unreasoning and untimely words, speaking like one in a dream, as he proposed the three tabernacles on the mount, "not knowing what he said." But this is no delirium, no ecstasy; his mind is clear as the sky overhead, his thought bright and sharp as was his sword just now. No, it was not a failure in the reason; it was a sadder failure in the heart. Of physical courage Simon had an abundance, but he was somewhat deficient in moral courage. His surname "Peter" was as yet but a forename, a prophecy; for the "rock"-granite was yet in a state of flux, pliant, somewhat wavering, and too easily impressed. It must "be dipped in baths of hissing tears" ere it hardens into the foundation-rock for the new temple. In the garden he was too ready, too brave. "Shall we smite with the sword?" he asked, matching the "we," which numbered two swords, against a whole Roman cohort; but that was in the presence of his Master, and in the consciousness of strength which that Presence gave. It is different now. His Master is Himself a bound and helpless Prisoner. His own sword is taken from him, or, which is the same thing, it is ordered to its sheath. The bright dream of temporal sovereignty, which like a beautiful mirage had played on the horizon of his thought, had suddenly faded, withdrawing itself into the darkness. Simon is disappointed, perplexed, bewildered, and with hopes shattered, faith stunned, and love itself in a momentary conflict with self-love, he loses heart and becomes demoralized, his better nature falling to pieces like a routed army.

Such were the conditions of Peter's denial, the strain and pressure under which his courage and his faith gave way, and almost before he knew it he had thrice denied his Lord, tossing away the Christ he would die for on his cold, impetuous words, as, with a tinge of disrespect in his tone and word, he called Him "the Man." But hardly had the denial been made and the anathema been said when suddenly the cock crew. It was but the familiar call of an unwitting bird, but it smote upon Peter's ear like a near clap of thunder; it brought to his mind those words of his Master, which he had thought were uncertain parable, but which he finds now were certain prophecy, and thus let in a rush of sweet, old-time memories. Conscience-stricken, and with a load of terrible guilt pressing upon his soul, he looks up timidly towards the Lord he has forsworn. Will He deny him, on one of His bitter "woes" casting him down to the Gehenna he deserves? No; Jesus looks upon Peter; nay, He even "turns" round toward him, that He may look; and as Peter saw that look, the face all streaked with blood and lined with an unutterable anguish, when he felt that glance fixed upon him of an upbraiding but a pitying and forgiving love, that look of Jesus pierced the inmost soul of the denying, agnostic disciple, breaking up the fountains of his heart, and sending him out to weep "bitterly." That look was the supreme moment in Peter's life. It forgave, while it rebuked him; it passed through his nature like refining fire, burning out what was weak, and selfish and sordid, and transforming Simon, the boaster, the man of words, into Peter, the man of deeds, the man of "rock."

But if in the outer court truth is thrown to the winds, within the palace justice herself is parodied. It would seem as if the first interview of Caiaphas with Jesus were private, or in the presence at most of a few personal attendants. But at this meeting, as the High Priest of the New was arraigned before the high priest of the Old Dispensation, nothing was elicited. Questioned as to His disciples and as to His doctrine, Jesus maintained a dignified silence, only speaking to remind His pseudo-judge that there were certain rules of procedure with which he himself was bound to comply. He would not enlighten him; what He had said He had said openly, in the Temple; and if he wished to know he must appeal to those who heard Him, he must call his witnesses; an answer which brought Him a sharp and cruel blow from one of the officers, the first of a sad rain of blows which bruised His flesh and made His visage marred more than any man's.

The private interview ended, the doors were thrown open to the mixed company of chief priests, elders, and scribes, probably the same as had witnessed the arrest, with others of the council who had been hastily summoned, and who were known to be avowedly hostile to Jesus. It certainly was not a properly constituted tribunal, a council of the Sanhedrim, which alone had the power to adjudicate on questions purely religious. It was rather a packed jury, a Star Chamber of self-appointed assessors. With the exception that witnesses were called (and even these were "false," with discrepant stories which neutralized their testimony and made it valueless), the whole proceedings were a hurried travesty of justice, unconstitutional, and so illegal. But such was the virulent hate of the hierarchy of the Temple, they were prepared to break through all legalities to gain their end; yea, they would even have broken the tables of the law themselves, if they might only have stoned the Nazarene with the fragments, and then have buried Him under the rude cairn. The only testimony they could find was that He had said He would destroy the temple made with hands, and in three days build another made without hands (Mark xiv. 58); and even in this the statements of the two witnesses did not agree, while both were garbled misrepresentations of the truth.

Hitherto Jesus had remained silent, and when Caiaphas sprang from his seat, asking, "Answerest Thou nothing?" seeking to extract some broken speech by the pressure of an imperious mien and browbeating words, Jesus answered by a majestic silence. Why should He cast His pearls before these swine, who were even now turning upon Him to rend Him? But when the high priest asked, "Art Thou the Christ?" Jesus replied, "If I tell you, ye will not believe: and if I ask you, ye will not answer. But from henceforth shall the Son of man be seated at the right hand of the power of God;" thus anticipating His enthronement far above all principalities and powers, in His eternal reign. The words "Son of man" struck with loud vibrations upon the ears of His enraged jurors, suggesting the antithesis, and immediately all speak at once, as they clamour, "Art Thou, then, the Son of God?" a question which Caiaphas repeats as an adjuration, and which Jesus answers with a brief, calm, "Ye say that I am." It was a Divine confession, at once the confession of His Messiahship and a confession of His Divinity. It was all that His enemies wanted; there was no need of further witnesses, and Caiaphas rent his clothes and asked his echoes of what the blasphemer was worthy? And opening their clenched teeth, his echoes shouted, "Death!"

The lingering dawn had not broken when the high priest and his barking hounds had run their Prey down to death--that is, as far as they were allowed to go; and as the meeting of the full council could not be held till the broad daylight, the men who have Jesus in charge extemporize a little interlude of their own. Setting Jesus in the midst, they mock Him, and make sport of Him, heaping upon that Face, still streaked with its sweat of blood, all the indignities a malign ingenuity can suggest. Now they "cover His face" (Mark xiv. 65), throwing around it one of their loose robes; now they "blindfold" Him, and then strike "Him on the face" (xxii. 64), as they derisively ask that He will prophecy who smote Him; while, again, they "spit in His face" (Matt. xxvi. 67), besmearing it with the venom of unclean, hissing lips! And amid it all the patient Sufferer answers not a word;

Henry Burton

He is silent, dumb, the Lamb before His shearers.

Soon as the day had fairly broke, the Sanhedrists, with the chief priests, meet in full council, to give effect to the decision of the earlier conclave; and since it is not in their power to do more, they determine to hand Jesus over to the secular power, going to Pilate in a body, thus giving their informal endorsement to the demand for His death. So now the scene shifts from the palace of Caiaphas to the Prætorium, a short distance as measured by the linear scale, but a far remove if we gauge thought or if we consider climatic influences. The palace of Caiaphas lay toward the Orient; the Prætorium was a growth of the Occident, a bit of Western life transplanted to the once fruitful, but now sterile East. Within the palace the air was close and mouldy; thought could not breathe, and religion was little more than a mummy, tightly bound by the grave-clothes of tradition, and all scented with old-time cosmetics. Within the Prætorium the atmosphere was at least freer; there was more room to breathe; for Rome was a sort of libertine in religion, finding room within her Pantheon for all the deities of this and almost any other world. In matters of religion the Roman power was perfectly indifferent, her only policy the policy of laissez faire; and when Pilate first saw Jesus and His crowd of accusers he sought to dismiss them at once, remitting Him to be judged "according to your law," putting, doubtless, an inflection of contempt upon the "your." It was not until they had shifted the charge altogether, making it one of sedition instead of blasphemy, as they accuse Jesus of "perverting our nation, and forbidding to give tribute to Cæsar," that Pilate took the case seriously in hand. But from the first his sympathies evidently were with the strange and lonely Prophet.

Left comparatively alone with Pilate--for the crowd would not risk the defilement of the Prætorium--Jesus still maintained a dignified reserve and silence, not even speaking to Pilate's question of surprise, "Answerest Thou nothing?" Jesus would speak no word in self-defence, not even to take out the twist His accusers had put into His words, as they distorted their meaning. When, however, He was questioned as to His mission and Royalty He spoke directly, as He had spoken before to Caiaphas, not, however, claiming to be King of the Jews, as His enemies asserted, but Lord of a kingdom which was not of this world; that is, not like earthly empires, whose bounds are mountains and seas, and whose thrones rest upon pillars of steel, the carnal weapons which first upbuild, and then support them. He was a King indeed; but His realm was the wide realm of mind and heart; His was a kingdom in which love was law, and love was force, a kingdom which had no limitations of speech, and no bounds, either of time or space.

Pilate was perplexed and awed. Governor though he was, he mentally did homage before the strange Imperator whose nature was imperial, whatever His realm might be. "I find no fault in this Man," he said, attesting the innocence he had discovered in the mien and tones of his Prisoner; but his attestation only awoke a fiercer cry from the chief priests, "that He was a seditious person, stirring up the people, and preparing insurrection even from Galilee to Jerusalem." The word Galilee caught Pilate's ear, and at once suggested a plan that would shift the responsibility from himself. He would change the venue from Judæa to Galilee; and since the Prisoner was a Galilean, he would send Him to the Tetrarch of Galilee, Herod, who happened to be in Jerusalem at the time. It was the stratagem of a wavering mind, of a man whose courage was not equal to his convictions, of a man with a double purpose. He would like to save his Prisoner, but he must save himself; and when the two purposes came into collision, as they did soon, the "might" of a timid desire had to give way to the "must" of a prudential necessity; the Christ was pushed aside and nailed to a cross, that Self might survive and reign. And so "Pilate sent Him to Herod."

Herod was proud to have this deference shown him in Jerusalem, and by his rival, too, and "exceeding glad" that, by a caprice of fortune, his long-cherished desire, which had been baffled hitherto, of seeing the Prophet of Galilee, should be realized. He found it, however, a disappointing and barren interview; for Jesus would work no miracle, as he had hoped; He would not even speak. To all the questions and threats of Herod, Jesus maintained a rigid and almost scornful silence; and though to Pilate He had spoken at some length, Jesus would have no intercourse with the murderer of the Baptist. Herod had silenced the Voice of the wilderness; he should not hear the Incarnate Word. Jesus thus set Herod at nought, counting him as a nothing, ignoring him purposely and utterly; and stung with rage that his authority should be thus contemned before the chief priests and scribes, Herod set his Victim "at nought," mocking Him in coarse banter; and as if the whole proceeding were but a farce, a bit of comedy, he invests Him with one of his glittering robes, and sends the Prophet-King back to Pilate.

For a brief space Jesus finds shelter by the judgment-seat, removed from the presence of His accusers, though still within hearing of their cries, as Pilate himself keeps the wolves at bay. Intensely desirous of acquitting his Prisoner, he leaves the seat of judgment to become His advocate. He appeals to their sense of justice; that Jesus is entirely innocent of any crime or fault. They reply that according to their law He ought to die, because He called Himself the "Son of God." He appeals to their custom of having some prisoner released at this feast, and he suggests that it would be a personal favour if they would permit him to release Jesus. They answer, "Not this man, but Barabbas." He offers to meet them half-way, in a sort of compromise, and out of deference to their wishes he will chastise Jesus if they will consent to let Him go; but it is not chastisement they want--they themselves could have done that--but death. He appeals to their pity, leading Jesus forth, wearing the purple robe, as if to ask, "Is it not enough already?" but they cry even more fiercely for His death. Then he yields so far to their clamour as to deliver up Jesus to be mocked and scourged, as the soldiers play at "royalty," arraying Him in the purple robe, putting a reed in His hand as a mock sceptre, and a crown of thorns upon His head, then turning to smite Him on the head, to spit in His face, and to kneel before Him in mock homage, saluting Him, "Hail, King of the Jews!" And Pilate allows all this, himself leading Jesus forth in this mock array, as he bids the crowd, "Behold your King!" And why? has He experienced such a revulsion of feeling towards his Prisoner that he can now vie with the chief priests in his coarse insult of Jesus? Not so; but it is Pilate's last appeal. It is a sop thrown out to the mob, in hopes that it may slake their terrible blood-thirst, a sacrifice of pain and shame which may perhaps prevent the greater sacrifice of life; while at the same time it is an ocular demonstration of the incongruity of their charge; for His Kingship, whatever it might be, was nothing the Roman power had to fear; it was not even to be taken in a serious way; it was a matter for ridicule, and not for revenge, something they could easily afford to play with. But this last appeal was futile as the others had been, and the crowd only became more fierce as they saw in Pilate traces of weakening and wavering. At last the courage of Pilate breaks down utterly before the threat that he will not be Cæsar's friend if he let this man go, and he delivers up Jesus to their will, not, however, before he has called for water, and by a symbolic washing of his hands has thrown back, or tried to throw back, upon his accusers, the crime of shedding innocent blood. Weak, wavering Pilate--

*"Making his high place the lawless perch*
*Of winged ambitions;"*

overridden by his fears; governor, but governed by his subjects; sitting on the judgment-seat, and then abdicating his position of judge; the personification of law, and condemning the Innocent contrary to the law; giving up to the extremest penalty and punishment One whom he has thrice proclaimed as guiltless, without fault, and that, too, in the face of a Heaven-sent warning dream! In the wild inrush of his fears, which swept over him like an inbreaking sea, his own weak will was borne down, and reason, right, conscience, all were drowned. Verily Pilate washes his hands in vain; he cannot wipe off his responsibility or wipe out the deep stains of blood.

And now we come to the last act of the strange drama, which the four Evangelists give from their different stand-points, and so with varying but not differing details. We will read it mainly from the narrative of St. Luke. The shadow of the cross has long been a vivid conception of His mind; and again and again we can see its reflection in the current of His clear speech; now, however, it is present to His sight, close at hand, a grim and terrible reality. It is laid upon the shoulder of the Sufferer, and the Victim carries His altar through the streets of the city and up towards the Mount of Sacrifice, until He faints beneath the burden, when the precious load is laid upon Simon the Cyrenian, who, coming out of the country, met the procession as it issued from the gate. It was probably during this halt by the way that the incident occurred, related only by our Evangelist, when the women who followed with the multitude broke out into loud lamentation and weeping, the first expression of human sympathy Jesus has received through all the agonies of the long morning. And even this sympathy He gave back to those who proffered it, bidding these "daughters of Jerusalem" weep not for Him, but for themselves and for their children, because of the day of doom which was fast coming upon their city and on them. Thus Jesus pushes from Him the cup of human sympathy, as afterwards He refused the cup of mingled wine and myrrh: He would drink the bitter draught unsweetened; alone and all unaided He would wrestle with death, and conquer.

It is somewhat singular that none of the Evangelists have left us a clue by which we can recognize, with any certainty, the scene of the Crucifixion. In our thoughts and in our songs Calvary is a mount, towering high among the mounts of God, higher than Sinai itself. And such it is, potentially; for it has the sweep of all the earth, and touches heaven. But the Scriptures do not call it a "mount," but only a "place." Indeed, the name of "Calvary" does not appear in Scripture, except as the Latin translation of the Greek Kranion, or the Hebrew Golgotha, both of which mean "the place of the skull." All that we can safely say is that it was probably some rounded eminence, as the name would indicate, and as modern explorations would suggest, on the north of the city, near the tomb of Jeremiah.

But if the site of the cross is only given us in a casual way, its position is noted by all the Evangelists with exactness. It was between the crosses of two malefactors or bandits; as St. John puts it, in an emphatic, Divine tautology, "On either side one, and Jesus in the midst." Possibly they intended it as their last insult, heaping shame upon shame; but unwittingly they only fulfilled the Scripture, which had prophesied that He would be "numbered among the transgressors," and that He would make His grave "with the wicked" in His death.

St. Luke omits several details, which St. John, who was an eye-witness, could give more fully; but he stays to speak of the parting of His raiment, and he adds, what the others omit, the prayer for His executioners, "Father, forgive them; for they know not what they do," an incident he probably had heard from one of the band of crucifiers, perhaps the centurion himself.

With a true artistic skill, however, and with brief touches, he draws for us the scene on which all ages will reverently gaze. In the foreground is the cross of Jesus, with its trilingual superscription, "This is the King of the Jews;" while close beside it are the crosses of the thieves, whose very faces St. Luke lights up with life and character. Standing near are the soldiers, relieving the ennui with cruel sport, as they rail at the Christ, offering Him vinegar, and bidding Him come down. Then we have the rulers, crowding up near the cross, scoffing, and pelting their Victim with ribald jests, the "people" standing back, beholding; while "afar off," in the distance, are His acquaintance and the women from Galilee. But if our Evangelist touches these incidents lightly, he lingers to give us one scene of the cross in full, which the other Evangelists omit. Has Jesus found an advocate in Pilate? has He found a cross-bearer in the Cyrenian, and sympathisers in the lamenting women? He finds now upon His cross a testimony to His Messiahship more clear and more eloquent than the hieroglyphs of Pilate; for when one of the thieves railed upon Him, shouting out "Christ" in mockery, Jesus made no reply. The other answered for Him, rebuking his fellow, while attesting the innocence of Jesus. Then, with a prayer in which penitence and faith were strangely blended, he turned to the Divine Victim and said, "Jesus, remember me when Thou comest in Thy kingdom." Rare faith! Through the tears of his penitence, as through lenses of light, he sees the new Dawn to which this fearful night will give birth, the kingdom which is sure to come, and which, coming, will abide, and he salutes the dying One as Christ, the King! Jesus did not reply to the railer; He received in silence his barbed taunts; but to this cry for mercy Jesus had a quick response--"To-day shalt thou be with Me in Paradise," so admitting the penitent into His kingdom at once, and, ere the day is spent, passing him up to the abodes of the Blessed, even to Paradise itself.

And now there comes the hush of a great silence and the awe of a strange darkness. From the sixth to the ninth hour, over the cross, and the city, and the land, hung the shadow of an untimely night, when the "sun's light failed," as our Evangelist puts it; while in the Temple was another portent, the veil, which was suspended between the Holy Place and the Most Holy, being rent in the midst! The mysterious darkness was but the pall for a mysterious death; for Jesus cried with a loud voice into the gloom, "Father, into Thy hands I commend My spirit," and then, as it reads in language which is not applied to mortal man, "He gave up the ghost." He dismissed His spirit, a perfectly voluntary Sacrifice, laying down the life which no man was able to take from Him.

And why? What meant this death, which was at once the end and the crown of His life? What meant the cross, which thus draws to itself all the lines of His earthly life, while it throws its shadow back into the Old Dispensation, over all its altars and its passovers? To other mortals death is but an appendix to the life, a negation, a something we could dispense with, were it possible thus to be exempt from the bond we all must pay to Nature. But not so was it with Jesus. He was born that He might die; He lived that He might die; it was for this hour on Calvary that He came into the world, the Word being made flesh, that the sacred flesh might be transfixed to a cross, and buried in an earthly grave. Surely, then, it was not as man that Jesus died; He died for man; He died as the Son of God! And when upon the cross the horror of a great darkness fell upon His soul, and He who had borne every torture that earth could inflict without one murmur of impatience or cry of pain, cried, with a terrible anguish in His voice, "My God, My God, why hast Thou forsaken Me?" we can interpret the great horror and the strange cry but in one way: the Lamb of God was bearing away the sin of the world; He was tasting for man the bitter pains of the second death; and as He drinks the cup of the wrath of God against sin He feels passing over Him the awful loneliness of a soul bereft of God, the chill of the "outer darkness" itself. Jesus lived as our Example; He died as our Atonement, opening by His blood the Holiest of all, even His highest heaven.

And so the cross of Jesus must ever remain "in the midst," the one bright centre of all our hopes and all our songs; it must be "in the midst" of our toil, at once our pattern of service and our inspiration. Nay, the cross of Jesus will be "in the midst" of heaven itself, the centre towards which the circles of redeemed saints will bow, and round which the ceaseless "Alleluia" will roll; for what is "the Lamb in the midst of the throne" (Rev. vii. 17) but the cross transfigured, and the Lamb eternally enthroned?

# CHAPTER XXVI - THE FIRST LORD'S DAY

St. Luke xxiv.

The Sabbath came and went over the grave of its Lord, and silence reigned in Joseph's garden, broken only by the mailed sentinels, who laughed and chatted by the sealed sepulchre. As to the disciples, this "high day" is a dies non to them, for the curtain of a deep silence hides them from our view. Did they go up to the Temple to join in the Psalm, how "His mercy endureth for ever?" Scarcely: their thoughts were transfixed to the cross, which haunted them like a horrid dream; its rude dark wood had stunned them for awhile, as it broke down their faith and shattered all their hopes. But if the constellation of the Apostles passes into temporary eclipse, with no beam of inspired light falling upon them, "the women" are not thus hidden, for we read, "And on the Sabbath day they rested, according to the commandment". It is true it is but a negative attitude that is portrayed, but it is an exceedingly beautiful one. It is Love waiting upon Duty. The voices of their grief are not allowed to become so excessive and clamorous as to drown the Divine voice, speaking through the ages, "Remember that thou keep holy the Sabbath day;" and even the fragrant offerings of their devotion are set aside, that they may keep inviolate the Sabbath rest.

But if the spices of the women are the spikenard and myrrh of a mingled love and grief, they are at the same time a tacit admission of their error. They prove conclusively that the women, at any rate, had no thought of a resurrection. It appears strange to us that such should be the case, after the frequent references Jesus made to His death and rising again. But evidently the disciples attached to these sayings of Jesus one of those deeper, farther-off meanings which were so characteristic of His speech, interpreting in some mysterious spiritual sense what was intended to be read in a strict literalness. At present nothing could be farther from their thoughts than a resurrection; it had not even occurred to them as a possible thing; and instead of being something to which they were ready to give a credulous assent, or a myth which came all shaped and winged out of their own heated imaginings, it was something altogether foreign to their thoughts, and which, when it did occur, only by many infallible proofs was recognized and admitted into their hearts as truth. And so the very spices the women prepare for the embalming are a silent but a fragrant testimony to the reality of the Resurrection. They show the drift of the disciples' thought, that when the stone was rolled to the door of the sepulchre it shut in to the darkness, and buried, all their hopes. The only Easter they knew, or even dreamed of, was that first and final Easter of the last day.

As soon as the restraint of the Sabbath was over, the women turned again to their labour of love, preparing the ointment and spices for the embalming, and coming with the early dawn to the sepulchre. Though it was "yet dark," as St. John tells us, they did not anticipate any difficulty from the city gates, for these were left open both by night and day during the Passover feast; but the thought did occur to them on the way as to how they should roll back the stone, a task for which they had not prepared, and which was evidently beyond their unaided strength. Their question, however, had been answered in anticipation, for when they reached the garden the stone was rolled away, and the sepulchre all exposed. Surprised and startled by the discovery, their surprise deepened into consternation as passing within the sepulchre, they found that the body of Jesus, on which they had come to perform the last kind offices of affection, had disappeared. And how? could there be more than one solution of the enigma? The enemies of Jesus had surely laid violent hands upon the tomb, rifling it of the precious dust they sorrowfully had committed to its keeping, reserving it for fresh indignities. St. John supplements the narrative of our Evangelist, telling how the Magdalene, slipping out from the rest, "ran" back to the city to announce, in half-hysterical speech, "They have taken away the Lord out of the tomb, and we know not where they have laid Him;" for though St. John names but the Magdalene, the "we" implies that she was but one of a group of ministering women, a group that she had abruptly left. The rest lingered by the tomb perplexed, with reason blinded by the whirling clouds of doubt, when suddenly--the "behold" indicates a swift surprise--"two men stood by them in dazzling apparel."

In speaking of them as "two men" probably our Evangelist only intended to call attention to the humanness of their form, as in verse 23 he speaks of the appearance as "a vision of angels." It will be observed, however, that in the New Testament the two words "men" and "angels" are used interchangeably; as in St. Luke vii. 24, Rev. xxii. 8, where the "angels" are evidently men, while in

Mark xvi. 5, and again in the verse before us, the so-called "men" are angels. But does not this interchangeable use of the words imply a close relation between the two orders of being? and is it not possible that in the eternal ripenings and evolutions of heaven a perfected humanity may pass up into the angelic ranks? At any rate, we do know that when angels have appeared on earth there has been a strange humanness about them. They have not even had the fictitious wings which poetry has woven for them; they have nearly always appeared wearing the human face divine, and speaking with the tones and in the tongues of men, as if it were their native speech.

But if their form is earthly, their dress is heavenly. Their garments flash and glitter like the robes of the transfigured Christ; and awed by the supernatural portent, the women bow down their faces to the earth. "Why," asked the angels, "seek ye the living among the dead? He is not here, but is risen: remember how He spake unto you when He was yet in Galilee, saying that the Son of man must be delivered up into the hands of sinful men, and be crucified, and the third day rise again." Even the angels are not allowed to disclose the secret of His resurrection life, or to tell where He may be found, but they announce the fact that they are not at liberty to explain. "He is not here; He is risen," is the Gospel of the angels, a Gospel whose prelude they themselves have heard, but, alas! forgotten; and since Heaven does not reveal what by searching we ourselves may find out, the angels throw them back upon their own recollections, recalling the words Jesus Himself had spoken, and which, had they been understood and remembered, would have lighted up the empty sepulchre and have solved the great mystery. And how much we lose because we do not remember, or if remembering, we do not believe! Divine words have been spoken, and spoken to us, but to our ear, dulled by unbelief, they have come as empty sound, all inarticulate, and we have said it was some thunder in the sky or the voices of a passing wind. How many promises, which, like the harps of God, would have made even our wildernesses vocal, have we hung up, sad and silent, on the willows of the "strange lands"! If we only "remembered" the words of the Lord Jesus, if they became to us real and eternally true, instead of being the unreal voices of a dream, those words would be, not "the distant lamps" of Heaven, but near at hand, lighting up all dark places, because throwing their light within, turning even the graves of our buried hopes into sanctuaries of joy and praise!

And so the women, instead of embalming their Lord, carried their spices back unused. Not unused, however, for in the spices and ointments the Living One did not need their own names were embalmed, a fragrant memory. Coming to the tomb, as they thought, to do homage to a dead Christ, the Magdalene, and Mary, and Johanna, and Salome found a Christ who had conquered death, and at the same time found an immortality for themselves; for the fragrance of their thought, which was not permitted to ripen into deeds, has filled the whole world.

Returning to the city, whither the Magdalene had outrun them, they announced to the rest, as she had done to Peter and John, the fact of the empty grave; but they completed the story with the narrative of the angelic vision and the statement that Jesus had risen. So little, however, were the disciples predisposed to receive the tidings of a resurrection, they would not admit the fact even when attested by at least four witnesses, but set it down as idle, silly talk, something which was not only void of truth, but void of sense. Only Peter and John of the Apostles, as far as we know, visited the sepulchre, and even they doubted, though they found the tomb empty and the linen clothes carefully wrapped up. They "believed" that the body had disappeared, but, as St. John tells us, "as yet they knew not the Scripture, that He must rise again from the dead" (St. John xx. 9); and as they leave the empty grave to return to their own home, they only "wondered at that which was come to pass." It was an enigma they could not solve; and though the Easter morning had now fully broke, the day which should light all days, as it drew to itself the honours and songs of the Sabbath, yet to the minds and hearts of the Apostles it was "yet dark;" the glory of the Lord had not yet risen upon them.

And now comes one of those beautiful pictures, peculiar to St. Luke, as he lights up the Judæan hills with a soft afterglow, an afterglow which at the same time is the aurora of a new dawn. It was in the afternoon of that first Lord's day, when two disciples set out from Jerusalem for Emmaus, a village, probably the modern Khamasa, sixty furlongs from the city. Who the two disciples were we cannot say, for one is unnamed, while the other bears a name, Cleopas, we do not meet with elsewhere, though its Greek origin would lead us to infer that he was some Gentile proselyte who had attached himself to Jesus. As to the second, we have not even the clue of an obscure name with which to identify him, and in this somewhat strange anonymity some expositors have thought they detected the shadow of the Evangelist, Luke, himself. The supposition is not an impossible one; for though St. Luke was not an eye-witness from the beginning, he might have witnessed some of the closing scenes of the Divine life; while the very minuteness of detail which characterizes his story would almost show that if not himself a participant, he was closely related to those who were; but had St. Luke himself been the favoured one, it is scarcely likely that he would have omitted this personal testimony when speaking of the "many infallible proofs" of His resurrection.

Whoever the two might be, it is certain that they enjoyed the esteem and confidence of the disciples, having free access, even at untimely hours, to the Apostolic circle, while the fact that Jesus Himself sought their company, and selected them to such honours, shows the high place which was accorded to them in the Divine regard.

We are not apprised of the object of their journey; indeed, they themselves seem to have lost sight of that in the gleams of glory which, all unexpected, fell across their path. It is not unlikely that it was connected with recent events; for now that the central Sun, around whom their lives revolved, has disappeared, will not those lives necessarily take new directions, or drift back into the old orbits? But whatever their purposes might be, their thoughts are retrospective rather than prospective; for while their faces are set towards Emmaus, and their feet are steadily measuring off the furlongs of the journey, their thoughts are lingering behind, clinging to the dark crest of Calvary, as the cloud-pennon clings to the Alpine peak. They can speak but of one theme, "these things which have happened:" the One whom they took to be the Christ, to whom their hearts had been so strangely drawn; His character, miracles, and words; the ignominious Death, in which that Life, with all their hopes, was quenched; and then the strange tidings which had been brought by the women, as to how they had found the grave empty, and how they had seen a vision of angels. The word "questioned together" generally implies a difference of opinion, and refers to the cross-questioning of disputants; but in this case it probably referred only to the innumerable questions the report of the Resurrection would raise in their minds, the honest doubts and difficulties with which they felt themselves compelled to grapple.

It was while they were discussing these new problems, walking leisurely along the road--for men walk heavily when weighted at the heart--a Stranger overtook and joined them, asking, after the usual salutation, which would not be omitted, "What communications are these that ye have one with another, as ye walk?" The very form of the question would help to disguise the familiar voice, while the changed "form" of which St. Mark speaks would somewhat mask the familiar features; but at the same time it would appear that there was a supernatural holding of their eyes, as if a dusky veil were wrapped about the Stranger. His question startled them, even as a voice from another world, as, indeed, it seemed; and stopping suddenly, they turned their "sad" faces to the Stranger in a momentary and silent astonishment, a silence which Cleopas broke by asking, "Dost thou alone sojourn in Jerusalem, and not know the things which are come to pass there in these days?" a double question, to which the stranger replied with the brief interrogative, "What things?" It needed no more than that solitary word to unseal the fountain of their lips, for the clouds which had broken so wildly and darkly over Calvary had filled their hearts with an intense and bitter grief, which longed for expression, even for the poor relief of words. And so they break in together with their answer (the pronoun is changed now), "Concerning Jesus of Nazareth, which was a Prophet mighty in deed and word before God and all the people: and how the chief priests and our rulers delivered Him up to be condemned to death, and crucified Him. But we hoped that it was He which should redeem Israel. Yea, and beside all this, it is now the third day since these things came to pass. Moreover certain women of our company amazed us, having been early at the tomb; and when they found not His body, they came, saying, that they had also seen a vision of angels, which said that He was alive. And certain of them that were with us went to the tomb, and found it even so as the women had said: but Him they saw not."

It is the impetuous language of intense feeling, in which hope and despair strike alternate chords. In the first strain Jesus of Nazareth is lifted high; He is a Prophet mighty in word and deed; then He is stricken down, condemned to death, and crucified. Again, hope speaks, recalling the bright dream of a redemption for Israel; but having spoken that word, Hope herself goes aside to weep by the grave where her Redeemer was hurriedly buried. Still again is the glimmer of a new light, as the women bring home the message of the angels; but still again the light sets in darkness, a gloom which neither the eyes of Reason nor of Faith could as yet pierce; for "Him they saw not" marks the totality of the eclipse, pointing to a void of darkness, a firmament without a sun or star.

But incidentally, in the swift current of their speech, we catch a reflection of the Christ as He appeared to their minds. He was indeed a Prophet, second to none, and in their hope He was more, for He was the Redeemer of Israel. It is evident the disciples had not yet grasped the full purport of the Messianic mission. Their thought was hazy, obscure, like the vision of men walking in a mist. The Hebrew dream of a temporal sovereignty seems to have been a prevailing, perhaps the prevailing force in their minds, the attraction which drew and cheered them on. But their Redeemer was but a local, temporal one, who will restore the kingdom to Israel; He was not yet the Redeemer of the world, who should save His people from their sins. The "regeneration," as they fondly called it, the "new creation," was purely national, when out of the chaos of Roman irruptions their Hebrew paradise will come. For one thing, the disciples were too near the Divine life to see its just and large proportions. They must stand back from it the distance of a Pentecost; they must look on it through their lenses of flame, before they can take in the profound meaning of that Life, or the awful mystery of that Death. At present their vision is out of focus, and all they can see is the blurred and shadowy outline of the reality, the temporal rather than the spiritual, a redeemed nationality rather than a redeemed and regenerated humanity.

The risen Jesus, for such the Stranger was, though they knew it not, listened to their requiem patiently and wonderingly, glad to find within their hearts such deep and genuine love, which even the cross and the grave had not been able to extinguish. The men themselves were true, even though their views were somewhat warped--the refractions of their Hebrew atmosphere. And Jesus leads them in thought to those "shining uplands" of truth; as it were, spurring them on, by a sharp though kind rebuke, to the heights where Divine thoughts and purposes move on to their fulfilment. "O foolish men," He said, "and slow of heart to believe in all that the prophets have spoken! Behoved it not the Christ to suffer these things, and to enter into His glory?" They thought He was some stranger in Jerusalem, yet He knows their prophets better than themselves; and hark, He puts in a word they had feared to use. They only called Him "Jesus of Nazareth;" they did not give Him that higher title of "the Christ" which they had freely used before. No; for the cross had rudely shattered and broken that golden censer, in which they had been wont to burn a royal incense. But here the Stranger recasts their broken, golden word, burning its sweet, Divine incense even in presence of the cross, calling the Crucified the "Christ"! Verily, this Stranger has more faith than they; and they still their garrulous lips, which speak so randomly, to hear the new and august Teacher, whose voice was an echo of the Truth, if not the Truth itself!

"And beginning from Moses and from all the prophets, He interpreted to them in all the Scriptures the things concerning Himself." It will be observed that our Evangelist uses a peculiar word in speaking of this Divine exposition. He calls it an "interpretation," a word used in the New Testament only in the sense of translating from one language to another, from the unknown to the known tongue. And such, indeed, it was; for they had read the Scriptures but in part, and so misread them. They had thrown upon those Scriptures the projections of their own hopes and illusions; while other Scriptures, those relating to the sufferings of Christ, were set back, out of sight, or if heard at all, they were only the voice of an unknown tongue, a vox et preterea nihil. So Jesus interprets to them the voices of this unknown tongue. Beginning at Moses, He shows, from the types, the prophecies, and the Psalms, how that the Christ must suffer and die, ere the glories of His kingdom can begin; that the cross and the grave both lay in the path of the Redeemer, as the bitter and prickly calyx out of which the "glories" should unfold themselves. And thus, opening their Scriptures, putting in the crimson lens of the blood, as well as the chromatic lens of the Messianic glory, the disciples find the cross all transfigured, inwoven in God's eternal purpose of redemption; while the sufferings of Christ, at which they had stumbled before, they now see were part of the eternal plan of mercy, a Divine "ought," a great necessity.

They had now reached Emmaus, the limit of their journey, but the two disciples cannot lose the company of One whose words have opened to them a new and a bright world; and though He was evidently going on farther, they constrained Him to abide with them, as it was towards evening and the day was far spent. And He went in to tarry with them, though not for long. Sitting down to meat, the Stranger Guest, without any apology, takes the place of the host, and blessing the bread, He breaks and gives to them. Was it the uplifted face threw them back on the old, familiar days? or did they read the nail-mark in His hand? We do not know; but in an instant the veil in which He had enfolded Himself was withdrawn, and they knew Him: it was the Lord Himself, the risen Jesus! In a moment the hush of a great awe fell upon them, and before they had time to embrace Him whom they had loved so passionately, indeed before their lips could frame an exclamation of surprise, He had vanished; He "became invisible" to them, as it reads, passing out of their sight like a dissolving cloud. And when they did recover themselves it was not to speak His name--there was no need of that--but to say one to another, "Was not our heart burning within, us while He spake to us in the way, while He opened to us the Scriptures?" It was to them a bright Apocalypse, "the Revelation of Jesus Christ," who was dead, and is alive for evermore; and all-forgetful of their errand, and though it is evening, they leave Emmaus at once, their winged feet not heeding the sixty furlongs now, as they haste to Jerusalem to announce to the eleven, and to the rest, that Jesus has indeed arisen, and has appeared unto them.

Returning to Jerusalem, they go direct to the well-known trysting-place, where they find the Apostles ("the eleven" as the band was now called, though, as St. John informs us, Thomas was not present) and others gathered for their evening meal, and speaking of another and later appearance of Jesus to Simon, which must have occurred during their absence from the city; and they add to the growing wonder by telling of their evening adventure, and how Jesus was known of them in breaking of bread. But while they discussed the subject--for the majority were yet in doubt as to the reality of the appearances--Jesus Himself stood before them, passing through the fastened door; for the same fear that shut the door would securely lock it. Though giving to them the old-time salutation, "Peace be to you," it did not calm the unrest and agitation of their soul; the chill of a great fear fell upon them, as the spectral Shadow, as they thought it, stood before them. "Why are ye troubled?" asks Jesus, "and wherefore do reasonings arise in your hearts?" for they fairly trembled with fear, as the word would imply. "See My hands and My feet, that it is I Myself: handle Me, and see; for a spirit hath not flesh and bones, as ye behold Me having." He then extended His hands, drew back His robe from His feet, and, as St. John says, uncovered His side, that they might see the wounds of the nails and the spear, and that by these visible, tangible proofs they might be convinced of the reality of His Resurrection body. It was enough; their hearts in an instant swung round from an extreme of fear to an extreme of joy, a sort of wild joy, in which Reason for the moment became confused, and Faith bewildered. But while the heavenly trance is yet upon them Jesus recalls them to earthly things, asking if they have any meat; and when they give Him a piece of a broiled fish, some of the remnants of their own repast, He takes and eats before them all; not that now He needed the sustenance of earthly food, in His resurrection life, but that by this simple act He might put another seal upon His true humanity. It was a kind of sacrament, showing forth His oneness with His own; that on the farther side of the grave, in His exaltation, as on this, in His humiliation, He was still the "Son of man," interested in all things, even the commonplaces, of humanity.

    The interview was not for long, for the risen Christ dwelt apart from His disciples, coming to them at uncertain times and only for brief spaces. He lingers, however, now, to explain to the eleven, as before to the two, the great mystery of the Redemption. He opens their minds, that the truth may pass within. Gathering up the lamps of prophecy suspended through the Scriptures, He turns their varying lights upon Himself, the Me of whom they testify. He shows them how it is written in their law that the Christ must suffer, the Christ must die, the Christ must rise again the third day, and "that repentance and remission of sins should be preached in His name unto all the nations, beginning from Jerusalem." And then He gave to these preachers of repentance and remission the promise of which the Book of the Acts is a fulfilment and enlargement, the "promise of the Father," which is the gift of the Holy Ghost. It was the prophecy of the Pentecost, the first rustle of the mighty rushing wind, that Divine breath which comes to all who will receive it.

    Our Evangelist passes in silence other appearances of the Resurrection Life, those forty days in which, by His frequent manifestations, He was training His disciples to trust in His unseen Presence. He only in a few closing words tells of the Ascension; how, near Bethany, He was parted from them, and taken up into heaven, throwing down benedictions from His uplifted hands even as He went; and how the disciples returned to Jerusalem, not sorrowing, as men bereaved, but with great joy, having learned now to endure and rejoice as seeing Him who is invisible, the unseen but ever-present Christ. That St. Luke omits the other Resurrection appearances is probably because he intended to insert them in his prelude to the Acts of the Apostles, which he does, as he joins his second treatise to the first. Nor is it altogether an incidental coincidence that as he writes his later story he begins at Jerusalem, lingering in the upper room which was the wind-rocked cradle of the Church, and inserting as key-words of the new story these four words from the old: Repentance, Remission, Promise, Power. The two books are thus one, a seamless robe, woven for the living Christ, the one giving us the Christ of the Humiliation, the other the Christ of the Exaltation, who speaks now from the upper heavens, and whose power is the power of the Holy Ghost.

    And was it altogether undesigned that our Evangelist, omitting other appearances of the forty days, yet throws such a wealth of interest and of colouring into that first Easter day, filling it up from its early dawn to its late evening? We think not. He is writing to and for the Gentiles, whose Sabbaths are not on the last but on the first day of the week, and he stays to picture for us that first Lord's day, the day chosen by the Lord of the Sabbath for this high consecration. And as the Holy Church throughout all the world keeps her Sabbaths now, her anthems and songs are a sweet incense burned by the door of the empty sepulchre; for, "The light which threw the glory of the Sabbath into the shade was the glory of the Risen Lord."

www.ingramcontent.com/pod-product-compliance
Lightning Source LLC
Chambersburg PA
CBHW032301150426
43195CB00008BA/533